JOSS ACKLAND

I must be in there somewhere

Hodder & Stoughton

LONDON SYDNEY AUCKLAND TORONTO

British Library Cataloguing in Publication Data

Ackland, Joss *1928*–
  I must be in there somewhere: an autobiography.
  1. Great Britain. Acting. Ackland, Joss, 1928–
  I. Title
  792'.028'0924

  ISBN 0-340-49396-8

Published by Hodder and Stoughton,
a division of Hodder and Stoughton Limited,
Mill Road, Dunton Green, Sevenoaks, Kent TN13 2YA.
Editorial Office: 47 Bedford Square, London WC1B 3DP.

Photoset by Rowland Phototypesetting Limited,
Bury St Edmunds, Suffolk

Printed in Great Britain by
St Edmundsbury Press Limited, Bury St Edmunds, Suffolk

I must be in there somewhere

To Pukk
and Melanie and
Paul and Irene
and Toni and David
and Penny and
Sammy and Paolo
and Kirsty and
Toby and Kandy
and Polly and
Sam and Ben
and Adam and
Tom and Emily
and Gianluca
and Romeo and
Daniel and
Abby
and
. . ?

The old actor was confused. Wearily, he prised open his old cigar box, pushed aside sticks of greasepaint, bottles of spirit gum, eyelashes, nose putty, odd pieces of crêpe hair and mumbled to himself, 'I must be in there somewhere.'

INTRODUCTION

The acting profession has always bulged at the seams. Today it is more crowded than ever. A steady stream of bright-eyed, optimistic youngsters flow in, as an almost equal number return to the world of normality – disillusioned, frustrated and often embittered.

My original purpose in writing this book was to encourage young actors, of both sexes, to persevere provided they feel it is their vocation and are prepared to gamble and accept disappointment, heartache and failure. If they seek stardom, bright lights and easy success – forget it. Only a secure, accomplished professional craftsman like Robert Mitchum can afford to say 'it is better than working'.

There is a famous story about Beethoven giving a lecture at a school in Germany. Afterwards one of the pupils approached him and said, 'I would like to be a famous composer. Do you think I should try?'

'No.'

'Why not?' asked the boy, 'You did.'

'Ah yes', said Beethoven, 'But I did not ask.'

An actor's life is a long game of snakes and ladders and consists of unknown paths and blind corners. Even during the ten years that this book has been in the writing, surprise has followed surprise. When I began in the business Hollywood seemed to be the bluebird of happiness but it has taken me forty years to touch the tinsel – and that is all it is.

ILLUSTRATIONS

Illustrations appear between pages 96 and 97, 160 and 161, and 192 and 193.

With the exception of the photograph from *A Little Night Music*, which appears by permission of Zoe Dominic, all the illustrations are drawn from the author's own collection. If copyright has in any cases been infringed the author and the publishers will be happy to make suitable acknowledgement in any future edition.

ONE

I remember fog and the pungent invigorating smell of the new-laid tar, while the great steamrollers clanked and clanked up and down like great lumbering giants, and the smell of black dusty sacks of coal drawn by heavy aged horses, forever clopping down the road. Horses were everywhere. Delivering milk and wood and coal and groceries and beer barrels. And horse troughs with the water slopping over the sides. But it's the fog I remember most. I loved the fog. Thick and grey and covering everything. To be in the fog was an adventure. Lost in the unknown. Sounds were both highlighted and distorted; and the imagination could stretch itself; houses and streets disappeared and one would be anywhere in the world. A lamppost would faintly emerge from the gloom and become a vessel with pirates on board. Footsteps in the dark could be the tread of a foreign spy. The fog wrapped around you like a magic cloak. There are no magic fogs nowadays. Not like then. Only Hollywood sees London with the eyes of a child. Hidden behind a thick blanket of grey mist. Unreal. Childlike. I remember fogs.

And I remember the little row of shops around the corner. The sweet shop with liquorice bootlaces – all different colours; Mickey Mouse toffees – twopence a quarter; packets of Imps – tiny sweets made from liquorice with menthol, with the kick of a mule; penny slabs of chocolate – brown and white; packets of sherbet with liquorice straws; bottles of Tizer and fizzy tablets that exploded in the mouth. There was a chemist that smelt of camphor and a grocer where the salty rashers of bacon blended with the sweet icing smell of biscuit animals, and a hardware store with bundles of wood to light fires and the smell of paraffin lamps, and, of course, the newsagent and toy shop with copies of the *Buzzer, Magnet, Gem, Champion, Film Fun* and many others, sometimes with magnificent free gifts – water pistols, Japanese flowers that erupted from their shells when put in water, and divers that bobbed up and down in the bath. And there were the soldiers and the cowboys made of lead – penny ones that stood; twopenny ones on horseback and sixpenny knights with removable swords – mounted, magnificent and unobtainable.

The very young are not aware of the roots from which they spring. Family is accepted like life itself. They are there. They are part of you and you are part of them. It is only when you spread your wings and fly away that you start searching for what you are leaving. But I was aware that we were not a normal family. I had a caring mother, strong and safe; a sister seven years older than myself and a brother, almost a man, thirteen years older than me, whom I worshipped from afar. But I was confused about my father. Even though Mother talked about him incessantly, only occasionally was he in the house, and then he would hum to himself with dreamy eyes, his mind elsewhere and only his body present.

Once in a while, when I climbed into my mother's bed in the morning, there he would be and I would gratefully crawl under the sheets and lie next to his warm body. Then when I awoke he would be stropping his razor on a leather strap, his face covered with soap, and he would hum away, tell me a joke, shine his shoes until they gleamed, put on his coat and away he would go with his fast military walk, head held high, and still humming. There were the odd occasions when my father would turn up for Sunday lunch. He would cut up my food, mix the meat and vegetables into a mush, divide it into four islands and pour gravy into the spaces. Then, leaving the largest until last, I would devour the islands, and nothing tasted more delicious.

My secret wish was for us all to be together at Christmas but when Christmas Eve arrived we would pack our bags and Mother, my sister and I would get the train to Birmingham, climb aboard the rickety tram to Erdington and join her mother and countless relatives for the festivities. For some reason Mother was always quiet on the journey.

Science has taught us that from the moment we spring from the womb, to the moment of death, we are forced by gravity and oxygen to live in this world. Whatever we do, unless we are one of the few astronauts who streak through space, briefly touching the dust of another planet and streaking back again, we are confined within the boundary walls of our existence. The world is our egg. Archaeologists and historians can show us faith and hope for worlds beyond, but actual, certain knowledge confines us within our shell. But there are many eggs in life – one inside the other – like a Matreshka doll. For some, more than others. It is bound to vary how many eggs we crack and break open in the search for broader horizons.

My birth was supposed to have taken place in hospital, but while my mother was in labour she heard there had been a mix-up of babies the previous day, so she fled in her nightdress and I was born, below the ground, in a basement flat in North Kensington on February 29th, 1928, so it was four years before I had my first birthday.

My first egg was a few rooms, grey buildings, shadows and strange people seen from the protective cocoon of a pram, and then a push-chair. I knew little of North Kensington where I was born, or the move we made when I was a toddler, but I remember the railway bridge over Ladbroke Grove, because every time a train thundered over I imagined it would come crashing down on top of me. And I remember sitting on the leads outside the windows, spending hours watching the back gardens, the houses and trains rushing past.

> Open the window very wide
> And take a look at what's outside.
> There you might see the fields of green
> With crushed down grass where man has been.
> Or maybe it's the sea you see
> Where all the sailors long to be.
> Or is that a train a-rushing past?
> It's hard to tell, it goes so fast.
> Or maybe you just see a yard
> With sticks and brooms and ground that's hard.
> But remember this – whatever you see
> The world is yours and it's all free.

I wrote that poem when I was eighteen but its origin stems from those early years.

My first friend was my age and lived in a flat in the next house and his name was Tino. He was very black and I, with my golden hair, was very white. Together we had great adventures, but one day his mother killed herself, and after that I didn't see him any more. Today we call those years the time of the Depression. Fortunes lost, poverty was accepted like life itself. Life and death were as close to each other as they are during war. Apart from Tino's mother, a woman who lived in the flat on the other side committed suicide, and across the road the body of a young boy was found under the floorboards. A friend of my mother's wrapped up all her belongings carefully, left little messages for all her friends and then jumped under a tube train. Another friend, a professional pianist, Mrs 'Bill' Williams, apparently made a suicide pact with her son, but did not go through with it. He took prussic acid, slashed his wrists and jumped from a window, only to land on a clothes-line which broke his fall, and he did not die for two hours. 'Bill', his mother, went straight off to America where she toured, and for many years, every week, I would get a letter with a token of love from her: different American flags or comics with Dick Tracey, Dagwood and Blondie, and Little Orphan Annie.

The colours of those years are brown and grey, but it was a rich brown and a rich grey, and although living through the middle of this century has been like going through a long, dark tunnel to the light – the light is electric and does not come from the sun. I was born only ten years after the First World War finished, but as a child of course it seemed a million miles away, as much a part of history as Trafalgar and William the Conqueror. By the time I had burst through to my second egg I was a young boy in West Hampstead where I could travel from my house to the foreign lands of Mill Lane – to the outer space of my primary school – with the exciting knowledge that the great planet of West End Lane was in the distance, and my spaceship was eventually able to take me by bus to the fantastic world of the cinema, near Golders Green, with the organist pounding away at the bellows, titillating the taste buds for the films which followed. And of course on Saturday mornings there was the Mickey Mouse Club with Flash Gordon serials, Buck Jones westerns and hundreds of cartoons.

After the umbilical cord was cut I was protected and safe until that sleight-of-hand moment of terror when I was left in a classroom full of strange children and my mother, nervous and smiling too hard, ran from the room while a strange adult creature guided me to my desk. Suddenly life was dominated by the strong smell of chalks grating harshly over the blackboard; indiarubbers broken up into dangerous missiles; and the tantalising, frightening odour of exercise books, filled with coloured paper stars and new things called words. And then running out of the grey, austere building into the stone courtyard where we played, fought, threw tennis balls, kicked footballs, and I discovered the trick of betting the other kids a penny they could not knock me down with one blow. I got quite a few pennies but I swear that the bone in my nose has not grown from that day to this.

Isolated moments leap out of the fog of recollection. Making little

Union Jacks for the Jubilee of George V and being given bright, decorative mugs, and periscopes to watch through the crowd. I remember intense emotions. Being scolded by my mother, seeing the hurt in her eyes after some act of naughtiness and knowing how hard she was fighting to make ends meet. The extraordinary pleasure of seeing her laugh until the tears rolled down her face and she collapsed weak and exhausted into a chair. Sometimes she would say, 'Let's see if we can't get to the pictures,' and we would rummage down the backs of chairs and sofas for the odd sixpence. Then off we would go and excitedly wait in the queue, while I thrilled with anticipation looking at the posters and the photos outside the cinema. Then, often wet and bedraggled, tickets tightly held, we would step into the magic world. The organ played while ice-creams were sold, then cartoons, the shorts, trailers of incredible films soon to appear, the second feature and then the big movie – to me, then, never short of wondrous.

But my first cinema visit had not been successful. *Min and Bill* with Marie Dressler and Wallace Beery. When the moment came that they threw chairs and tables at each other, I burst out crying and had to be taken sobbing uncontrollably from the cinema.

Sometimes at the Gaumont State, Kilburn, as well as all the other goodies before the main feature there would be a bonus of an hour's variety, and I can still vividly remember seeing the hilarious Wilson, Keppel and Betty with their Egyptian dance in front of a shaky Pyramids backcloth; Teddy Brown, a gargantuan man playing a delicate xylophone; Harry Tate with his exploding car; the Nicholas brothers all the way from America, who must have been made of indiarubber, leaping higher than Nijinsky and further than Jessie Owens, bouncing off and around the entire auditorium. Then there were ventriloquists, high wire acts, musical saws, conjurors and always lines of beautiful, high-kicking girls.

On the way to and from school I would play marbles or conkers, according to the season. Marbles were of two sizes – ordinary ones and slightly larger and very precious ones. Sometimes I would risk playing one of the latter, over the pavements and along the gutters, and, after losing the game, would watch sadly as the favourite green and yellow bauble would disappear into some rotten boy's canvas bag. The conkers I would saturate in vinegar and leave in front of a fire to harden, in the hope that one might have become a seventy-eighter, leaving other boys' seventy-sevener conkers shattered along the road. I cannot remember ever just walking to school without some kind of activity. If there were no marbles or conkers

13

I would make sure never to step on the lines of any paving stone lest some catastrophe occurred; and there were railings to be rattled with twigs, leaves to be blown with pursed lips, making incredibly rude noises, and creeping plants you could put up your shirt-sleeves while you waited for them to work their way out of your collar.

One Sunday morning, after buying a penn'orth of sweets at the corner shop, I was walking home when three boys I knew came tearing up behind me. 'Look what we got,' said one excitedly, and he held up a half-pint carton of cream. At this point a heavy, florid, middle-aged man came panting round the corner shouting 'Stop thief!' and the boys fled. I walked on, but within seconds felt my ear being tugged painfully by the furious, panting giant.

'Where's the cream then?' he roared.

'I didn't take it,' said I.

'We'll see about that,' he bellowed. 'Where do those boys live?'

'I don't know,' I lied, and I felt myself being yanked down the road.

Eventually we reached the doorway to an apartment in a huge luxury block of flats. 'Right, where do you live?' demanded the gross apoplectic. I gave him a false address. 'Well, I want that cream back on this doorstep within half an hour or I call the police and it's off to prison with you, my lad.'

Distraught, I ran off home and my mother, who could see I was upset, asked me what was wrong. I told her, and my father, who strangely was at home banging on an old typewriter, overheard. 'My God,' he roared, with his Irish temper rising, 'how dare the man. I'll soon settle his hash. Show me the way.'

He grabbed me by the hand, led me at the double back to the block of flats, and rang the bell. I waited with bated breath for my father to render the man unconscious with one blow. After a few seconds the door was opened, not by the monster, but by his wife. She was very beautiful. I looked at my father and could see he had noticed. His anger dissipated in a moment, a strange light came into his eyes, he apologised for coming and I knew that I would get no retribution that day.

One morning I got to school early and I was playing quite happily in the yard when a girl, older and bigger than myself, started making fun of me. Eventually the rotten thing went too far and we started fighting. The other kids stood around and laughed as we prodded and thumped each other until, suddenly, the viciousness escalated and we were fighting savagely, rolling over and over on the ground. But the mean, stupid girl was too old, too big and too strong, and eventually she was straddled across me and holding my wrists with an iron grip while the other kids stood around me in a circle guffawing and cheering. My eyes were red with tears and I hated her silly pretty face and I hated her silly stupid body which encased mine. We were both panting from our exertions and were taking breaths in unison and the more I tried to break free the tighter she forced me down with her thighs. Her eyes blazed with triumph and then something extraordinary happened. The triumph faded from her eyes and was replaced by uncertainty and a mixture of fear and elation, and through my body passed a sensation so rich and pleasurable that for a long moment in time gone was the pain, gone was the circle of raucous onlookers, gone was the enemy sitting astride me, and in her place was a creature of beauty who had magic in her eyes, her smell and above all in her feel. We stared at each other in confusion; she released her grasp and then together we rose silently to our feet, averting our eyes as we did so. The bell had rung and we joined our separate groups and quietly trooped into school. I never knew her name or ever really saw her after that – perhaps we subconsciously avoided each other because we shared a guilty secret. One thing I had discovered.

Girls could be jolly interesting.

Today it is very complex for the young to have ideals and aspirations. What is their Utopia? Capitalism and Communism and Socialism and Liberalism and Fascism and Marxism have all rubbed off on one another and made a rather tasteless stew. But for the young in the thirties it was very easy to have ideals. The world was split. Communism had triumphed in Russia. Fascism had triumphed in Germany. In China, Spain and elsewhere the two ideologies were fighting it out to the death, and gradually it seemed inevitable that the whole world must choose between one doctrine or the other. Labour or Conservative were just watered-down versions.

To be a child in London in the thirties was to be a child in the largest city in the world – the capital of England – the capital of the British empire, still invested with the arrogance and quiet self-assurance of the Divine Right of Victorianism. Our comic strips and exciting yarns encouraged us to beware of sly Chinese devils, scalp-hunting redskins, greasy dagoes and the Russian anarchists. Even if we tied cans to cats' tails we should be kind to dogs, and we should take care of Little Black Sambo as long as he remained faithful. Armed with a good straight left and a stiff upper lip anything could be achieved.

'Wider still and wider, shall our bounds be set – God who made thee mighty, make thee mightier yet,' we sang at school; while in Germany *'Deutschland Uber Alles'* was sung fortissimo. Not only was the world around me dividing into two – something else was happening. I have never understood why kids had to belong to groups, or adults come to that; they clung to each other, wore the same clothes, supported the same football team and hated outsiders. In a way this was only an extension of Nationalism. Their inability to reach out and discover new worlds and excitements bred suspicion, hatred and fear of anyone outside their group. They had to retire inside their uniform. Today there is no change and whether the uniform is a bowler hat, football colours, safety-pins in the ears and bovver boots, or torn jeans plus Gucci shirt and cordless telephone it is still a uniform. Even fashion and the length of hair is aligned to this. In the thirties, with massive unemployment and insecurity rampant, people huddled together desperately forming their groups and throwing on political uniforms. The division between Left and Right widened and tempers shortened. Scapegoats were necessary and, as in Nazi Germany, the Jews came under the hammer. It got so bad at school that I got a gang to help stop victimisation of Isaacs, Cohen and one little chum called Sammy Shitlemits. You can imagine what hell he went through! The absurdity of children playing at politics is difficult to imagine. I called our gang the Clenched Fist Gang because we had little transfers of two hands, firmly grasping each other, stamped secretly on various parts of our small anatomies. Transfers were the rage in the thirties.

At weekends I would go with my brother, my sister and their friends to Trafalgar Square with our banners, 'Stop Hitler Now', 'Down with Fascism', 'Up the Republicans' and soon the inevitable 'Workers Unite', and from one meeting we would move to another to boo Oswald Mosley with his right-arm salute and goosestepping followers. 'Down with the Jews', 'Stop the blacks' they would roar while thousands applauded and we heckled. As time went by Mosley's Fascists and the establishment seemed to take on the same face. Chamberlain, Halifax, Hore-Belisha and Simon seemed to don the same uniforms as Hitler, Mussolini and Franco, even if the colours of the uniforms were of lighter hue. These meetings invariably ended in bloodshed as tempers frayed and stones and bottles were thrown, and the strongarm tactics of the Fascists were in no way impeded by the police who, like Nelson, all seemed to possess one blind eye. 'Attention must be paid,' we yelled. 'Stop Hitler', 'Stop Franco', 'Stop persecuting the Jews', but all our isolated cries were lost in the wind and the only solution seemed to lie in Marxism. The Russians had achieved their aims by revolution. Equality of man. Fair shares for all. Unity is strength. This was the answer. No more crying in the wind. Together our voices would make an enormous din of protest. Comrades. Workers unite. Intellectuals guide the way. The Left Book Club was formed and became diet for the thinking man. Spender, Isherwood and Auden were to become my heroes. Bright young men who could link arms with the unemployed, and like Don Quixote join the International Brigade and fight the windmills in Spain. Positive thinking was the answer. Black and white became easily defined. Greys were unnecessary. Stick to the simple rules. Any variation must be reactionary. Stalin was the positive, straightforward peasant – the salt of the earth. Trotsky and Koestler were deviationists. Orwell and T. S. Eliot were Fascists. I wore no bowler hat, no football colours, no bovver boots, but without knowing it I was mentally putting on a uniform.

For my first theatrical experience I played the title role in *The Sleeping Prince*. This was not in the comedy by Terence Rattigan, but a twenty-minute piece at junior school, a sort of *Sleeping Beauty* in reverse. The cast consisted of twelve boys and girls as the different hours of the clock, myself, and a little Scots girl who dazzled me with her radiance. The chief object of the plot was to teach us to tell the time, but the play finished with the little beauty waking me with a kiss and I declared my love for her. I think somehow I must have lacked authority because the moment the play finished she departed for the wilds of Scotland and I never saw her again. I remember well the preparation for the piece. Going with my mother to Marks and Spencer's to buy a new pair of flannel pyjamas because the ones I possessed were a little threadbare, and the making of the crown with cardboard, gold paper and a paper doily stuck in the middle. My next part was a cardinal in a piece which I remember not at all. There obviously was no beautiful Scottish girl around at the time. But I do remember the anguish as my mother had to find some cheap material to make the rich voluptuous robes. Shortly afterwards my father got me a ticket to the Press Club party which was fancy dress, so the cardinal's robe got an extra airing. In my flowing robes my father collected me from home and took me by bus to Mayfair where he deposited me in the flat of a mysterious, haughty lady with her mysterious, haughty little girl, who showed me a children's book full of photographs of herself modelling with soldiers in busbies outside Buckingham Palace. Then on with the mother and her child to the Press Club – and we went, marvel of marvels, by taxi. But my magnificent robes now made me self-conscious and their magnificence seemed a little gaudy. I didn't like the girl.

Throughout my childhood I had suffered from migraines which kept me in a dark room for long periods of time while my head ached and I brought up everything I ate. One day when I was very young I was ill in bed when my mother got a precious ticket for Priestley's *Johnson over Jordan* with Ralph Richardson and Edna Best at a West End theatre. Leaving me in the care of my brother and sister she went off to see the show, and afterwards went round to the stage door to get them to sign her programme. Edna Best signed without a word and then shot away in a chauffeur-driven limousine, but Ralph Richardson touched my mother's heart by asking her where she had been sitting and if she had heard everything clearly. After chatting for a while he stomped off into the night. I had never been to a theatre then, and when my mother returned home, told me the story and gave me the autographed programme, I was strangely fascinated by it and kept it for many years as a treasured possession.

My first theatre visits were to the Golders Green Hippodrome – first to Gilbert and Sullivan's *Iolanthe* and I wished I had gone to the pictures, and then to *Golden Boy* by Clifford Odets with the wonderful Group Theater from New York. Open-mouthed I gazed in wonder as a new world opened up before me.

My brother and his friends were closely linked with the little Unity Theatre in the hinterland between Euston and St Pancras stations. (It didn't seem little then, of course – it would have been Drury Lane on ice.) It was very much a people's theatre. I saw the superb Paul Robeson in *Plant in the Sun* and his enormous lovable personality filling the small auditorium as it did when I saw him later in the vast hall at Olympia, and there I saw *Aladdin*, with the Dame and Wishee Washee gleefully singing 'Strike While the Iron is Hot' and 'Let's All Linger Under Ladders', and we all joined in with

> Heigh ho, hi ho, we'll fight the Fascist foe
> And down the drain with Chamberlain
> For Chamberlain must go!

Great-Aunt Annie had travelled a lot, spoke seven languages and was the most formidable woman I ever met. Charles Dickens could have created her. In a movie Edna May Oliver would have played the part. A true eccentric, in spite of her skill with languages she always called Maison Lyons – Maison Lee-on, turning dear old Joe Lyons into a Frenchman. She loved the pianola, and in a rare moment of generosity had given the family her old one. I loved it and would sit like Walter Mitty pressing the keys and straining the footpedals as the cylinder revolved and imagine I was Rubenstein while 'Liebestraum' or the William Tell Overture reverberated through the house. On the few occasions when she visited us, I would sit at the pianola with my hair combed and wearing a clean shirt and wait for her august person to arrive. When the bell rang I would beat out 'Liebestraum' until she appeared with her pince-nez and tightly rolled umbrella. Then she would sit majestically and wait to be served scones, blackcurrant jam and cream. When she lay dying I still remember the awful moment I had to kiss her bearded face.

Aunt Annie had been very angry when I was born. 'Two children is enough for anyone,' she said, so in her will she left a little money to my brother and sister but none to me. My mother did not want to hurt me, so she gave me six whole shillings which she said Aunt Annie had left me. Never had I seen so much money. Elated, I ran from the house straight to the magic shop where I had spent long hours gazing wistfully through the frosted windows at the wonders within. The bell clanged excitedly as I leaped into the shop where monsters, clowns and witches stared down at me with bulbous eyes, and S. K. 'Cuddles' Zakall came out of the shadows to serve me. I bought a rubber face which could twist into incredible and horrid shapes; and a matted straw tube which could hold your fingers like a vice and never let them free; and three tin boxes each inside the other, each secured and yet in a moment a marked coin could be transported magically into the very innermost box; and card tricks; and three shells with a disappearing pea; and other incredible discoveries. Then with a bag full of goodies and an empty pocket I rushed home and delighted my mother with surprise after surprise. But by the end of the day, when my elation had died down, I lay in bed and thought of what else I could have done with the money. I could have taken the whole family to the pictures. I could have given it to my mother for a rainy day. Overwhelmed by guilt I lay awake for hours and my pillow was wet with tears.

And I remember one Christmas Eve, when we did not go to

Birmingham, being woken by Paddy, my brother, cursing to himself because he could not get the top of my Christmas stocking over the bedpost. 'Try the other one,' I whispered.

'Thanks,' he whispered back, and slowly the situation dawned on him. 'Shut up and go to sleep,' he grinned sheepishly.

When I was born, Paddy was nearly thirteen and he always seemed a man to me. Even when he was at school he appeared to be strong, secure and wise, and when I teased him it was with respectful awe. His rugby cap had dangling gold tassels. Like a crown. He was always getting knocked out playing rugby and would lose his memory for two days at a time. Then everything went back to normal. When he left home he worked for several newspapers and he would bring me home posters of movies, which I proudly hung in my room.

Apart from movies I discovered another great excitement – the public library. Hour after hour I would spend there, with its pungent smell of print and warm leather, trying to decide which two books to take home – one fiction and one non-fiction. At home I had discovered A. A. Milne, the Brothers Grimm and Kenneth Grahame – how I had wept after reading *The Piper at the Gates of Dawn* from *The Wind in the Willows* – and thanks to the library I travelled through Richmal Crompton, G. K. Chesterton, H. G. Wells, Hilaire Belloc, Charles Dickens, Jack London, John Steinbeck, Tolstoy, Ilya Ehrenburg and all the marvellous American plays of the thirties – a golden period.

As my father led another life away from home, my mother could never afford holidays, and as a child, except for the annual trip to Birmingham, we never travelled far. Once in a while, however, we got on a bus and visited Mr and Mrs Santa in Harrow. Behind their house they had a lovely garden full of apples and pears and plums, which I gathered to take home, and the back gate of the garden opened on to a common where I spent many happy hours rolling down mountainous hillocks and chasing squirrels and rabbits. Mrs Santa was very talkative and Mr Santa was very mild. Mr and Mrs Santa were not young and had no children but they had a permanent lodger, Mr Watcyn Watcyns. Mr Watcyn Watcyns was very large, very amiable and he had a deep bass voice and sometimes sang on the radio. When Mr Watcyn Watcyns came home Mr Santa, whose first name was Monty, would always fetch Mr Watcyn Watcyns's slippers for him and make him high tea. Mrs Santa confided in Mother that she had been left three thousand pounds by her aunt, which was a lot of money in those days, and had bought herself a new hat. The rest of the money she had put in the bank and would not touch, she said, as long as they lived. Mrs Santa also confided in my mother that she and Mr Santa made love once a year; they did not enjoy it, said Mrs Santa, but it was the thing to do. Mr and Mrs Santa and Watcyn Watcyns had a large cigar-store Indian holding an ashtray and I liked them very much.

The wireless was comforting and secure. Mabel Constanduros as Mrs Buggins, *Children's Hour* with Uncle Mac, *Toytown* with Larry the Lamb and Denis the Dachshund, Harry Hemsley the ventriloquist and his 'family', Elsie, Winnie, Johnny and Horace, Jeanne de Casalis, Ronald Frankau and Tommy Handley as Murgatroyd and Winterbottom, Gracie Fields endlessly singing 'Little Old Lady Passing By' and horrifying suspense serials like *The Gang Smashers* with Ivan Samson and the wicked Tortoni and *Number 17* with Leon M. Lion – and the gramophone.

We had a wind-up gramophone and you had to turn the handle twenty-six times for each playing, and needles which you changed every two sides. For a concerto or a symphony you would need six twelve-inch records which was very expensive. His Master's Voice records – ten-inch records – cost ninepence, but from Woolworths you could buy a small record for sixpence. We had records by Jack Payne and Jack Hylton and their bands, Layton and Johnstone singing 'Life is Just a Bowl of Cherries', Jack Hulbert and Cicely Courtneidge singing 'A Fly Crawled Up the Window' and 'Why Has a Cow Got Four Legs?', Gigli singing 'Your Tiny Hand is Frozen' and a merry chorus singing 'Live, Love and Laugh'. Sometimes I would only turn the handle twenty-two times and the record would grind to a heavy cacophonous halt. But it was excitement.

In 1938 the newspapers, the wireless and the neighbours all talked of the possibilities of war with Germany, and men who had been so long on the dole now found work digging air-raid shelters. One day I had to go to a large grey building where I was fitted for a gas mask. Then, with the grotesque black rubber Martian face with its huge perspex eyes and metal Schnozzle Durante nose tucked inside a cardboard box hanging by a string from my shoulder, I went home to imagine the worst. That evening Mother took me to see the Alexander Korda movie of H. G. Wells's *Things to Come*. Open-mouthed and round-eyed I watched the dreadful results of the holocaust, with the little boy, with his tin drum hanging by a string from his shoulder, lying dead in the rubble. Later that night

I knelt by my bed and prayed long and hard. 'Please don't let there be war. Please! Please!' The fear I felt during those few hours never returned – not even when war did break out, or during the chaos that followed.

In spite of my love of films I had never shown any interest in the theatre, but one day early in 1938 my father saw an advertisement in *The Times*: 'Wanted – twelve-year-old fair-haired boy for leading part in West End play', and for no logical reason he arranged for me to meet the director. I was to go for the interview immediately after school, and on the morning of the great day as I was wearing my best grey shorts and clean white shirt my mother would not allow me to go to school until the last possible moment. I must not dirty or damage myself. However, during break a few of the boys and myself had to practise running in the road outside the school. The running was fine but on the way back I slipped on the newly tarred road and a pointed stone stuck in my knee-cap. When I arrived home with a gaping hole in my knee and blood pouring down my leg my mother nearly had a fit, and on the way to the interview we had to stop off to have the wound dressed by a doctor and covered with large strips of plaster. I still have the scar.

I remember little of the interview. The play was *On Borrowed Time* and had run for a year in New York. The plot concerned a small boy trapping the Devil in a tree, and while he was trapped no one could die. The director was the tall, elegant Philip Holmes and he was also the star. He had just had a great success in the play *Ten Minute Alibi*. I remember he was very kind and that they had seen two hundred boys for the role, and that is all I remember. But I got the part, and was about to enter a new world. I would have to leave school, have private lessons, rehearse the play at the Comedy Theatre and open at the Theatre Royal, Haymarket. Life would have been transformed. However, one day I returned from school to find my mother looking strained and worried. 'I have some bad news for you,' she said quietly. She then told me she had received a letter from the London County Council who had discovered that I was under twelve years of age and therefore not allowed to work in the theatre. She thought I would be broken-hearted, but, quite unconcerned, I went out to meet some friends on the green where we played and wrestled and laughed and the 'tragedy' was forgotten. Rehearsals were held up as a court case decided my future. We lost the case and life went on as usual.

Today I am very grateful. The theatre is no place for children. If you are going to go mad – at least develop first. Despite its success in America, *On Borrowed Time* only ran for six performances. For me there was no new world and life at school was the same, but somewhere, tucked inside my skin, a tiny little acting bug had become imbedded, lying dormant for many years before it exploded into that absurd, lunatic disease.

When I hurt my knee on the day of the interview we had been practising for the final of the North London under twelves' hundred-yard relay – and what an important race that was! Somehow my mother persuaded or coerced my father to come to the sports and when the big race started there he was waiting by the final tape and humming to himself.

In the relay I was the last of the four members of our team to run because I was the fastest. Small for my age, in those days, I could belt along like greased lightning, and I was determined to show my father what an athlete his son was. The race was on but by the end of the third leg our school was not doing too well – we were last of the six teams. As the baton was thrust into my hand I just had time to see that my father was standing with a teacher and watching attentively. With heart pounding, chest thrust out and little arms flailing like windmills, I caught up with number five boy, passed number four, number three, number two, inched my way past the leader and threw myself at the winning tape. Gulping great chunks of air and with eyes sparkling with pride I looked up to catch my father's eye, but he was no longer there. Then I saw him, away from the track, walking with his back to me and with his arm around the teacher, deep in conversation. She was very pretty. After that I ran a little slower each year.

Later in 1938 we moved to a flat in Fordwych Road, Kilburn, where we lived above a Mr and Mrs Staples and their ten-month-old baby whom I played with at every opportunity. 'Sweet,' said everyone, 'to see a young lad showing such affection for a baby.' It was all hokum of course. I was secretly in love with the mother. When the child cried Mrs Staples would rush out to the pram, golden hair flowing in the North London breeze, and her high heels clicking sideways in a very feminine motion down the garden path. I watched her every movement with rapt adoration.

The following year brought my next major step in evolution. Choosing a school – even finding a school. After several entrance exams, which I failed, I eventually got a place at Dame Alice Owen's in Islington, and so we moved again, this time to Stoke Newington which was only a short bus ride away. While I waited I joined another local council school, and then came the holidays, after which would come the day when I first set foot inside Dame Alice Owen's.

Little did I know that day would never come.

During the holiday period, my mother, sister and I were to have a great adventure. We were to visit my mother's youngest brother and his wife for two weeks – across the sea in Ireland. Until that time I had never seen the sea, and it was in great excitement that we got the train to Holyhead and in the middle of the night boarded the *Innisfallen* and sailed to Cork. It was so late and so dark and I was so seasick I still did not catch sight of the wondrous waves, but it was not long before I did.

Aunt Eva and Uncle Jim and their year-old son Paddy lived in the village of Ballintemple a few miles from Cork. Blackrock Castle was nearby; the air was clear; there was a donkey in the garden; and it was magic. Uncle Jim had a car and he drove us to the beach and I smelt the salt and the spray and splashed about in the most enormous bath in the world. The beaches were deserted except for an occasional horse and cart which would drive up to the water's edge, and the carts would always carry one husband and one wife. The husband would sit and puff away at his pipe while the wife ran, backwards and forwards, into the sea collecting great clumps of seaweed and filling the cart with the green slime. Then they would take it back to their home and scatter it over the rocky ground, instead of precious earth, to grow potatoes.

The holiday was drawing to an end, and then one Sunday morning we heard there was to be a very important message on the wireless and everyone was to listen. Just as the Prime Minister, Mr Chamberlain, was about to speak the baby Paddy started to cry, and I had to take him into the next room. By the time I had quietened him and carried him back to join the others I just managed to catch the words, '. . . and consequently we are now at war with Germany'.

INTERLUDE
A Scots Girl in Africa

In 1929 or 1930 a girl child was born in Blantyre in the heart of British Central Africa. The record of birth registration was lost in a fire and the child's grandmother had written the birthdate as 1930 in her bible, but the child's mother thought it was 1929. The child's grandmother had been one of the first white women to go to Central Africa towards the end of the last century and had made the journey by paddle steamer from Beira to Chiromo, and, from Chiromo, carried by machila across the Zambezi through the bush to the village of Blantyre which had just been named by Dr Livingstone after his birthplace in Scotland.

The child's father had gone to Africa after the First World War, married the child's mother and become a trader, shop-owner and eventually mayor of the new town of Blantyre. The girl child had a brother and a sister, but when war broke out one was fighting in Burma and the other was at school in England, and as the father and mother were always busy with business the girl child spent her time playing with the African children, riding bareback over the red earth and under the warm skies, and dreaming of Sabu whom she had seen in a movie.

Two

The west coast of Ireland was a million miles from the war. Our two-week holiday stretched to three months, and I went to the Cork Grammar School and started to learn Gaelic. The postmistress at Ballintemple had ears and eyes larger than the whole village and she knew every bit of gossip before even the closest relatives. It was she who told us my father had joined the army and my brother had joined the army and my brother who had been going to marry Freddie, married her sister Zena and my brother's friend Jack, who had been going to marry Zena, married Freddie.

I caught wasps in jars, shot flies with a pop gun, learnt painfully to play hurley, saw Jimmy O'Dea in variety, John Wayne in *Stagecoach* and revelled in the crisp fresh air, the open fields and the salty sea. Early in 1940 we returned to England but not on the *Innisfallen* because it no longer existed. We had to travel across Ireland, to Dublin, by train and then the journey to Holyhead was only a short one. In Dublin we stayed with my father's father. In his middle seventies he drank a bottle of whisky and swam in the sea every day. He had a maid, Molly, whom he woke every morning with a cup of tea, then she would go off to Mass while he, a Protestant, prepared a large breakfast for them both.

The trip back across the channel (I was nervous with the tensions of war but still standing like a greyhound in the slips) was short but memorable. Late at night the boat zigzagged to avoid possible torpedoes and the tough, grey, sea-sick bags were used en masse. Strangely enough, this time mine stayed empty. At the next table four nuns sat with heads permanently bent in prayer and for the first time I smelled the odour of war. When we boarded the train to London the odour grew even more pungent. The only light in the compartment came from a sinister little blue bulb and people moved like black shadows silently along the corridors and whispered to each other, careful not to wake the sleeping dragon. All the shades were down over the windows but beneath them I saw the strange criss-cross of sticky brown paper which was to become so much a part of life for the next six years.

In London there was a feeling of limbo, but as the weeks went by everyone threw off their skins of insecurity and found a new skin underneath. A tougher skin, ready to adapt for what was to come. People learned to laugh and live together, war became a natural state of existence, a rich protective humour grew from nowhere, class barriers crumbled and, as in a chess game, bishops, knights and pawns linked arms to create a unity which I have not known before or since.

We were ready.

My new school had been evacuated to Bedford, so before joining it, once again I went with my mother and sister to Birmingham for a week or two. Once again we boarded the rickety tram to Erdington where aunts and uncles and cousins and family friends accumulated like bees in a hive. The Queen Bee was my grandmother, and everything revolved around her. We played endless games of cards whose names I cannot remember and always with ten or twelve of us around a table and laughing hysterically at anything whatsoever. Then we had bread and cheese, pickled onions and Ovaltine and went to bed.

Then suddenly, what we had been subconsciously preparing for happened. The air-raids started. The wail of the sirens brought us down from our beds and once again we played cards – this time in pyjamas – and the hilarity grew even more frenetic as the dull thuds of falling bombs continued at regular intervals. Sometimes the thuds got louder and we would pause a brief moment waiting to hear where the next nasty would drop. One night the thuds grew really loud and we waited a long moment in time before the final thud, which seemed to have an orchestra with extra instruments, and the criss-crossed French windows had shattered glass all over the floor.

Back to London. Back to Green Lanes, Islington, where we had moved from Fordwych Road so that I would be near my new school. But now the school had been evacuated to the country so the move seemed unnecessary. In retrospect, however, it proved fortunate because years later I went to visit the house in Fordwych Road to be greeted only by an empty space. The house had received a direct hit. I enquired after the delectable Mrs Staples and was relieved to hear that she and her family had also moved away in time.

So with my clothes and toothbrush in a case, a satchel full of books, my gas mask hanging from my shoulder, and accompanied by my mother, I boarded a train and travelled the fifty miles to the little market town of Bedford. There I was deposited with my 'billet lady' Mrs Rogers and her husband, and, after a brief chin-up,

27

tearless, smiling, lying farewell, my mother returned to London.

For ten shillings a week Mr and Mrs Rogers sheltered me, fed me, put a warming pan in my bed, and we all played with their budgerigar who could talk and ring bells.

Dame Alice Owen School shared with Bedford Grammar School, and we would have our lessons in the morning and they had theirs in the afternoon. The pattern of my life at school was formed on my first day when the headmaster showed me to my classroom and, because I had recently come from Ireland, jokingly searched me for bombs in front of my new classmates. I became a loner. Every day my body sat on the school bench but my mind stayed outside the school precincts. I was a fringe member. Recently Owen's School and their Old Boys gave a dinner for Lord's Taverners, and together with England cricketers, Denis Norden, Hughie Greene, Peter Cook and Dudley Moore, etc., I was invited as a guest. When the present headmaster said, 'Will the school rise and toast the guests?' I said, 'What do I do – half rise?' He gave an embarrassed smile. He had no idea that I was an Old Boy.

But outside the school there were books to be read, and the Granada Cinema and the Plaza and the Picturedrome on opposite sides of the River Ouse, and the little cinema directly opposite the school which changed programmes twice a week and which we fondly called 'the bug house', and, joy of joys, there was the Bedford County Theatre with its live touring shows, saucy shows, variety shows, revues, melodramas and Phyllis Dixie. The winter of 1939 and early 1940 was severe. Apart from Ireland I had never been outside London and now we would walk to school through deep snowdrifts, and the snow crawled over the top of wellington boots and froze crunchily around the toes. On arrival we would change into precious leather shoes, but sitting inside the classroom the snow would melt inside the socks, leaving them damp and putrid and the toes would ache as chilblains developed. As we rowdily ran from the school we pelted each other with snowballs, rolled down hills and arrived wet, bedraggled and shivering back at our billets to be cared for by people unused to young monsters. At night the warming pan was placed on sheets stiff with cold, and I would throw off my garments and leap into the warm patch, snuggled up like an unborn babe.

After a few months my mother left the rented flat in Green Lanes and rented a flat in Clapham Road, Bedford. My sister joined us for a while but then went off to university at Oxford. My brother went to Sandhurst on an Officer Training Course and my father, who had run the gauntlet in the First World War from ship's purser to fighting in the trenches, started off with a commission and was fighting in France. 'We're going to hang out our washing on the Siegfried Line, Have you any dirty washing, Mother dear?' we sang with confidence, and 'Run, rabbit, run, rabbit, run, run, run . . .' with even more. After all, the Maginot Line was invincible – the Germans would never get through it.

We were right. It was strong enough – but not long enough. The Germans quietly slipped around the sides and pushed the French and English back towards the sea.

After school one day, I ran home to lunch, rushed through my homework and then raced off to the Plaza to see *The Wizard of Oz*. Judy Garland sang 'Over the Rainbow' in sepia, Billie Burke and the Munchkins in colour, Frank Morgan in confusion. I took the film home with me exploding in my head, my brain not working by computer but rather by reels of celluloid. The projector of my mind whirred on through the night and in the morning when the bell rang I raced downstairs with the film still playing. There, at the door, was my father, messy, dusty, unshaven and fatigued. 'I've just come from Dunkirk,' he said. After days on the beach and hours in the water he had been picked up by a fishing boat and brought back to England. My mother helped him off with his clothes, laid him down on the bed and fed him some soup. 'I've had an exciting time, too,' I said, and proceeded to tell him the story of *The Wizard of Oz* shot by shot. He sat up in bed, smiled, and for one of the few times in his life listened avidly with total concentration.

On another day my mother was called to the door. Standing there was a small boy but two years older than me and therefore important with a cocky pathos. 'You're my new billet lady,' he said. There had been a mistake. We already had a small boy evacuee staying with us for the customary ten shillings a week, but my mother felt sorry for the little newcomer and Geoff Rowley shared a room with me. His brother had been killed and his father with the AFS had died fighting fires in the London blitz. The two-year age difference was so enormous we could never be close friends, but I respected him and at night when we lay in our beds he would tell me of his meetings with the local girls and I listened with rapt attention. There was Eileen Tysoe and Joan Collins and, above all, Aileen Smith. Aileen Smith was Lana Turner – she even played a Lana Turner role. Thirteen or fourteen years of age, like a ripe cherry, she looked ready to be swallowed, pips and all. I learned her pattern of movement, what time she left school, when she would meet her friend Pam, when they would wander through Woolworths, at what time Aileen would ride back over the railway bridge to her house, and I followed her everywhere, pushing or riding my pedal bike so that I could always keep up with her. Breathlessly I waited for her appearance in her little white riding mac with collar turned up seductively and my heart would leap with excitement when she came into view. Never once did I have the courage to approach her. Never once dared I venture a smile or a word. Eventually she became aware of my regular appearances, would give a little knowing smile and avert her head. One night Geoff Rowley told me how he had walked with Aileen through the park that evening. Walking arm in arm eventually they had sauntered along with their hands in each other's pockets. Overcome with jealousy and erotic joy at the thought I put my head under the pillow, but the vision stayed clear in my mind for hours before the layers of sleep blanketed it from my mind.

We were only a few miles from Cardington airport with its green and yellow camouflage trying to hide it from the enemy above, but no bombs ever fell on Bedford. However, the wail of air-raid sirens continually broke the sleep of the night and we would rise from our beds and assemble in what we thought was the safest part of the house and once again play cards until the drone of the 'All Clear' wound its way through the blacked-out windows.

There were queues for everything. Our meagre weekly food rations would barely do for one meal today but with reconstituted egg powder, dried milk, vegetables with curry powder or a three-penny piece of haddock, skate or cod and two penn'orth of chips we managed to keep healthy. On the odd occasion rumours would go around that a particular tobacconist would have cigarettes, and early in the morning the queues would grow in the hope that ten cigarettes would come their way. Sweets were strictly rationed and I am sure my generation benefited with strong healthy teeth. I remember once hearing a news flash on the wireless asking for a banana for a child in hospital with some rare disease, which apparently could only be cured by this unobtainable fruit. Queues everywhere, and I particularly remember with pride one Christmas my present for my mother was the result of many hours of queuing over a period of three months – six boxes of matches.

The wireless was a great joy. Laughter all the way. *ITMA* with Jack Train as Colonel Chinstrap and Funf the German spy, Dorothy Summers as Mrs Mop, Horace Percival selling dirty postcards, and an absurd submariner who would appear anytime, anywhere, with his 'Don't forget the diver, sir, don't forget the diver', and of course the incomparable Tommy Handley holding the lunacy together. I recall Clay Keyes with his 'penny on the drum' game; Arthur Askey and Richard Murdoch in *Band Wagon*; Jack Warner in *Garrison Theatre* with his catch-phrase 'Mind my bike' and his 'little gel' Joan Winters selling 'chocolates, cigarettes' before she joined the ATS; *Workers' Playtime* with artists such as the great Robb Wilton, Sandy Powell, Tessie O'Shea, Issy Bonn and Elsie and Doris Waters, and the appalling *Works Wonders* from factories 'somewhere in Britain'. The most untalented collection of artists ever to appear before a radio audience referred constantly, it seemed, to the factory foreman, thereby ensuring gales of laughter from his colleagues in the audience. Now I can only remember it with affection.

Popular music was supplied by Harry Roy, Roy Fox, Nat Gonella, Geraldo and Ambrose and their bands with songs sweetly sung by Anne Shelton. Songs like 'A Nightingale Sang in Berkeley Square', 'There'll be Bluebirds Over the White Cliffs of Dover', 'In Room 504', 'The Last Time I Saw Paris' and 'London Pride' sung by Noël Coward, provided nostalgia and an undercurrent of sentimental sadness. But Vera Lynn perpetually singing 'We'll Meet Again' seemed cloying to a young sophisticate like myself until my brother, home on leave on a thirty-six-hour pass, gently rebuked me with 'Sentimental it may be, but – you'd be surprised – it can mean a lot to us.'

Every night Dick Barton spent fifteen minutes fighting his way out of trouble; *Monday Night at Seven* was promoted to *Monday Night at Eight*, and each Saturday the mighty roar of London's traffic – on disc – was stopped to introduce some famous celebrities. American comedy shows with Jack Benny and Rochester, Bob Hope, and Edgar Bergen and Charlie McCarthy were brilliant, but the funniest comedy show of all from abroad was the nasal Lord Haw-Haw broadcasting from Berlin each day and telling us our position was hopeless. Once in a while, when the situation looked blackest, we would hear the rumbling voice of Winston Churchill injecting us with adrenalin. Every few hours there was the drama of the news, with armies advancing; armies retreating; convoys attacked; battleships sunk; the long-drawn-out excitement of the sinking of the *Graf Spee*; the bombings and casualties in London, Coventry, Berlin, and the incredible day-by-day accounts of the Battle of Britain with details of planes shot down like massive football scores; the ups and downs of the Desert Army; the insane attack of the Germans on Russia; the advance to and defence of Stalingrad – and all read by Bruce Belfrage, Alvar Liddell or Joseph McLeod, who told us their names in case German parachutists had taken over the BBC.

When Mother found it difficult to pay the rent each week, she took in lodgers. First came three Indians on short government courses: Mr Singh, a Hindu with a turban which when unravelled revealed hair so long he could sit on it, Mr Bari, a tubby Mohammedan who was always laughing, and Mr Chita, a friendly little man who was an Untouchable. Individually life was fine with them, but when together the air grew tense with friction and no way could we reconcile the Mohammedan and the Hindu with the Untouchable. I learned that prejudice and class consciousness were not confined to the white man. After three months they completed their training course and left for fresh fields. They were followed by a nasty piece of work who sniffed around after my sister like a nervous ferret, but luckily he soon departed. Then Don arrived, a pleasant young man, who met and married a local girl and together they opened a dry-cleaning shop in Bedford.

Another evacuee from the London bombings was the BBC. We took in as lodgers two members of the BBC Symphony Orchestra, Joe Young who played violin and Jack Mackintosh who played the cornet. It was fascinating to hear them discussing the idiosyncrasies of their various conductors, Sir Henry Wood, Malcolm Sargent, Thomas Beecham and Adrian Boult, who was a great favourite. Once in a while I would see Boult, with his walrus moustache and wearing gum boots, walking through the Bedford streets, and I was as thrilled as I had been in even younger days on seeing the actor Conrad Veidt walking arm-in-arm with his wife down Platts Lane in Hampstead when I raced up to the Heath on Sunday mornings. Occasionally Jack and Joe would play tennis with Kay Cavendish and I went with them to act as ballboy. Kay Cavendish was well known at the time for her radio programme *Kay on the Keys*.

I have always held a grudge against Woolworths. In those days its proud slogan was 'nothing over sixpence' and one day while wandering through, possibly looking for Aileen Smith, I saw a salesgirl playing with a matted straw finger tube similar to the one I had bought after Aunt Annie died. That had disintegrated years before, but this was one of the six articles in a magic box which cost the top price of sixpence. So I ran home and collected sixpence that I had saved, rushed back to Woolworths and bought a box. Back home again I opened it and found five magic tricks but, alas, only an empty space where the finger tube should have been. Then I remembered the salesgirl playing with a tube. Furious, but uncertain how to cope with the situation, I returned to Woolworths and when the salesgirl's back was turned I took a finger tube from another box and put it in my pocket, but I was seen by the store detective and taken off to the manager. He lectured me for about twenty minutes, threatened me with the police, and said he would report me to my school. Desperately I proclaimed my innocence and told them what had occurred, but no one showed a glimmer of belief, and when I was released I had to wait with trepidation for several days, sure that I would be called forth by my headmaster and expelled. I was never called, but I did not have the matted straw finger. I have avoided Woolworths ever since.

In spite of the lodgers it was still difficult to make ends meet. I tried to help out by making calendars from cardboard, glue and pictures taken from art books; and during the holidays I did a paper round. The distance I had to cover was over six miles, and I dared not tell the newsagent that I did not possess a bicycle at that time or I would never have got the job. So I am afraid some unfortunate householders did not receive their morning papers until the afternoon. It was weeks before my pretence was discovered and I lost the job. At school it was proving more and more difficult to concentrate on work. The sixth formers were going straight off into the forces and when the Battle of Britain started they queued to get into the RAF. All too often only a few weeks after they had taken off their school caps for the last time the headmaster would read out their names among the latest casualties. Peter Senn was a tall Anglo-Indian and although I was a junior when he was a sixth former he was always friendly and treated me like an equal. It was not long after his leaving school that I saw him back in Bedford, elegant in his officer's uniform, covered in plaster and walking on crutches. His Wellington bomber had been hit and crashed. Luckily for him he was in the correct crouching position when the plane hit the ground, was thrown clear and was the only survivor. After the war he became a journalist, for some years on the William Hickey column on the *Daily Express* and I still see him from time to time.

'Lend a hand on the land,' said the posters everywhere, so during the holidays I would get up at dawn and clamber aboard a lorry with a group of Amazons who were the toughest collection of women I ever worked with. Always cheerful and telling filthy stories, which grew me up fast, they would lead the way collecting potatoes in the hard earth or the squelchy mud or threshing the hay, heaving the great piles into ricks.

> Roll me over – in the clover,
> Roll me over – lay me down
> And do it again

they sang with the fervour of anticipation. They taught me many useful things – like urinating on my hands to prevent blisters.

Gradually I started meeting girls. When I had a bicycle and dusk had fallen I would ride up to Russell Park with other boys and we would grin sheepishly and make remarks at giggling clusters of schoolgirls until gradually we found our partners and walked off together, pushing our bikes, chatted, kissed and cuddled surreptitiously and then rode off home. One evening I went to the Granada Cinema with my mother and joined the customary queue. Fortunately we had to wait for over an hour, because a beautiful young thing in a perky hat arrived with her mother and stood behind us. It started to rain and the long mass of people pressed together, sheltering against the wall. With furtive manoeuvring I managed to stand with the back of my hand gently touching hers. After a few minutes we drew even closer, both of us talking to our respective mothers as if unaware of any intimacy. Our bodies touched more frequently now, and we experienced little tremors of excitement. The queue moved inside the cinema and the magic was broken. We were ushered to different rows. When the film finished my mother and I were walking home when I saw the little girl in the perky hat and her mother on the other side of the street. Kismet. I could not let the opportunity pass. 'I'll catch you up in a minute,' I said to my mother, and ran across the road waving to the girl. She left her mother and approached me.

'Can you come to the pictures with me?' I asked, with nervous bravado.

'Next Monday at the Granada,' she replied, just as nervously.

'Seven thirty,' I said.

'Seven thirty,' said she.

And I ran to catch up with my mother.

The following Monday I was waiting in the one and ninepenny queue – I had chosen the most expensive seats to impress her – when she arrived. We introduced ourselves then silently waited in the queue, silently sat through the movie, and I silently walked her home. 'Goodnight,' she said.

'Goodnight,' I replied – and left.

A few weeks later I was walking through the rain from the Picturedrome when I saw her perky little hat, almost hidden under a large umbrella, going in the opposite direction. 'Hello,' I said.

'Hello,' said she.

'Can I walk you home?' I said.

'If you like,' said she. A few yards from her home she said, 'You had better leave me here.'

'All right,' I said. 'Can I kiss you?'

'If you like,' said she.

Fumbling nervously I squeezed under the umbrella and passionately held her to me. I pressed my mouth on hers. She reciprocated.

'Goodnight,' she said.

'Goodnight.'

I never saw her again.

Then, suddenly, there was Mary Collins. I had never met her – never even seen her – when she sent me a note inviting me to her party. She was very pretty and vivacious with red hair and freckles and a younger brother. Her father was a musician playing for the BBC. The party was a success. We spent many evenings at her house, flirting quietly while her younger brother made jokes about us. We got on well and never argued, but then went our separate ways.

Zena, my brother's wife, came to stay with Mother and me while Paddy was away. His weekend leaves were very rare, but having her near was a great comfort. Then she became pregnant and my nephew Richard was born and she and my brother got a flat in Brentwood in Essex, where he was stationed. Sometimes Mother and I would visit her and listen to records of Jean Sablon and Bing Crosby. I grew older, more sophisticated and met friends at the Kardomah Café for coffee. My only schoolfriend was Vivian Moses, and he and I would cycle along together and talk with great assurance about life and the future. Recently I met up with him again and felt the same easy relationship we had felt before. He is now a professor of biochemistry, but at the time neither of us had a clue which direction our careers would take.

I met Jill, Anne and Liz who could say 'Anyone for tennis?' without sounding jokey. If there had not been a war they would have been skiing in Switzerland or at finishing school in France. Jill's father had been head of ICI in Japan and had a country cottage a few miles from Bedford where they ate jugged hare and drank Pimm's. I spent more and more time at the cottage while other boyfriends stood on their heads a great deal of the time. We would listen to records of Glenn Miller and Tommy Dorsey with the young Frank Sinatra warbling away as part of a backing group. 'Perfidia' became my favourite song. It was a new world for me and, despite a feeling of guilt, with my mother scrimping away at home, I enjoyed it. Glenn Miller and his orchestra were stationed nearby and his piano player was a frequent guest at the cottage.

I remember saying goodbye to him when the orchestra was flying off. 'Is Glenn Miller going with you?' I asked.

'No,' he replied, 'he's gone on ahead.'

Of course we heard later that he never arrived.

By now the tide had turned. The invincible Third Reich was skidding on thin ice and it was our turn to cross the Channel. When D-Day arrived my brother's company headed the first attack – but without Paddy. He had to stay behind to have his appendix removed. By this time he was a first lieutenant about to be made captain, and he felt a strong bond with his comrades. Most of them were killed during those first few days in France and Paddy felt strangely guilty. We thought it was fate. But he had only a few days to convalesce and then he would be going over to France. He spent a few days with Zena and Richard and one morning he took Mother and me to see an early show in London – Walt Disney's *Dumbo*. It was too sentimental by far:

> Baby Mine, don't you cry,
> Baby Mine, dry your eye,
> Rest your head close to my breast . . . Baby of mine

sang the mother elephant to the lonely Dumbo. Mother's eyes glistened suspiciously. Then we went off to a late lunch. It was a good day. Paddy crossed the Channel, my father was a major in India and Mother and I went back to Bedford.

Mother received a letter from Paddy. A pacifist, he fought only because he felt Hitler and his followers had created an evil that had to be stopped. In his letter he wrote that probably a few yards from him was a German soldier who was as much against war as he was. 'Yet if either of us raises his head,' he wrote, 'the other has to kill. It is sad and crazy that it should come to this.'

Mother was very superstitious and convinced she had second sight. 'I heard an owl hoot last night,' she said at breakfast one morning. She had reason for her superstitions. In the First World War, Paddy, then a baby, was asleep in his cot during a Zeppelin raid. In the next room Mother was supposed to be playing cards with her friends, but, increasingly agitated, she could stand it no longer and ran and grabbed the sleeping baby out of the cot. As she did so a bullet from our own guns shot through the open window; the cot was in the firing line. Apparently, my mother fainted. Years later when Barbie, my sister, was also a baby my mother and Barbie shared the same bedroom. Paddy usually slept on the floor below, but one night my mother made him sleep in the same room. That night there was a gas leak on the floor below and Paddy's room was thick with gas before it was discovered.

One morning, shortly after the hooting of the owl, I was cleaning my shoes when my mother called me. Very white and calm she handed me a telegram. 'We regret to inform you that your son is missing.' I remember the feeling of numbness and strange dispassionate disassociation as I went back to polish my other shoe. After a few more days Zena received another telegram. This time it said, 'Missing believed killed' and that was the end of official communications. For many years Mother believed Paddy could still be alive. She talked of the times at school he had been concussed and lost his memory for long periods. Maybe he was still alive somewhere – the past forgotten. Years later Zena was contacted by a corporal who had been with my brother on that last day. They had been on reconnaissance in a minefield when they had been picked up by a party of Germans. Impulsively my brother socked one on the jaw, kicked another in the balls, jumped over a hedge and was never seen again. The corporal was taken prisoner and so it was long before he could tell the story. After the war Zena moved with young Richard and her family to America. It was fourteen years before she married again. She met Ken Fitzgerald when they were both working for the *New York Herald Tribune*. He is a tall, gentle man with a wry sense of humour. He and Zena make a delightful couple, and he has been a good father to Richard.

School had become very heavy going and I was determined to get into the theatre. After all, I thought, that was the best way to get into films – my real love. It was the Lewis Milestone movie of *Of Mice and Men* which had decided the issue. I had seen it eight times in one week. One day I hitchhiked up to London and went to *Gone with the Wind*, which I have since seen several times and is now one of my favourite movies. But the first time I had to pay six

37

shillings to get in and my feelings of guilt clouded my appreciation of what I was seeing. As a child I was never interested in collecting autographs, although I did once send off for a glossy photo, with a stamped signature, of Olivia de Havilland which I kept under my pillow at night for a time. At school the only subjects I showed any real interest in were English and art. The latter I did as an alternative to chemistry and I used to sit in a class where I was the only pupil. I even got an offer to go to the Slade School of Art which was then in Oxford, but the magnet of show business was pointing my way. I scraped through mock matriculation except for Latin, which was essential, and then went to see my headmaster and told him I wanted to leave school to be an actor. I was fifteen. He was flabbergasted. 'But you have never been in any of the school plays,' he said. It was true – the Dramatic Society would never take me on; I could not even get into the chorus of *Cyrano de Bergerac*. I told him that even that enormous obstacle would not deter me.

'Well, I think you are very unwise,' he said, 'but if you are determined let me give you a piece of advice. Let me put it this way. Recently I had to go to a tailor for a new suit, and he took far more measurements than were actually necessary.' He paused and took a breath while he waited for the enormity of this to sink in. 'There are a lot of people like that in the theatre!'

And that was that. I left school. I was free. Today, of course, I regret it. I regret not learning languages. I regret not going to university. But they were unusual times. And I thought I might be able to earn a little money to ease my mother's burden. As it proved I was never much help.

I went to work in a brewery – Mitchell and Butlers in Bedford – heaving barley sacks and cleaning up mess. We were given eight pints of beer a day free – two before breakfast. I have never been able to drink beer in England since. The majority of workers there were a tough bunch of Liverpool Irish. Whereas they downed their beer quota on the spot, I used to take mine home. I was ignored and made to feel like a creature from another world, which I was, until by chance I tipped them a horse which came in at thirty-three to one. Then on my way to the brewery one day I crashed my bicycle and had to spend some time at home recovering from my bruises. Farewell Mitchell and Butlers. So I got another job, in a tomato processing factory, putting permanganate of potash in the soil to make the fruit a deeper red. Next I worked in a dairy cleaning bottles. I wore a long leather apron which gradually congealed with stale milk until the smell became overwhelming. 'Ah me,' I thought grandly, 'this is the experience of life. This is the way I learn to act.'

Then, joy of joys, I got a job backstage at Bedford's Royal County Theatre, working in the flies, which gave me an aerial view of the stage, and then spending all Saturday night and the weekend getting shows in and out. My first smell of greasepaint. My first contact with the absurd, lovable world of the theatre. How lucky to start with the world of variety – a world now gone alas! – where the people were the warmest, friendliest, the most conscientious and hardworking I have ever known. And what pride they had in their jobs. The first revue I worked on was *Soldiers in Skirts*, perhaps the original drag show, done by members of the American forces. I am sure my former headmaster would have thought it was a company of tailors. Maybe it was fortunate I was up in the flies. I remember the camp way the soldiers danced the 'Floradora', pursing their lips and twirling their skirts.

> Oh tell me, pretty lady – are there any naughty things you do?
> Well just a few, kind sir – and some of them are just for you.

And the title song went thus:

> Night after night in the army
> I dream such a lonely dream,
> It's not that I miss the cup final,
> Or strawberries and Devonshire cream.
> It isn't the lights of the city,
> So maybe I should explain
> What's on my brain.
> I keep dreaming of skirts-da-de-da-de-da,
> Skirts-da-de-da-de-da.
> Through a thousand alerts,
> But it's plain old GI whackie I see all day.

It was monstrous and adorable.

Soldiers in Skirts was followed by a series of touring revues. The sets were tatty, the costumes gaudy and the make-up heavy. But the lighting with the follow spots, the floats, the blues and ambers, the raucous brassiness of the band, the shrill voices of the cheerful, high-kicking chorus line, and the wicked humour of the North Country comics with their outrageous rapport with the delighted audiences, created an aura of sheer uncomplicated fun and friendship we rarely see today. It is hard to imagine Noël Coward's sad, sophisticated 'Poor Little Rich Girl' sung by a group of slightly off-key semi-strippers in blue tinsel as a moving experience. But it was. In one show I was besotted by a young girl who sang 'Wrong, Would it be Wrong to Kiss' in the first half, and 'Ave Maria' in the second. She had a high-pitched, whiny voice, was always nervous before she went on, and I adored her. But her glance never strayed up into the flies. As the girls left the stage door each would be grabbed by either arm by pairs of American soldiers who were waiting outside with their cartons of cigarettes, silk stockings and tins of coffee, and the next day I would listen open-mouthed as the girls boasted to each other of their conquests.

By the time the Americans had come into the war all that the young English could remember was a utility existence. Utility clothes. Utility food. No fruit. No cigarettes. No coffee. Queues for everything. We were used to a simple life of order and managing to do without. Our colours were greys and browns, serviceable and dull. Like living in an outdoor prison. Then the Yanks arrived with their packets of goodies, undisciplined and easy-going, brash and confident. The older generation regarded them with narrowed, suspicious eyes. The young girls saw them as Clark Gable, Gary Cooper or John Garfield. They were supermen with humour. They were different and with their packs of goodies they were wealthy. The English had spent the last century as leaders of an empire and had developed a natural superiority as if the whole country had been schooled at Eton, but now lease-lend was on the way, a great psychological change was taking place. And barriers were tumbling, within the country itself. Early in the war the lady of the manor would help out at Toc H, pouring tea or dressing wounds in hospitals, but as the years went by their daughters worked as landgirls or in the factories alongside their former servants. And people could no longer afford to have or to be servants. There is a story told against himself by a famous actor, now dead. He was travelling alone in a non-smoking, first-class train compartment. A soldier got in, unshaven and dishevelled, with his knapsack, and lit up a cigarette. The old actor leaned forward and pointed to the 'No Smoking' sign. The soldier looked at the sign, looked at the actor, then opened up his shirt and jacket revealing makeshift bandages and a badly stitched wound. Then he buttoned up his shirt and calmly continued with his cigarette.

One memorable week Tod Slaughter appeared at the County

Theatre in his most famous role – and the one that had inspired his name, *Sweeney Todd*. Lit by white or green spots, he would hiss at the audience and they, with relish, hissed back. The rest of the company were pretty dreadful, but he skilfully skated between the boundaries of comedy and horror and took his bows at the end of the evening to loud applause. When the reception died down he would step forward and make a speech to the audience and I suspect he enjoyed this more than the show itself. One night, as he stepped forward, I pressed the wrong button, the theatre curtains (or tabs as we called them) were drawn across him, and the theatre band played 'God Save the King'.

Tod Slaughter stood on the stage, cursed and shook his fist at me, and it was thirty minutes before I dared to come down. By that time I knew it was safe – because the pubs were closing.

How was I to embark on my career? I had no contacts. No idea where to start. My father had always claimed that the well-known playwright Rodney Ackland was a cousin, so one day I hitchhiked up to London, looked up his telephone number in the directory, and nervously called him. 'I'm Jocelyn Ackland,' I said, 'and I'm your cousin. Is it possible for me to come and see you?'

'Of course,' he replied. 'Come around and have a drink.'

He lived at Albany with its exclusive bachelor pads, off Piccadilly. Other theatrical celebrities who lived there were Terence Rattigan and Edith Evans. Rodney, a gentle, kindly, nervous man, ushered me into his elegant apartment, introduced me to a couple of Australian flight lieutenants and handed me an enormous pink gin which I casually accepted as if it were my fifth that day.

Before I had finished my drink the Australians fuzzily took their leave and Rodney said, 'Now sit down and tell me what it is you want.'

'I don't want anything,' I said. 'I'm your cousin.'

'That's strange,' smiled Rodney, 'my real name isn't Ackland.'

I wanted to sink through the floor. Silently I wanted to curse my father's blarney. 'I'm sorry – I'd better go,' I said.

'Just relax and sit down,' said Rodney, and he generously topped up my unfinished drink.

I sat down. I told him what my father had told me, how it had all been a mistake and how I wanted to get into the theatre. Rodney said perhaps we were related, because the name Ackland came from his mother's side of the family and maybe we were second cousins. Then he told me it was possible he could help me get started in the theatre, and he sat down and wrote a letter to

41

Gwyneth Thurburn, the new principal of the Central School of Speech Training and Dramatic Art. He told me he had been a student there just after Laurence Olivier and Peggy Ashcroft, but he was so nervous as an actor he had been made to say his lines in rehearsal lying flat on his back on the stage. He also mentioned a movie, to be called *Hungry Hill*, with Robert Newton, and said he would suggest me for the young boy's part. With eyes like saucers I thanked him, left the flat, and walked out into a muzzy, whirling Piccadilly.

That night I stayed with my sister Barbie in town without being aware that I had taken my first step towards being an actor. Life changed very suddenly and very drastically. I had to go for my interview and audition for the Central School. As usual I hitchhiked to London from Bedford, and was given a lift in her little car by a woman in the uniform of the Women's Voluntary Service. As we drove through the open farmland, along a small rough road, I caught sight of a man cutting his way through the corn – a lonely figure amidst hundreds of acres of empty fields. He was clutching a bottle and singing with all the fervour and freedom of drink. 'Good grief,' I said to the driver, 'do you know who that was?' By this time we had left the fellow along with the corn and the open sky.

'Who?' she said.

'Robert Newton,' I said, still amazed at the sight of the great actor. 'I'm probably going to be in a film with him,' I added grandly.

'Which film is that?' asked the WVS lady.

'*Hungry Hill*,' I replied.

'That's interesting,' she said. 'My cousin wrote that.'

'Who is your cousin?' I asked.

'Daphne du Maurier,' said she.

Later she sent me a copy of the book signed by her cousin and I said I would return it. I have always had a feeling of guilt that I lost her address and was unable to do so. And I never did get the part. It was played by a young boy, Peter Murray, who for many years now has been the well-known disc jockey. In the film he played opposite a young actress called Jean Simmons, then in her teens.

Getting into the Central School in those days was simple. I was given a form asking me if I could afford to pay. I wrote 'no' and became a drama student. Then I discovered why. As it was wartime there were two hundred and fifty girl members of the school and four men. Such was the shortage of manpower that for actual productions we had to recruit amateurs from outside to fill some of the roles. So just after my fourth real birthday, I left my mother in Bedford and moved into a flat with my sister in North London, in Belsize Park. Barbie had come down from Oxford. Always active politically, she had been secretary of the Communist Party as a student and was now sub-editor on the *Daily Worker*. Barbie shared the flat with her friend, Eve, and Eve's younger brother Mark, both of them also journalists on different newspapers. The Central School in those days was situated within the Albert Hall in Kensington. Because of our BBC lodgers in Bedford I had been able to attend concerts there and watch the great conductor; now I could continue to do so as the glorious sounds reverberated through the massive building.

Once I started at the Central School I experienced a strange feeling of guilt. What was I doing there? I had been alive sixteen years and now I was surrounded by sophisticated young ladies who were either treating the time as their finishing school because they couldn't get to Switzerland, or dedicated young ladies who were eager to become speech therapists and teachers, and of course the few ambitious young actresses. Of the men, George Rose left as I arrived; George Cooper, who loved the traditions and greasepaint of the theatre, had come from a Cockney family and changed his natural speaking voice to the deep tones of a Henry Irving by listening to records of John Gielgud; Maxwell Reed, from the Merchant Navy, who shaved his eyebrows, looked good and had been put under contract by Alexander Korda; and Jack Taylor, a lovable character in his thirties, who ran a devious business in Soho and whose friends were villains in black cars with sliding windows. With his Gioconda smile and slightly American George Sanders-type drawl, he was obviously a man of know-how who regarded the theatre as an amusing *divertissement*. And why was I there? I was ambitious, but I always felt that I was there by chance, not through talent. It was a fluke. I was a huckster. Pure luck. Forty years later I still have the same feeling.

I enjoyed the Central School. Lucky I may be, but at last I felt I belonged. An entirely new world. My mother moved back from Bedford and took a flat in Marloes Road, opposite St Mary Abbot's Hospital, just off Kensington High Street, so I was able to walk to the Albert Hall in a few minutes. By this time my mother and father were no longer married. He had obtained the divorce to marry an eighteen-year-old girl, but instead returned to his Irish mistress of many years in Maida Vale. Once again my mother took in lodgers: Hugh Sibley, a photographer; Alison Browne, who became a stage manager; and Yolande Bird, who had been up at Oxford with my sister and today works for the National Theatre.

Owing to the shortage of men at the Central School, there was little chance for me to do my full quota of studying theatrical history or learning to speak clearly by placing little pegs between my teeth. I enjoyed improvisation and being a teapot or a three-legged camel, but I never found out what to do with my diaphragm – I still breathe out when I should breathe in. It was a consolation when I heard that Ralph Richardson did the same. Most of the time I was learning plays – Restoration, modern, Shakespeare – and gradually my legs and arms became less and less impediments attached to a nervous, shaking body.

I have read Stanislavsky's *My Life in Art* three times. Once before I went to the Central School, and found his reasoning difficult to follow; once when I was there, when I thought, 'Ah, now I understand; what brilliant logic!'; and once, a few years later, when I thought, 'What a naïve, heavy-handed way of stating the obvious!' But I realise now it was a natural process. One should never forget or despise that marvellous feat of learning to tie a shoelace.

Not only was I lucky enough to be in so many plays – there was another bonus. I used to slip along to watch rehearsals, at the New Theatre, of the Old Vic Company, and there could have been no finer training ground for any actor. I watched the creation of Ralph Richardson's Falstaff and Cyrano de Bergerac, Laurence Olivier's Richard III, Oedipus and Hotspur, the superb ensemble playing in *Arms and the Man*, the wiles and wickedness of that great director Tyrone Guthrie at work. And what a company! Sybil Thorndike, Joyce Redman, Harry Andrews, Margaret Leighton, George Relph, Alec Guinness, Nicholas Hannen, Sidney Tafler, Michael Warre among them.

Meanwhile at the Central School we decided to put on a revue, and I wrote a golfing sketch which I started to rehearse. One day, Maxwell Reed was watching and he said, 'You can't do that – everyone will know you copied it from Sid Field.'

'Who is Sid Field?' I asked.

'He's in *Strike a New Note* at the Prince of Wales,' he said.

So I queued to see it and experienced an evening of perfection that I shall never forget. From the first moment the amiable bear of a man walked on stage he held the whole audience under his control. It was impossible not to love him. Impossible to define his timing, his warmth and above all the extraordinary rapport he seemed to have with every individual in the house. His photographer's sketch, his golfing sketch, his cinema organ sketch and his Slasher Green sketches left everyone weak with laughter. Night after night I stood at the back to see the show and the ones that followed. *Strike It Again* and *Piccadilly Hayride*. At one performance I remember the entire audience were standing, holding their sides with laughter, and the man next to me was carried out by medical attendants, literally ill with paroxysms of mirth.

I never did do my golfing sketch.

At home, as usual, Mother struggled to make ends meet, and so, quite against the Central School rules, I got a late afternoon and evening job washing walls at the American Services Club in Hans Crescent, Knightsbridge. For a thirty-hour week I earned thirty shillings, but the canteen food contained goodies I had never seen and occasionally I was given a packet of cigarettes to take home.

After a year at the Central School, Julian Somers, the actor, who was directing a play at the school, took a few of us along to meet Michael Powell the film director. He told me that there would not be much opportunity for me in movies, because I looked too like a rising young actor called Gordon Jackson.

A short time later I was asked if I would like to carry a spear with the Old Vic Company. While I was thinking about it I heard through Rodney Ackland that *The Hasty Heart*, a new play by John Patrick, was being cast at the Aldwych Theatre, and with Rodney's recommendation, and without telling anyone at Central, I applied for an understudy. One morning I stood backstage with a group of out-of-work actors. My name was called and for the first time I stepped out on to a proper stage, with a single working light, and looked out into the blackness behind the floats where, somewhere hiding between the empty seats, were two or three people who would settle my fate. A voice called up from the darkened auditorium. 'You're very young. Can you do an American accent?'

'Oh yes, sir.' After all, I had not washed walls in Hans Crescent for nothing.

'Right, you had better read Yank. Read away.' A script was thrust into my hand, and I read. There was a pause – then a muffled discussion. Another pause, then, 'Thank you, young man. Wait behind, will you?'

I waited. When all the readings were over a tubby man with an eye that seemed to revolve uncontrollably called me over to the side of the stage. 'Right,' he said, 'you can understudy Yank and Kiwi. Have you got an agent?'

'No, sir,' I said, scarcely daring to draw breath.

'Well, that's lucky,' he said. 'You don't have to pay commission. A tenner all right for you?'

'Fine, sir,' I said.

'Right,' he said, 'we'll give you a contract.'

I walked out of the stage door, down towards the Strand, and started to cross the main busy thoroughfare. 'Ten pounds a month, that's more than I get at Hans Crescent.' Then I realised it was not ten pounds a month – it was ten pounds a week. I stopped dead in the middle of the road and cars shrieked to a halt all around me. Ten pounds – a week! I continued my way towards the safety of the pavement and I had just reached there in time when my legs started to shake as the real impact hit me.

I was an actor.

THREE

The war was over. We gathered together *en masse* at Piccadilly Circus and danced and sang and cheered. The last shot had been fired, but the war had really ended earlier when the Americans dropped the most powerful bomb ever on Hiroshima. An atom bomb it was called. When we heard what damage was done we were very sad. But it was worth it. There would be fewer casualties in the long run, because it would hasten the conclusion of the carnage. So we believed. We had no conception that from the moment the first atom was split the world would never be the same again.

No longer was the human race indestructible. The new generation of children grew up with the knowledge that their planet could destroy itself at any time. There was no definite future. No God. No conscience.

The first days of peace brought no reward. There was no victory parade. We did not grow rich as our soldiers returned with their spoils of war. The country was bruised and lame and poor and tired. Churchill, a giant in war, was now an embarrassing reminder of pomp and circumstance and had been thrown aside in the elections as people chose quiet normality after years of combat.

The world seemed to consist of would-be actors, who flocked out of the services, men much older than myself, their careers having been curtailed by six years of waste, many who just wanted a life without regimentation. Once again I had the sensation of being a fraud, of being an actor simply because there had been no competition; because I had been lucky enough to be young. I was unaware at the time that I had learned much at the Central, but all the improvisation, breathing exercises, playing diverse roles – old, young, funny, sad; plastering my face with sticks of greasepaint; conquering nerves, and turning cardboard sets into reality in my mind – had unknowingly given me that sixth sense: a sense of theatre.

Working in the Albert Hall environment watching rehearsals with the fiery bombastic Sir Thomas Beecham and the precise dandy Malcolm Sargent was bound to have some influence and I began to relax and meld with different groups. Mentally I developed the habit of playing different roles all the time. I could not stop acting.

47

On buses I would talk to conductors in a foreign accent. If I saw an attractive girl I could not let her go by and would walk up to her either shyly or with confidence, with sophistication or with an accent or a dialect – whichever I felt would be effective. Often I would be a lonely American. Even after the war this often paid dividends. Then, if a relationship grew, I would have to keep up the pretence until the relationship petered out or I lost confidence. I could play Don Juan but I could never live the part. Beneath the façade was always the boy who was lost in awe at the beauty of the opposite sex. I could never be dispassionate. I could never forget the hurt in my mother's eyes on those trips to Birmingham.

However, I was in the theatre and I was working. I had left the Central School after only eighteen months convinced that more training was not necessary. I was at the Aldwych and was ready for the big time. Success lay ahead. So many possibilities . . . *The Hasty Heart*, a sentimental piece about a dying Scottish soldier, clutched at the heart-strings and the turnstiles clicked for eighteen months.

Apart from understudying, for an extra pound a week I started off as assistant stage manager and call boy. Not very successfully, because I was gently relieved of the responsibility and the pound. At the theatre I got dreadfully bored. Night after night at the Aldwych plus two matinées sitting in a dressing-room in case either John McLaren as Yank or Nicholas Parsons as Kiwi did not turn up. Mornings and afternoons I would sneak across Covent Garden into the back of the New Theatre to watch Richardson and Olivier rehearsing and I kicked myself for not joining the company.

On February 13th, 1946, I arrived at the Aldwych fifteen minutes before the play was due to begin. A stern-looking stage director stood outside the stage door with various members of the management. "Cripes," I thought, "I'm for it." But the stage director put his arm around me. 'Take it easy, lad,' he said. 'John McLaren is ill – you're on.'

I was in a dream. Everything, everybody, appeared unreal. I was led into a strange dressing-room. In front of the mirror were sticks of greasepaint which I wiped over my cold face. Strange figures helped me into pyjamas and directed me on to the stage. The action of the play took place in an army hospital ward in Burma so I was helped into bed and tucked up under a mosquito net. Through the tight mesh I stared blankly at the heavy curtain which protected me from the thousand people who chatted gaily in the auditorium. Their enthusiasm might have been a little dampened if they had realised that the thirty-year-old Yank, perhaps the longest part in the play, was to be performed by a totally inexperienced seventeen-year-old. The curtain rose. The final curtain fell. In between those two moments I remember little. A strange numbness seeped through my body as if I had been tranquillised before an operation. Even Jerry Verno, who played the Cockney soldier in the next bed, did not fluster me when he tried to help by hissing or prodding me whenever I had to speak! Apparently I remembered my lines, got my laughs and did not fall over the furniture.

John McLaren returned the next day and I never played Yank again, but later I played the dull role of Kiwi for three weeks when Nicholas Parsons was ill.

After some months with *The Hasty Heart* I directed *Winterset* by Maxwell Anderson for one matinée performance at the Twentieth Century Theatre, Notting Hill Gate. Most of the cast were junior members of the Old Vic with Jane Wenham as Miriamne and George Rose as Mio. Apart from directing and producing the piece I also played the tragic gangster Shadow, covered in tomato ketchup for my death scene. After many months in *The Hasty Heart*, I had managed to save eighty pounds. This I spent putting on the show, but one reasonable house would get my money back. However, London's premier management, H. M. Tennent, tried to stop me putting on the play as they had plans for a London production, and the only way that I could avoid this was by doing the show for charity. I even had a telephone call at the Aldwych threatening me with being blacklisted in the theatre if I continued with the production. It was a dilemma, but the cast had learned their lines.

We did it for charity and I lost all my savings.

Some years later *The Hasty Heart* was filmed. I besieged Bob Lennard, the casting director, to see if I could get the part of Yank. It was decided to have an American flown over to help distribution in America. Not a star necessarily, but they did want a recognisable name. Anyway they wanted someone much older than me. They got Ronald Reagan.

After a year I had to leave *The Hasty Heart*. I had received my call-up papers and at the age of eighteen I was made to swell the army ranks. The morning after a farewell party I left to join my platoon in Brentwood in Essex. Then I had to return. I had misread my papers. I had gone a day early.

49

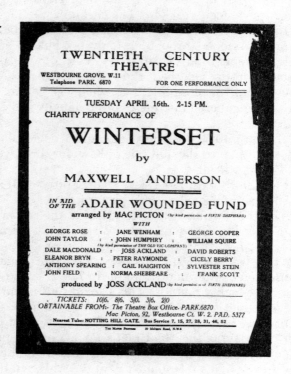

My army life bombed. Scheduled to last for eighteen months, it proved to be a very short run. In the theatre I have been in an abundance of flops, but this was a lulu.

Being one of the lads came easier to me now. Unlike school, where most of the boys had come from a similar background, my platoon was a very mixed bunch. I was able to observe and absorb, and meld into this mixed bag, with mates who varied from a Middlesex lad who had volunteered as a regular in order to play the saxophone, to a Glaswegian from the Gorbals with a razor-blade concealed in his boot for 'emergencies'.

However, after only a few weeks I was threatened with imprisonment, after a contretemps with a young lieutenant during a half-hour political discussion – officially without rank. The discussion turned out to be a lecture proposing we made use of the atom bomb before the Russians could develop one. When I suggested that this would be following Hitler's example the trouble started. Two weeks later I was interviewed by the Personnel Selection Officer.

'Would you like a commission?' he asked.

I paused before replying. It meant a further six months in the army – but the hell with it. 'Yes, sir,' I replied.

'Would you like to go to Palestine?'

'No thank you, sir.'

The eyes facing me froze. 'Are you a Jew?'

'No, sir.'

'Is it because of religious reasons?'

'No, sir.'

The eyes narrowed. There was a pause. 'Come back this afternoon and see the psychiatrist.'

I did. A woman. The same questions. The same replies. A very unusual psychiatrist – I thought she would froth at the mouth. The sergeant standing behind her gave me an encouraging wink as she gave an apoplectic scream and asked me to wait outside. I did. After a few minutes the PSO stormed up to me. He was very angry. 'If you want to be an officer, you will be an officer! If we want you to go to Palestine, you will go to Palestine! Is that understood?'

'Yes, sir – but you did ask.'

A few days later I was told to report to the medical officer who informed me that I was discharged from the army.

I was shattered and confused. Relieved but embarrassed. There were many who made it a full-time occupation trying to get out of the army, feigning madness, homosexuality and even stabbing their hands and feet with bayonets – to no avail. I was out. Not only without effort but also unprepared. I had been fired. Returning to Civvy Street was a treat, but I did not care for the form of transport. Back home, armed with a demob suit, an honourable discharge and a hat two sizes too large, the dangerous military anarchist became an uncertain shy boy seeking a path into the theatrical wilderness.

Never for a moment did I consider the possibility of failing as an actor. This was neither confidence nor vanity. It was blind optimism. I was a gambler perpetually putting my wage packet on a blind number on the roulette wheel – except that I had no wage packet. The insecurity of my childhood had denied me firm roots. I have always been a maverick revelling in changes, crossing my fingers as I round a corner but excited at the prospect of new horizons. Never have I understood the joy in being a caterpillar, confined and secure; to me the magic of life starts with the butterfly colourfully soaring through its brief existence.

I needed work.

Each day I would walk and bus into town, bombarding every agent's office around Wardour Street. An actor's only contact with work is through an agent, and the first big hurdle is to obtain a sole agent, someone who has your name on his or her books, who works for that list of names alone. Some agents dealt only with small projects such as Ministry of Information shorts or one-line parts in second feature movies. Occasionally the word would get around that a dockyard or a courtroom scene was being shot that day and the office of the agent concerned, and the stairs leading up to it, would be crowded with eager desperate thespians laughing and joking and saying they didn't know why they bothered to come as they did not really need the job anyway and they had something good coming up. Then a figure would appear, glance quickly around the assembled throng and, with a muttered, 'You-you-you and you', would depart with the few chosen lucky ones. Gradually I discovered which agents would tolerate my perpetual visits, even if no work ever materialised. Felix de Wolfe and Richard Stone became quite friendly and I would sit in their office and listen to them arranging deals with actors who actually worked.

Much time was spent in writing off to the hundreds of repertory theatres which flourished in the forties. Every small town possessed one as well as a variety theatre. Every week a different play was presented. Audiences liked the familiarity of seeing the same actors trying their hand at different roles. A relationship was formed across the footlights and much loneliness was relieved that way. Today audiences watch their weekly rep on television with *Coronation Street, Eastenders, Neighbours, Dallas* and *Emmerdale Farm*, but instead of seeing a broad spectrum of plays, it is the same never-ending saga and the eyes no longer meet over the footlights. Audiences are no longer participants – merely voyeurs.

For the actor reps were a wonderful training ground. He was for ever playing a diverse selection of roles in farce, tragedy, drama, sophisticated comedy, the occasional Shakespeare or Restoration pieces, even pantomime. He could make mistakes and learn by them. Of course there were dangers. Only the surface of a good play could be acquired in a week – it was difficult enough to learn the lines in such a short time. Mannerisms could be acquired and insecurity could lead to a desperate search for cheap laughs. But if an actor could progress to two-weekly, or, the much sought after cream of the provinces, three-weekly rep there could be no finer way to learn his craft.

The young man with strange, faintly Asiatic features stands back-stage in the cramped passage of the tiny Arts Theatre off Leicester Square, nervously adjusts his toga and adds little strokes of white greasepaint beneath his cat's eyes. Surreptitiously I take note and determine to do the same in the future. Paul Scofield is preparing for a performance of Christopher Fry's *A Phoenix Too Frequent*, running alternately with *The Rising Sun* by Herman Heijermans in which I play a small part. My director is the intelligent actress Beatrix Lehmann who is to lead the following summer's Shake-speare season at the Stratford Memorial Theatre. Her friend Walter Hudd is in charge of the company and he asks me to audition. I do not take it too seriously. My ambition is to work in a modern group theatre similar to the one in New York that I have just read about in Harold Clurman's *The Fervent Years*.

It is November 1946. I read a passage from *Macbeth* and one from *Romeo and Juliet*. I do not even learn them. They must be very late in casting, because in January 1947 I join the grey figures fighting through the snow and, with my duffel coat and scarf tightly wound around me, I bus and walk to cold rehearsal-rooms in Holloway, North London. The icy cold winter might be an omen. Rain, snow and hailstones fall thick and turn to slush in the grey streets. Food is still strictly rationed and people move aimlessly through biting winds in heavy utility clothes and Tootal ties. Like an army of ants the war has broken our formation and now, in a confused mass, we strive to find some sort of direct line. Men and women pour out of the forces and find their dreams of the security of home shattered. Promises made by former employers are not kept. Business is business. But the war has paid its toll. People are not angry. They are confused, hurt and disillusioned.

The enormous hall is heated only by a couple of stoves set apart from each other. Around them huddle clumps of actors – dozens of them. I am part of a massive company. Is it going to be like school again? But these are different creatures from yet another world. They appear casual and unimpressed. Once again I realise that I am one of the youngest, yet the director of *Romeo and Juliet* and *Love's Labour's Lost* is only two years older than I. He is small and his large collar seems to envelop his birdlike, bespectacled face. But his nervous blinks and high, overexcited stammer do nothing

53

to lessen his obvious intelligence and assurance and I become more conscious of my arms and legs which seem to be pinned incorrectly on to my body. The aged boy is Peter Brook and other directors include Tyrone Guthrie's disciple Michael Benthall from Eton, Oxford and the army; Nugent Monk, the aged amateur from the Maddermarket Theatre in Norwich; and of course Walter (Dickie) Hudd, pert and precise. The leading actor is Robert Harris, world-weary and casually dressed, but his shoes look handmade. The ice on the overcoats begins to melt, the steam rises and I realise that I am working with the boffins of the boards.

The small town of Stratford is a smug and pretty possessive mother which sells its cream teas and pictures of its favourite son to the world's visitors. Those less fortunate creatures born outside its environs it treats with compassion and sympathy. The Memorial Theatre is a family album of their son's work and any actor should be proud to have walked its boards and stood in William's aura.

The snow has turned to heavy slush and the frozen River Avon has burst its banks. The only way to reach the theatre to rehearse is by rowboat. Gradually the company sorts itself out into groups and we click the shutters of our camera and take our personal pictures of the rest which are liable to stay imprinted in our minds for ever. I share a dressing-room with five others: John Warner, full of fun and friendly exuberance; David Oxley, smooth, good-looking and obviously plays tennis at Roehampton; Julian Amyes, older, wiser, who twinkles sardonically; George Cooper – *the* George Cooper who stayed for long periods with my mother and myself at Marloes Road but who is now aloof and distant; and a boy actor who has a cat which eats my greasepaint.

Again I am a fish out of water. I become an extrovert loner and retire outside myself. Everything I do is disastrous. If I touch a piece of scenery it falls down. If I take a step I fall over. If I run on stage I am too early or too late. The more I try to control events the bigger the disaster that follows. Even the most tolerant members of the company sigh as I approach. I try to cover up with laughter and jokes and the atmosphere fogs up even more, and I go through hell.

And what snapshots is my little camera taking? Beatrix Lehmann twinkling benignly when I trip her on stage. Duncan Ross, red-haired and older, who buys me a cup of tea and sympathetically asks me if I realise what opportunities there are for a greengrocer;

Daphne Slater, young and aloof straight from RADA, with stars in her eyes, to play Juliet; Laurence Payne, her Romeo, experienced, with a friendly grin and a nervous air; Miles Eason who knows Noël Coward and is very witty – one day in a heavy blizzard he sees me approaching down Stratford High Street, throws his duffel coat over his head, flails his arms wildly and desperately screams, 'Heathcliff, Heathcliff!'; Douglas Seale who closes his eyes and grits his teeth nervously when I come near; Margaret Courtenay, who was a sergeant in the ATS, outrageous and ebullient and leaping at life; David Hobman, full of practical jokes, the life and soul of the company; and the three bright young men from Birmingham Rep: John Harrison, Donald Sinden and Paul Scofield, all three aged twenty-five and doing their second year at Stratford. Paul, the young man with the white liner at the Arts Theatre, has extraordinary stage magnetism and stardom looms ahead. He is gentle and retiring, as is his pretty wife Joy who is in the company and whom I quietly fancy. They have a four-year-old son Martin who does imitations of Dickie Hudd. John Harrison is an ex-school-teacher and for a time we share digs at the Rose and Crown. One day I buy two records, one jazz and one classical, and John says, 'If you like one why pretend to like the other?' I leave the Rose and Crown. Donald Sinden is good-natured, sounds as if he has swallowed a prune, forgets to shave and is late for rehearsal, but no one sighs when he approaches.

As the season progresses I make two friends. Ken Wynne is much older than I. He started at Stratford as a very old call-boy and worked up. Small, dark and Italian-looking, he has a marvellous sense of comedy and an almost too strong ability to laugh at himself. Herbert Roland is a gangling red-haired Austrian Jew who as Herbert Schacter became a refugee with those of his family who avoided the concentration camps at the beginning of the war. We have discovered that during the 1914–1918 conflict his father and mine were in opposing trenches.

In the theatre I remain a dead weight. Understudying is a nightmare and I cannot learn the part of Aguecheek because I am not playing the role. I need impetus. Elizabeth Ewbank is one of the Thorndike family – Sybil is her aunt and Eileen is her mother. Elizabeth is in digs two doors away from mine. One morning my landlady wakes me before breakfast to tell me that Elizabeth is at the door.

The girl stands there bleary-eyed. 'Sorry to trouble you but I have been up all night learning Juliet. Can you hear me?'

55

'Are you understudy?' I asked.

'No, but Daphne Slater is not feeling well and if her understudy is not able to go on I could help out.'

A little shamefaced I hear the exhausted girl through the part that neither she, nor the understudy, will ever be called to play. I have witnessed the Thorndike dedication – I hope it rubs off.

Tea and cakes at the Hathaway, beer at the Dirty Duck, coffee and cakes at the Cobweb. Life is a great whirligig of excitement. Smiling, satisfied faces beam through beams and leer through leaded windows. I long for the confusion and noise of the city and every possible weekend I board the train which sets out from Stratford before midnight, and seems to stop every few yards before it draws into Paddington station before dawn. The all-night bus drops me at the Lyons Corner House in Coventry Street and I wait there for the Sunday morning tube trains to start running.

At five a.m. the Piccadilly Corner House is a hive of devious activity. Beneath the neat tablecloths can be heard the sound of pound notes passing from hand to hand as prostitutes by the score settle the dealings of the night with their ponces. One weekend a very pretty pro chats for hours over coffee and do I want a quick one up against the wall for nothing? On another occasion the train journey itself becomes a meeting, a romance, and a hasty farewell as a gangster boyfriend arrives with chums to meet the train.

Some weekends I get a lift by car, either from Dudley Jones, the small friendly Welsh singer who plays Feste in *Twelfth Night*, or, on a couple of occasions, from Michael Benthall, the director. Nervously I sit quietly in the front of the car as he speeds through the night, every few seconds wiping the mist from the windscreen and cursing with frustration at the car's inability to go at ninety miles an hour through the country lanes. I pluck up the courage to ask him why he is rushing. His eyes twinkle, blink and the Eton drawl informs me that he must get back to his wife.

It is not until later that I learn that he is not married and that he shares a flat in Belgravia with Robert Helpmann.

The girl I am missing is the stunning Eunice Gayson whom I met in the street in London and followed to Derby where she was playing principal girl in *Aladdin*, but at Stratford I have a brief romance with a fair and fuzzy-haired young journalist. Much of the icing falls off the cake when my landlady walks into my room one day, without knocking, and drops a tray.

The long hot summer continues. I have an understudy rehearsal on Monday morning so this weekend I do not go home. On the Sunday I wander over to the theatre as I intend to go punting on the Avon and then for a swim. During the season we have had a tragedy. A couple of young actors were brought in from Birmingham Rep to swell the company for *Richard II*, and after only a day of rehearsal one of them, a fair-haired nineteen-year-old, went out in a punt, dived in the river, hit his head, and was drowned. That night the show was a subdued affair and the next day some of the locals told me that they thought it was me who had died. For the first time it hit me what a precarious activity was the process of living. When I was a very small child I had been thrown in the deep end of a swimming pool by other boys and nearly drowned. The fear of water stayed with me and I never learned to swim. The day after the accident, in the firm belief that lightning never strikes twice in the same place, I went out on the Avon, jumped from the boat, made a few furious, pathetic breast strokes and swam for the first time.

As I reach the theatre this Sunday morning five American visitors approach me and ask if there is any chance of their seeing inside. Are they tourists? There is something different about them – young, gregarious, full of fun and life. I take them inside and learn that they are members of the cast of *Oklahoma!* which has opened at the Theatre Royal, Drury Lane, and taken London by storm. They are Betty-Jane Watson who plays Laury, Harold Keel who plays Curly, his girlfriend Gemze de Lappe who is principal dancer, Dorothy McFarlane (Ado Annie) and Beatrice Lynn, 'the girl who falls down'.

We all become friends and I arrange to see Beatrice in London when I have free weekends.

On another occasion the film star Lizbeth Scott arrives from Hollywood, accompanied by two cameramen who click away perpetually. She is a human freeze frame, which makes conversation tedious; every two words the cameramen shout 'Hold it' and she wets her lips and goes rigid like a puppet. The play that evening is *Love's Labour's Lost* and when she suggests that during the performance she walks on to the grassy set and says 'Hello to the folks in the audience', Walter Hudd and Peter Brook turn very pale and suggest that perhaps it would not be advisable.

Meanwhile my life on stage grows more precarious. Scarcely a performance goes by without disaster.

*

57

In *Richard II* I play the small role of Lord Ross. At the end of one act Richard abdicates to Henry Bolingbroke and says 'Go we toward London, cousin, is it so?'

'Ay, my good Lord,' says Henry.

'Then I must not say no,' says Richard and in dignified silence, I, heavy with emotion, step forward, take Richard's arm and lead the pathetic creature to the back of the stage as the lights change and the stage starts to revolve for the next scene.

However . . .

One night Robert Harris as Richard says, 'Go we towards London, cousin, is it so?'

'Ay, my good Lord.'

'Then I must not say no,' and I step forward to take his arm, but unfortunately the revolving stage gives a little jerk. I am on the wrong foot. I crash to the ground in my very heavy armour. The clanking metal reverberates throughout the theatre. The magic is broken. This would not have been so bad if the joints of my armour had not stuck, and I am carried, by several actors, like a sardine can from the stage.

In *Doctor Faustus* I play Beelzebub. At the end of the first half Paul Scofield as Mephistopheles follows Lucifer and myself up a long line of steps at the back of the stage, to a platform eighteen feet above the ground. Robert Harris plays Faustus and utters a long terrified moan as the music rises to a crescendo of drums and I appear, thrust out my wings and roar mightily.

My costume for Beelzebub includes six-foot wings and a heavy mask with horns. Gauze over the eyes does not help anyone as short-sighted as I. One night as Robert Harris is moaning and the crescendo is mounting I climb the steps to make my entrance. I sense that Paul Scofield is not behind me. "Oh God, Paul is off," I think, and take a step back to look. I fall eighteen feet. Luckily my wings act as a parachute and I float gently down to the ground. The crescendo wears itself out and there is silence apart from Robert Harris's desperate elongated moan. In panic, I run up the stairs, half-heartedly lift my wings and go 'humph'.

In *Romeo and Juliet* I play a citizen of Verona. Peter Brook has organised a very effective street fight. The Duke Escalus enters to stop the brawl. As he sweeps majestically onstage, as part of the background action I receive a slight wound and fall from a tiny rostrum, while the actors retreat in silence, leaving Escalus downstage centre to make his severe threatening speech. Then he turns, clutches his train and makes a long dignified exit.

However . . .

One night Escalus, played by Robert Harris (who else) makes his entrance and I fall wounded from the tiny rostrum. Unfortunately, I am wearing a large black and gold hat with coloured feathers and as I hit the floor the hat falls off and gently rolls across the vast stage as Escalus advances. Eventually it lands on his train, and when his speech is over he turns and sweeps with dignity, majestically upstage – with my hat with its long feathers firmly planted in the middle. This would not have been so bad, but my wig is still inside the hat. Not unnaturally the audience and the cast all burst into peals of laughter.

After the performance, Robert Harris solemnly hands me the hat, the wig and a photograph of Eunice Gayson which, for some reason, I had secreted inside the hat.

'I believe these are yours,' he murmurs impassively.

In *Twelfth Night* I am one of Orsino's court and this production opens with Viola and the sea captain downstage and Orsino and his court, hidden behind a gauze, upstage. As the first scene ends Viola and the sea captain exit, the lights go up behind the gauze, the gauze rises and Orsino goes into 'If music be the food of love' as another actor and myself throw a large ball to each other.

However . . .

One evening I am a little late and cannot find my tights which I wear with a frilly blouse, velvet waistcoat, billowing trousers and a large hat. The other actors go downstairs to wait in darkness behind the gauze, while our dresser, having searched unsuccessfully for my tights, gives me a pair of black stockings. Hurriedly I throw on my costume and rush down to join the others behind the gauze.

The first scene ends. The lights go up. The gauze rises. Michael Golden, an Irish Orsino, starts, 'If music be the food of love, play on' – and bursts into suppressed laughter. The other actors join in. So do the audience. Tossing the large ball back and forth downstage centre I fail to see the humour. Then I feel cold. First physically – then with terror. I have gone on without my trousers. Between the frilly blouse and the black stockings there is a considerable gap. Desperately, a half-naked actor flees to the comfort of concealment.

On the first night of *The Merchant of Venice*, I am playing Portia's servant and I have the line, 'Madam, I go with all convenient speed', and I have been told that if you say the line disdainfully and make a slow exit, you receive a guaranteed round of applause. This I do. Sure enough the audience clap but unfortunately the enormous umbrella that I am carrying gets stuck in a doorway and I cannot leave the stage. Eventually I slide off behind a flat – leaving the umbrella firmly embedded in the doorway.

There is no respite. I am punished until the end. On the last night of the season we are doing *Pericles* and I play a pirate chief. At one moment I charge offstage fighting with cutlass and knife. Then after a brief scene I return to sell Marina to the bawd.

However . . .

I cut and thrust offstage then wait in the wings with the other actors who shake their heads at me and say, 'Last night or no, you have gone too far.' I glance down. The cutlass has cut my finger and thumb to the bone. My chest is covered with blood.

'It's me,' I cry. 'It's blood!'

'Don't fool around,' they say, and we sweep on and I play the scene in a dizzy haze and then have to go off to have stitches.

At last it is over. The season has ended. Goodbye purgatory. Redemption is at hand. I shall start afresh! The past will be forgotten. I have received one lifeline. I might give up the theatre after such a battering, but one day near the end of the season, Robert Harris, who has suffered so much from my indelicate behaviour, takes me aside and says, 'You know, my boy, you are a very good listener. That is a fine quality in an actor.'

The door has not slammed shut. A spark of light. Put on blinkers. Forget 1947 and go forward.

In 1948 I did not get one day's work.

FOUR

Two old actors met in Shaftesbury Avenue.

'What are you doing here, dear boy? I thought you were at Scunthorpe.'

'I have lit up the boards at the theatre there for the last twenty-seven years but I received a letter inviting me to participate on the West End stage from a Mister Hugh Beaumont Esquire.'

'Well done, old chap. What sort of gratuity are they paying you?'

'To be honest, my dear, I had not thought about it. At Scunthorpe I have always received a remuneration of eight pounds a week.'

'Eight pounds! My dear old fellow, this is the West End of London. The least they should pay you is thirty pounds.'

'Thirty pounds . . . thirty pounds. Do you really think so?'

'Not a penny less, dear boy.'

So the old actor went up in the lift at the Globe Theatre to a small office where Binkie Beaumont sat behind a desk.

'Do sit down,' said the impresario. 'I have heard great things about your work and I would like you to consider playing a role in this new play by Terry Rattigan.'

'Frightfully decent of you,' said the old actor as he settled back in his chair.

'There is only one problem.' Binkie smiled benignly. 'It is a wonderful role – not all that big, but very showy – but the cast is very large. Paul Scofield is playing the lead and unfortunately there is very little money to spare. I'm afraid it all depends on what sort of salary you were expecting. What did you have in mind?'

The old actor leaned forward and gesticulated with his hand. 'Well I rather thought a reasonable stipend would be – th . . . th . . .' He coughed gently. 'How do you feel about th . . . th . . ?'

Binkie raised his eyebrows.

The old actor coughed again. 'I thought perhaps – thweight!'

As the days move inexorably by, the prospects of ever working in theatre or film grow fainter day by day. Every inch of the area around Wardour Street is known to me. Every dingy backstreet

61

agent's office and every manicured, glossy, patronising, secure receptionist and secretary becomes as familiar as the closed doors, which they guard, threatening and uncompromising. Some are sympathetic and develop a bantering humour, others are cool, callous and unconcerned – but all follow the same maxim, 'Thou shalt not pass.' Behind the closed doors the small-time cigar-chewing agents sweat and fast-talk into telephones which seem to be extensions of their bodies.

Throughout the long depressing months, my mother (whom I now call Muzz) scrubs, irons, cooks, cleans and comforts, without criticism. She seems to accept that an actor does not actually work and with a warm hug accepts all my disappointments and near misses.

I join up with Beatrice Lynn and the *Oklahoma!* crowd and see the show several times. Always the audience become hysterical with excitement and literally dance up the aisles in the interval. How I long to be part of the musical world. Betty-Jane Watson is still playing Laury even though she is very obviously seven months pregnant. When she sings 'People Will Say We're in Love' the song takes on a different meaning. Before Harold Keel had understudied Curly in New York he had struggled unsuccessfully in Hollywood. After his success in London he is offered an English thriller movie playing a convict on the run. This leads to an MGM contract, his name is changed to Howard and he is taken back to make musicals in Hollywood where he began. Dorothy McFarlane is as crazy offstage as she is on and Beatrice is always ebulliently different and attractive.

Many evenings are spent with Barbara Davies and Laura Cook-man, two Canadian girls who were in the forces show *Meet the Navy*. I met Barbara at the Central School. They have a flat in Kensington and when they move to Barnes I still continue to see them. They share the flat with Paddy Stone from the Sadler's Wells Ballet who is now being spectacular as the Indian dancer in *Annie Get Your Gun* at the Coliseum where he met the fourth inmate, Irving Davies, who plays the juvenile lead opposite Wendy Toye. The star of this enormous hit is Dolores Gray who plays the gun-toting Annie. Despite her success she enrols at RADA, where she has speech lessons and also appears as Regina in Lillian Hellman's *The Little Foxes*, their end-of-term production. Paddy, Irving and I go to see her. Her performance as the wicked sophisticate is very broad and at any moment I expect her to whip out a pistol and fire away. That evening I stand at the back of the crowded Coliseum Theatre as Dolores demurely enters. Somehow I feel she has been caught between two stools.

Barbara and Cookie are confident, crazy, experienced and full of bubbling life. Barbara has Red Indian blood and, with her attractive slanting eyes, looks oriental. Later she and her two brothers appear in a play written for them by J. B. Priestley. Cookie is plump and effervescent and bursts into hysterical laughter as we joke together. She is a great cook and spends a lot of time in the kitchen complaining that nothing exciting will ever happen to her. Later she goes to India to sing at the Taj Mahal Hotel in Bombay, slims down until she looks like Ava Gardner and makes her permanent home there.

I have come to accept that banging perpetually on agents' doors does not result in eventual success of any kind. I retreat into childhood, and inertia and stagnation overwhelm me. Ken Wynne, Herbert Roland and I, all out of work, meet up and derive pleasure playing simple games with cards and even football with pennies. When work finally does come it is in dribs and drabs, odd days on documentary films and plays at try-out theatres which do not survive very long – the plays or the theatres. I succeed in closing two of the theatres myself. The Torch Theatre is so small that when we do a play about Henry VIII with a large cast, the three-piece orchestra have to play in the lavatory and the lady cellist sits astride the loo, scratching away with the door open.

During the run of this play I appear on television for the first time – in fact I have not even seen a television set. I am employed for a semi-documentary about juvenile delinquency to play a policeman chasing Anthony Wager across the studio rooftops. This television play is performed live on Sunday and then on Thursday when the cast and unit have to go back and do it all again. For this one performance I have to be released from the play at the Torch Theatre so Herbert Roland says my few lines on that day. For eight performances at the Torch I receive thirty shillings, but for the television I earn seventeen pounds.

Arnold Ridley, who wrote *The Ghost Train*, has written a play called *Easy Money* and I get the part of the comedy juvenile in a production for the English troops in Germany. Arnold Ridley and Doris Hare play the leading parts and for the first time since my trip to Ireland as a child I go abroad. Germany is devastated. Throughout the days we wander through the bruised and battered streets and confusion, depression and desperation pervade the sweet-and-sour-smelling bombed-out cities. The people are drab

63

and grey, queues are everywhere, food is difficult to find and coffee and cigarettes can only be obtained on the black market. In Minden, the home of Eva Braun, there is still much antagonism and the locals refuse to walk on the same pavements when they see us approach, but the theatre is a gem, built at Hitler's instigation for his mistress, with every conceivable facility backstage. However, in Hamburg, where the destruction has been appalling and the city almost flattened by the RAF, the people are cosmopolitan and tolerant. One day I go for a haircut in the hotel and, speaking no German, I point vaguely at my head.

'Short back and sides, sir?' says the barber. He is a Cockney who has been living in Hamburg since he fought in the First World War and who carried on between 1939 and 1945 as if nothing had happened.

We share each theatre with German companies who perform their shows for civilians, after we finish at eleven at night. Doris Hare has been a great favourite with the forces throughout the war on the radio, and after our play finishes, our adrenalin still high, she and I go off to different nightclubs and usually find our way on to the small stages where we sing 'Buttons and Bows' – more for our own pleasure than anyone else's. Occasionally, we come across an American company entertaining their troops and I meet two of the Hollywood stars I used to queue to see on the magic silver screen, Constance Bennett and Charlie Ruggles.

Easy Money is a very light entertainment about football pools, but for the first time I feel the extraordinary bond that humour can create across the footlights. The delicate joy of timing a laugh. Like a juggler you toss a line into the air, hold your breath, your body poised at the correct angle, your thought sincere behind an expressionless mask and you press an invisible button and, if all co-ordinates with precision, you know – as you count quietly to yourself – you know with absolute certainty when the audience will erupt into uncontrollable laughter.

And I experience my first stage practical jokes. Our stage manager, John Hewitt, is likeable, bizarre and at any moment liable to break off into madness. At one point in the show the stage is very quiet as Arnold Ridley reads a newspaper, Doris Hare knits and I stare gloomily out of the window. 'It must be getting late,' says Arnold, and, as if in reply, a small carriage clock chimes nine times.

One night, in the silence, Arnold murmurs, 'It must be getting late,' and the whole stage shakes and reverberates with shattering, deafening noise. In the wings John Hewitt stands, naked, beating an enormous J. Arthur Rank gong.

Towards the end of the tour we are the first show to be asked to go to Berlin during the air lift. Unfortunately some lucky ones in the cast have other contracts and we have to refuse.

The most famous 'tatty' agent in London is Miriam Warner. One of the great eccentrics, her huge frame fills her tiny office, hanging obesely over her chair and cluttered table, a cigarette permanently between heavy lips, the thin line of smoke forcing her to half close her currant eyes which disappear behind mounds of flesh. 'Hello, dear,' she says without looking up. 'What can we do for you?' The answer to this rhetorical question is invariably nothing, and indeed it is always some time before she is able to see through the smoke whether I am male or female, young or old.

One day, however, when she gets me in focus, she tells me that the part of Dougall is going in *Little Lambs Eat Ivy* at Wolverhampton Rep. They have a regular company, but an extra male is needed for the one play – a 'special week' as it is known in the trade. My train fare paid for, I excitedly get the train to Wolverhampton with my eyes glued to the French's copy of the play. Dougall is the leading role and if I can get through the interview it will be the best part that I have played. Basil Thomas runs the rep and he sees me in his office. 'Are you a bowler or a batsman?' he asks.

'I beg your pardon?'

'You do play cricket, don't you? Do you bowl or bat?'

'I bowl,' I reply, utterly confused.

'Thank God for that. The part is yours.'

Confused and elated I relax back into my seat, only to learn that Miriam Warner had got it all wrong. The part is not the lead, Dougall, but the dreary juvenile, McGill. However, it is work, a week rehearsing and a week playing, and it is only later that I learn that Basil Thomas is cricket mad and insists that the company's unbeaten team is always kept at full strength. If I had been a batsman I would not have got the job. Two weeks later that is what I am – without one game of cricket.

A long pause follows before I go off to Great Yarmouth to join the company which is not only weekly rep, but also twice nightly. Twelve performances a week which leave very few hours to rehearse and play. Any free time is very valuable, because there is a beach to lie on, bloaters to eat and a very attractive girl who is totally preoccupied with sex. However, even I know that the standard of work is dreadful and when we open my first play, *A Soldier for Christmas*, in which I play the soldier, not only are we under-rehearsed but the lines are still unfamiliar. Before the first performance I am so nervous I do something that I shall never do again. I take a Benzedrine tablet and the play flies by at breakneck speed. All the voices, including my own, sound like the Munchkins in *The Wizard of Oz*. Eventually I dry up – forget my lines – and there is an interminable pause. Half a century goes by before we are able to pick up roughly from where we stopped.

During the interval I rush to the corner to find out why the assistant stage manager, who was on the book, had failed to prompt me. I learn that when I had dried up the ASM had burst into uncontrollable laughter, turned to the person behind him, pointed to the script, and gurgled, 'This is what he should be saying!'

Weekly rep, twice nightly, is beyond my powers, and I leave the company. As the months go by I get odd days on documentary films and an occasional play at the Q Theatre, near Kew Gardens.

Eventually the magic moment arrives. I hit the jackpot. I am offered a role in a major movie. It is only one day's work as a policeman in the Boulting Brothers' film *Seven Days to Noon*, but it is a good scene and I know that this is the breakthrough I have longed for. I could be a star. The film is about a mad professor who wants to blow up London, and in my scene I have to rush from the telephone to my sergeant, with the following words, 'I say, Sarge, I've got a message here from Mrs Emily Georgina Pickett of 70 Clesby Road. She has got a lodger who has been acting queer and putting the wind up 'er. Here's his description. Small, bald with a dark brown overcoat. I think it's this bloke who wants to blow up London.' And the sergeant says, 'What do you expect – a medal?'

I learn the piece and get a very early tube train to the studios where I rehearse the scene with Roy Boulting the director. He seems very pleased and I even have the courage to put in a comedy trip on my exit. 'Very good,' he smiles. 'Now we'll break for lunch and then shoot the scene straightaway.' I turn to go, but he calls me back. 'Oh, by the way, there are one or two little changes in the script. Perhaps you can tidy them up over lunch. It is not Pickett – it is Peckitt. It is not Clesby – it is Clisby. It is not 70 – it is 13, and it is not a dark brown overcoat – it is a light grey raincoat. See to that, will you?'

Boggle-eyed I go off to lunch and concentrate on the changes.

After lunch I stand on the set in uniform, my make-up is powdered down and my hands clenched tight with concentration.

'Action,' says Roy Boulting.

I open a door, and enter the office energetically. 'I say, Sarge, I've got a message here from Mrs Emily Georgina Peckitt of 13 Clisby Road. She has got a lodger who has been acting queer and putting the wind up 'er. Here's his description. Small, bald with a light grey raincoat. I think it's this bloke who wants to blow up London.'

Breathlessly I stopped speaking and stared at the sergeant whose eyes glazed over.

'I'm terribly sorry – I've dried,' he said.

'Never mind,' said Roy Boulting. 'Take two.'

Once more I was powdered. Once more I opened the door. Once more I tore through my speech with all the correct changes.

'Hold it,' called Roy Boulting. 'Cut. Will someone paint those white drawers – they are too light.'

The drawers were darkened, my face was powdered and my confidence wilted.

'Action,' said Roy Boulting.

I rushed through the door. 'I say, Sarge, I've got a message here from Mrs Emily Georgine Peckett of 13 Clesby Road – sorry Clisby.'

'Take four.'

'I say, Sarge, I've got a message here from Mrs Emily Georgina Pickett – er Peckett.'

'Take five.'

'70 Clesby – sorry 13 Clisby.'

Take after take. Worse and worse. The sweat drips from me. After take twelve Roy Boulting suggests we stop and have a cup of tea. He comforts me by telling me that Orson Welles had an incredible number of takes for one line in *The Third Man*. We start again. Despite the tea my mouth is dry and my speech becomes a series of anagrams.

The studio door opens and John Boulting leads in a group of men and announces, 'Normally we do not allow visitors on the set, but today we have twenty members of the Australian parliament and they have never seen any filming before.'

'Take twenty-five.'

John Boulting discreetly leads twenty members of the Australian parliament out of the studio.

I babble on.

After forty-eight takes we stop. They have two possibles in the can. I leave the studios, get on a tube train and fall asleep. When I awake the train has gone back and forth on its journey.

My life in the movies is over.

The next day I meet an actor in the street and he asks me if I am working.

'Oh I've just done a bit on *Seven Days to Noon*,' I say grandly.

'Really,' he says. 'Do you know, I believe there was some poor devil there yesterday who had forty-eight takes?'

My life in the movies is definitely over.

The years 1949 and 1950 seemed to last for ever. Like an over-eager butterfly I flew from flower to flower desperate to find good pollen, but each landing was so brief that every flower became a different adventure. At the Q Theatre each play ran for only one week. On two occasions the time I spent there was even shorter when I turned up at the first rehearsal to find someone else playing my role. One American director, Robert Henderson, was in the habit of handing out scripts to any actor who happened to be around, and promising them parts.

Rehearsals were made more complicated by the management cutting down the expenses by giving us cue scripts, so that instead of having the entire play, you only had your own individual lines and the few words that preceded them. The actors had to sit in rehearsal with their eyes glued to their script until someone came up with their cue. This could lead to complications and it was very near the end of the week's run of an Agatha Christie play that a sweet old actress came up to me and said, 'Sorry to trouble you, dear, but do tell me – who killed me?'

It was after *Appointment with Death* that I swore never to play in an Agatha Christie play again. One of my lines had been 'No, no, a thousand times, no', and another, 'She is dead, but she won't lie down!'

My most challenging role at the Q was in *All My Sons* which the director insisted we play without make-up. As I was playing a thirty-nine-year-old I gave him a stooping back and a rasping voice. At Q I met the director Chloe Gibson, who ignored my clumsy, gauche confusion, and treated me as an equal. She lived at Pembroke Studios in Kensington where she would sit on the floor with hawklike intensity, waving her perpetual cigarette like a conductor's baton, and discuss philosophy, politics and religion until the early hours of the morning. There was no conceivable subject which she could not treat with passionate fervour and devouring interest, and she had an endearing habit of pausing in full flight, her eyes would glaze over, a little friendly smile would play around her lips as she became conscious of your presence and she would glide down to earth for a few brief seconds before taking off once more, perusing and devouring every detail of whatever enthusiasm absorbed her at the time. She had recently directed *Power Without Glory*, by Michael Clayton Hutton, in London and New York, which had launched both Dirk Bogarde and Kenneth More on their successful careers. Her husband had left her and had set up with another woman in the next street where their bedroom backed on to the studios.

It was through the eccentric and lovable Chloe that I became part of the bizarre world of the Embassy Theatre at Swiss Cottage where I was employed, on and off, for the next eighteen months.

Tony Hawtrey ran the Embassy Theatre and the repertory theatres at Croydon, and Buxton in Derbyshire. Occasionally new plays were tried out at Buxton, and, if successful, they would be done again at Croydon and with luck might move to the Embassy. From the Embassy there was always the faint hope of the play moving to the West End and an even fainter hope of the play not being recast with well-known actors. Even though I spent so much time in the company, Tony Hawtrey remained an enigma. I hardly ever spoke to him and rarely saw him. Steeped in theatrical tradition – his father was Charles Hawtrey, the first of the underplayers, and his mother the niece of Ellen Terry – he was tall, handsome and invariably booted like a 1920s film director. He played the actor living impulsively in his own dream world with various girlfriends and balancing precariously on a tightrope. Before a matinée at the Embassy he would scoop up the box-office takings and go off and bet them on the racecourse. His wife Margerie was warm, understanding and had a boyfriend who was the theatre chef and very temperamental. Every so often, as in *Alice in Wonderland*, a crashing and banging and screaming would come from the kitchen and pots, knives and pans would follow.

When I was at Buxton, Terence de Marney of *Count of Monte Cristo* fame and his wife, the brilliant actress Beryl Measor, joined the company for two plays. They owed Tony money; he said, 'All right come and work it off.'

Chloe Gibson was directing a new play, *The Beautiful World* by Ian McCormick. It was yet another allegorical piece based on *Romeo and Juliet*, set in Berlin with Christian Democrats and

Social Democrats representing the Montagues and the Capulets. After auditioning I was told that I was likely to get the Romeo part opposite the Juliet of Carol Marsh who was well known from films such as *Brighton Rock* and *Alice in Wonderland* in which she played Alice.

A great opportunity. But one afternoon I persuaded the author to join me and stand at the back of the theatre to watch a little of the matinée of *Rain before Seven* which starred Marian Spencer. She was playing a scene with a young man, Lyndon Brook, who was the son of Clive. Ian McCormick stood silently beside me and after a few minutes left the auditorium. When the act finished I also left to find that during that time the Romeo role had been offered to Lyndon.

I played the Mercutio part but, alas, there was no Queen Mab speech.

Carol became a friend and I spent two happy Christmases dividing my time between my home and hers where we had fun and festive meals with her mother and sister.

The main fare at Buxton and Croydon was a mixed bag of light comedy, thrillers and, most popular of all, farce. The latter was not only the most difficult to play, but also proved to be an invaluable training ground for an actor. The experienced farceur learns the importance of discipline, delicacy, pace and, most vital of all, no matter how outrageous and unreal the situation, truth. If you believe – the audience believe with you. If you are only working externally the audience, subsconsciously, become aware that you are striving for effect, and lose interest. Sadly there is no similar training ground today.

After some weeks at Buxton I was to play the leading part in *The Gioconda Smile* by Aldous Huxley, but despite long hours of study not one line had stuck in my brain. So the day before rehearsals were due to begin I telephoned Tony Hawtrey in London and said that I would not be able to cope. 'Never mind, old boy,' said Tony. 'I'll come and play it.' And he did.

The most familiar question actors ever hear is, 'How on earth do you manage to learn all those lines?' It is also the most boring. It is as relevant as asking a painter, 'Where on earth do you find all that paint?' or a musician, 'How do you learn all those notes?' Learning lines is a chore but it is just part of the complicated process. As I have always been very slow, weekly repertory was agony. After opening in play A on Monday you set the moves for play B on Tuesday, rehearse act one of play B on Wednesday, act two on Thursday and act three on Friday. Meanwhile there are eight performances of play A, including a mid-week matinée and another on Saturday. On the Sunday the scenery for play A comes down and goes up for play B. The following Monday a dress rehearsal of play B is followed by the opening night and the next morning play C goes into rehearsals. As learning was such a slow process for me I would prepare a week in advance. In other words while I played in play A and rehearsed play B, I would be learning play C, so I found myself studying until two or three in the morning.

The other most common questions asked of an actor are, 'What is your proper job?' and 'What do you do during the day?'

These also rank pretty high in the boredom stakes.

At Croydon, Buxton and the Embassy, the director that I worked with most of the time was an immensely tall country squire-like man, who looked perpetually confused as his arms and legs moved in competition with his body. He was the Hollywood version of an Englishman who stuttered and apologised with gentle charm. On the rare occasions when he acted in a play he looked like a square peg in a round hole. Bad puns fell from his lips in a never-ending stream. He was also the finest director of farce that I have ever known, and one of the warmest, most generous men. His name was Shaun Sutton, who was to go on to become the BBC TV's head of plays, and he and his wife Barbara have remained my friends ever since.

In *The Happiest Days of Your Life*, a clever farce by John Dighton, I played at Buxton, Croydon, the Embassy as well as at Hayes in a new theatre which Shaun helped through its teething days. In each production (all by Shaun) I worked with a different cast which was very useful, because it was similar to playing tennis with different players and on each occasion timing, approach shots and strokes varied accordingly. At the Embassy the monstrous schoolgirl Colquhoun – pronounced Cahoon – was played by Ba Sutton. In those days we did not have the luxury of a backstage Tannoy system linked to every dressing-room. Actors were in the hands of a call-boy, or girl, knocking at your door and yelling, 'Your call, please.' But it was an unwritten rule of the theatre that this was never an excuse for being off. You were master of your own fate. However, at one matinée of *The Happiest Days* the call-boy forgot to knock on Ba Sutton's door for her entrance. Robert Perceval as Pond, the headmaster, Dennis Ramsden and myself as the masters Billings and Tassell, were on stage rattling through fast repartee which culminated in my unlikely line, 'Ah well, homo in omnibus.' At this point the door opened and Ba thrust her head inside and surprised us – or should have done. Alas, not at this matinée.

Silence.

The three of us stared at each other with glazed, horror-stricken eyes. After an interminable pause Dennis Ramsden said, 'What do you mean, Tassell, by homo in omnibus?'

I felt the audience look in my direction, and I started to babble, 'Well, why take it for granted that only heterosexuals travel on buses? Come to that, why only people?' and then I proceeded to ramble on about various occasions when giraffes, kangaroos and even elephants were inclined to use London Transport. Finally I ran out of steam and said, 'But surely you know all this?'

Both men gravely shook their heads.

'I had no idea,' said Robert Perceval.

'Nor had I,' said Dennis Ramsden. 'Do tell us more.'

Meanwhile the ASM glanced up dreamily from her prompt book, saw I was babbling on with a stiff body and a high voice, sidled from her seat and slowly walked up eight flights of stairs to Ba Sutton's dressing-room. Instead of screaming, 'You're off,' which was the traditional cry of panic, she knocked gently, opened the door, gave a friendly smile and said, 'Hi, Ba. I think that you had better pop down soon.'

'Thanks,' said Ba, and continued adjusting her make-up. She walked slowly down the eight flights and stood in the wings listening for her cue. From the stage came the sound of unfamiliar gibberish.

After some confusion she entered and three schoolmasters collapsed into exhausted hysteria. We had been stranded for three minutes – half the length of a variety act. But this variety act was not only unrehearsed, but also unlikely ever to be repeated.

Lovers Leap, Love's a Luxury, The Perfect Woman, Job for the Boy, Mountain Air, Wasn't It Odd? Today these plays are not likely to make your heart skip a beat, but in the forties they were all guaranteed money-makers and moving from rep to rep I not only found myself repeatedly appearing in the same plays, but also playing different parts, depending on the average age of the company.

Mostly these were comedies and farces that had run successfully in London, but some were new plays which we tried out, but never transferred. One such example was *The Lady Purrs* by Ted (later Lord) Willis. The plot consisted of the blackmailing of an alderman's household by their cat after she had turned into a human being.

Eleanor Summerfield was the cat, Charles Heslop was the alderman and the household included Dandy Nichols as an enthusiastic member of the Salvation Army. I was the 'straight juvenile' and my understudy was Roger Moore, who surprised me recently by quoting from the play – I cannot even remember the name of the character. The play was directed by that lovely comedian Henry Kendall who remained a friend until he died.

During rehearsals I wore a voluminous duffel coat and one day Harry K. paused reflectively and then said, 'I'm not sure whether to raise the curtain on act two or get Joss to take off his coat.'

On the day of the opening something occurred which helps explain why an actor needs the philosophy of a clown and the resilience of an acrobat. In the second act a new character appeared, played by an actor who had been Robertson Hare's understudy for years. His appearance was similar, his mannerisms were similar and his voice had the same sound of a confused foghorn. But in *The Lady Purrs* he had his opportunity. At the public dress rehearsal, which preceded the first night, he worked his way frenetically through the role to the delight of the audience, and when he made his exit through the window there was a great round of applause. That evening his wife and family all had seats for the first performance. Unfortunately, in the sixty minutes between the two shows, the director and the author felt the play was overrunning by half an hour so they cut out his part completely. While his family were waiting for him to appear he was drinking quietly in a nearby pub.

It was at the Embassy that I played to my smallest house ever. Before one hot mid-week matinée, as I was applying five and eight Leichner to my face and placing dabs of carmine in the corners of my eyes to give me glamour, the front of house manager appeared to say there was only one person out front. Equity rules were different in those days. I may be wrong but I think if the cast outnumber the audience they do not have to perform. However, at the matinée concerned the cast stood anxiously behind the curtain as the manager stepped through and explained the situation to the confused man.

'As you are the only person here, perhaps you would like to

get your money back from the box-office and come another time?'

The entire audience paused, folded his arms, and said, 'I've paid me money to see a show and that's what I am going to see.'

So he did.

FIVE

The old actor was recalling, with misty eyes, a production of *Hamlet* in which he had appeared.

'My God, that was a company. I played the gloomy one, my good lady wife was Gertrude, 'Phelia was the girl I was living with at the time – I forget her name now – and Laertes was Walter Farnesbarnes and (lifting three fingers in the air) – and you don't get him for that!'

My love-life was hardly bursting at the seams. Girl after girl had caused minor firework displays in the solar system, and time after time I found myself stranded on the outskirts of London in the early hours of the morning having, somehow, to find my way home. A student at St Martin's School of Art, an ice skater, a fighter pilot's widow, young actresses, all made brief entrances, but, despite an intense romantic yearning within me, I always had a warning bell in my computer system which stopped me taking full advantage whenever the opportunity presented itself. I had discovered by this time that my father had always leapt with eyes shut and trousers open at every sexual possibility without thought of consequence. He truly loved women. So did I, but I was always restricted by the fear of causing pain. The sadness in my mother's eyes was always there.

This could lead to complications. One day I idled into an amusement arcade in Charing Cross Road where the attendant was a stunning redhead aged about twenty. As I placed my penny in the fruit machine she came up behind me, turned my face with her hand and kissed me full on the lips. I had heard of fast girls – but this was ridiculous. We arranged to meet at eleven o'clock that night when she finished her work.

When she emerged from the arcade, with her red-gold hair flying and her cheeks gleaming with innocence, I took her arm and walked with her to a nearby café. She had just arrived from Portsmouth and was looking for a proper job and a place to stay. My house was full of lodgers and I did not fancy surprising my mother with an extra visitor at one o'clock in the morning so I was sorry, but I had to get the last tube back to Earl's Court and maybe we could meet the next day and I might be able to come up with some ideas. She said, 'Earl's Court fine, maybe I can find something there.'

We found a seat on the crowded Piccadilly platform and I was busy expostulating on the possibilities of searching for a future when I discovered that my flies were undone and her hand had settled comfortably inside, searching for something quite different. My soldier snapped to attention and, with a red, excited face, I covered myself with a newspaper as the crowds jostled around. The train drew in. I was saved by the bell and retired to a neutral corner. As my attractive opponent stood close to me, grinning wickedly, I wondered how to face the next round. Should I fight or take a dive in the second?

She was still clinging to my arm, at Earl's Court, as we left the station and walked up the alley leading to Marloes Road. Suddenly she pushed me into a corner, flung her arms around me, and said, 'Surely you can find a place for me in your bed?'

'It's not possible,' I gasped.

'Do you want to bet?' she said, and grabbed my soldier, who remained on duty, and violently forced me to my knees.

In agony and ecstasy I had to grab her by the throat before she released her hold. The fight was over and I had won a victory – or had I? After lending her my coat she disappeared from view with a cheerful wave. The next morning I waited outside the penny arcade at eleven thirty and she arrived with a big smile, my coat hanging decorously from her shoulders and followed by a white-faced, shattered young sailor.

Patricia Plunkett was playing *The Girl Who Couldn't Quite*, at the St Martin's Theatre, and Herbert Roland and I got complimentary tickets. I found the fey, dark, strange creature very attractive and, as Herbert had known her at RADA, we went backstage to see her. There followed a romantic fling that went on for eighteen months. We had little in common, argued a great deal, and were perpetually breaking up, but after interminable telephone calls that contained long silences and heavy breathing duologues, we became reconciled.

Pat had been lucky (unlucky) to find success early. Straight out of RADA, she was understudying Jessica Spencer who played the leading part in *Pick Up Girl* at the Gateway Theatre in Notting Hill Gate. Jessica Spencer fell ill, Pat took over, Queen Mary saw the play and gave it considerable publicity, *Pick Up Girl* moved to the West End and Pat's name was up in lights before she knew what hit her. A film contract followed and she joined Michael Denison, Dulcie Gray, Richard Todd, Stephen Murray, Joan Dowling under contract to Associated British at Elstree Studios. She was paid very little, but her contract involved non-stop publicity appearances in clothes hired for the occasion. She was photographed in sexy poses behind balloons, on giant Christmas cakes and sitting on Mr Universe's muscles. She attended gala performances and, when a dress suit was not required, I would sometimes be in tow. But this ambitious young actor did not play his part well. I was not resentful but, as I was invariably out of work, I grew more frustrated. The situation was not helped by Pat's mother, who lived in a tall, sombre house in Half Moon Lane in Herne Hill, where I spent many evenings with her and Pat's two sisters. Large and foreboding, her mouth tightened at the edges as she tried to force herself into a welcoming smile, but her disapproval could not be concealed. Riches were what she wanted for her daughter and it was plain that these I could never supply. She was much happier when Pat was on a magazine cover than when she was successful in a play or film.

Pat and I began to squabble, invariably over petty jealousies. One New Year's Eve, at the Vic Wells Costume Ball, ended in a disastrous emotional argument. I was dressed as Billy the Kid which proved my undoing. Booted and spurred with a white neckerchief and a large sombrero, and throwing a tantrum, I only succeeded in emphasising the trivial pettiness of the row and the absurdity of the situation.

How different to the year before, when the Vic Wells Ball became an unexpected thrilling event.

Ken Wynne, Herbert Roland and I were absolutely penniless but, like Cinderella, were determined to go to the ball dressed as the Marx Brothers. Ken Wynne looked very like Chico and needed only a loose bow tie and a floppy hat. Herbert's hair was powdered and we made him up, and with the appropriate clothing he became Harpo. With the help of a burnt cork moustache, a false putty nose, a floppy suit and a wig I had kept from Spaans the wigmaker, I was transformed into Groucho. We borrowed three shillings and took a Number 9 bus to the Strand. Transferring to a taxi, we drove the few remaining yards around the corner to the Lyceum where the crowds gathered to welcome the celebrities.* We paid the driver and clambered out to roars of applause from the crowd. The uniformed ticket collectors laughed as we approached. Groucho-like I circled them as Herbert hooted his horn. 'He's got the tickets – no, he's got the tickets – no, he's got the tickets!' I rasped, raising my eyebrows and shaking ash from a stale cigar. The officials joined in, even more, with the merriment of the crowd. We made dizzy circles around them and, suddenly, we were inside.

The evening could not have been more successful. Smoked salmon was thrust upon us, and every time we passed a table with a surfeit of champagne I would say, 'You're too old to drink – you ought to be ashamed of yourselves – do your wives know about this?' and grab a bottle and everyone laughed more heartily than ever. We entered every competition, even the beauty competition and won several prizes. Harpo chased every beautiful girl in the place, Chico ended up under a table with a girl dressed as Dorothy Lamour and I was kissed by Vivien Leigh – not *a* Vivien Leigh – *the* Vivien Leigh – who embraced me and told me that I was her favourite actor.

The only blot on the evening was a man, high in his cups, who followed me everywhere, saying, 'I know you – you're Hoopo; no, you're Jicco; no, you're Bobbo.' I began to insult him Marx-fashion. When a passing reveller patted him on the back and said, 'Hi, Tolly', light began to glimmer. The drunken pest was Anatole de Grunwald the famous film producer. Behind the mask I was an out-of-work actor. It was my turn to follow him. 'Okay. Guess who I am – guess who I am,' I purred with eyes rolling non-stop.

One thing I learned that night. Anarchy can get you anywhere. After a long spell I got a movie. Well, a sort of movie. It was a documentary in three sequences sponsored by British European Airways. Mine was a two-hander with a fantastic original plot. My wife and I go on honeymoon in Jersey, have a row and make up. However, it proved a most enjoyable little job. My wife was the very attractive Canadian actress Patricia Owens, later to play opposite Marlon Brando in *Sayonara*, and travelling with the unit,

* This was not the shortest taxi ride that I ever took. On one occasion I was looking for a street in Hampstead and walked for miles, getting hopelessly lost. Eventually a taxi drew up and I got in. The driver said, 'Where to, guvnor?' and pressed down the flag. I gave him the address. The taxi driver raised his eyebrows and pointed to the nearest house. 'There she is, guv,' he said witheringly. Shamefaced, I handed him the minimum fare and clambered out of the other door.

as chaperone, was the BEA representative, Guy Challis, a funny, charming man who looked like Sid Field.

Filming in Jersey was always eventful and often hilarious.

One day I made a *faux pas* that might have made John Gielgud blink. An infection developed in one eye and it became very inflamed, so before filming began, together with Pat Owens I visited an island chemist. The shop was crowded, but when I finally got the girl assistant's attention I pointed to my sore eye and, as she was French, I spoke in English in a very loud voice. 'Excuse me,' I said, 'I am sorry to trouble you but I don't know what to do with my eye. Do you have some Durex?'

Pat collapsed on the floor and a look of cool resignation appeared on the assistant's face. Her thoughts were quite clear – another kinky Englishman.

The day we were due to shoot the reconciliation scene outside a large hotel, grey weather held up the shooting so I sat down with some of the unit and played poker and drank Pernod. During the forties this drink was nearly pure absinthe and was later taken off the market because small men had been known to rape large trees. Eventually the sun shone bright and we made our way to the hotel courtyard to shoot the scene.

The action consisted of Pat and I sitting at a table looking lovingly at each other, a waiter arriving, opening a bottle of champagne, pouring two glassfuls, me sipping one, nodding approval at the waiter and Pat and I clasping hands and staring even more lovingly at each other as we drained our glasses. We rehearsed a few times and as champagne was so cheap on Jersey the director insisted we open a new bottle on each occasion. The light was now as hazy as we were, so we broke for lunch at the hotel and the management gave us all an aperitif followed by an enormous meal with different wines for each course – even the dessert was rum baba – then coffee and a large brandy. After lunch we rehearsed once more and then did three takes. 'Great,' said the director. 'It's a wrap.'

Unfortunately what he failed to notice was that everyone in the unit, including himself, the cameraman, Pat and I, were all pissed out of our minds, and it was not until we viewed the rushes in London that we saw the results.

TAKE I

Pat and I stare lecherously at each other, the waiter arrives, pours the champagne, eventually the glass finds its way to my lips, I nod my head like Stan Laurel, Pat and I grasp each other's hands

79

like drowning creatures and stare at each other through a sea of alcohol.

TAKE 2

Was worse.

TAKE 3

As before except by this time my feet could be heard stomping beneath the table and I was frothing at the mouth which emitted a long low growl.

On our return, at Heathrow Airport, Guy Challis stood nervously by as Pat Owens and I declared various leather goods which we had collected as presents. After all, he was the BEA representative and it was important that all went smoothly. The customs official shook his head and suggested that we all move into a small back room which was deserted except for an empty bench. There he held aloft a half-empty bottle of Pernod which he had found in my luggage. 'Pernod,' he said. 'We are not too keen on this stuff coming into this country.'

'Perhaps I should leave it here,' said I.

'Do you know,' said the customs officer, 'I have been working here for five years and I have never tasted this stuff?'

'Why don't you taste it?' I suggested.

He produced a couple of tumblers and poured a large measure for him and myself. 'Cheers,' he said and raised his glass.

'You have to mix it with water,' I said.

'Oh no,' he said, 'I always like my drinks straight.' He drained his glass, and I sipped mine delicately and very slowly the heat from the drink created a firework display in my brain. Guy Challis hummed nervously. 'We might as well finish this off,' said the customs official as he replenished his glass and topped up mine. 'It's rather hot in here,' he said. 'Let's sit down.' He sat on the bench and I stood by, sipping gently. Then he started to chat about the film unit for *The Blue Lagoon* which had just gone through and 'What a pretty girl that Jean Simmons is –'

In mid-sentence he collapsed on to the bench and passed out cold. The inhabitants of the room looked at each other in amazement. Then we picked up our luggage and walked outside to the waiting cars and drove off. By the time I reached home, where my mother and Pat Plunkett were waiting, the Pernod had hit me, despite my attempts to sip it carefully and when I rolled heavily into the room, I was hardly the prodigal son or Ashley Wilkes returning to Tara.

Shortly afterwards Pat and I finally split after a passionate row in her hotel bedroom at Elstree, where she was filming, and I stomped out into the dark night and the pouring rain. For a few weeks I was sad and angry, and then the hormones adjusted themselves.

Whatever happened, I decided, I was not going to get heavily involved again. Shakespeare came back into my life in the shape of an Arts Council tour of *The Tempest* for schools, performances twice daily at nine thirty a.m. and two thirty p.m. I was to play Ferdinand whom I thought to be a dull young man. Unfortunately this filtered through to the audience who were only too keen to agree. After a dress rehearsal at Toynbee Hall in London a young girl visited Marten Tiffin who played Stephano. She had worked with him in *Charley's Aunt* at the Piccadilly Theatre when he was the bogus aunt and she played his girlfriend, Ela. When he asked her what she thought of the show she said that she loved it, but how an actor like the fellow playing Ferdinand was allowed on to a stage she could not imagine! Of course Marten did not tell me this. She did. Long after we married.

The Tempest tour proved great fun. We played small towns and unlikely venues, and it was never easy making up in the corridors of school halls or tatty dressing-rooms with broken mirrors, at nine o'clock in the morning to the music of *Housewives' Choice*. But the evenings were free, even though this proved fatal to some of the older actors because the pubs were open. For the first time I discovered the wonderful world of theatre digs where almost all the landladies turned out to be bizarre, eccentric characters with outsize personalities.*

Alas, it is a world of the past but I am grateful not to have missed it. Every 'date' had its list of digs and the experienced pros would book them well in advance. If digs were not known by the regulars there was a good way of sussing them out. I would ring the bell and ask to see the room. On the way upstairs I would glance at the 'visitors" book which was always to be found in the hall. If the previous occupants had written 'Fantastic', 'Wonderful food', 'Really comfy' or the like – book in. But if they had written 'Never known anywhere quite like it', 'Extraordinary' or 'Unrepeatable, and what food' – get the hell out of there fast.

And joy of joys. Sharing the digs would be variety artists doing their spot at the local Hippodrome, Palace or Empire, and I got to know the people I had idolised at the Gaumont State as a child.

* Painted lovingly and accurately by J. B. Priestley in his novel *Lost Empires*.

The Ganjou Brothers and Juanita, the Radio Revellers, high wire acts, comics, conjurors, ventriloquists, dancers; wonderful, warm, friendly dedicated creatures who squeezed their efforts and non-stop rehearsal and practice into seven minutes of talented, concentrated essence on stage. They could be wickedly funny about each other. If an act they did not like had not gone well they would shake their heads and say, 'Bad – I'll say he was bad – you could hear him walk off.'

When the world of variety ended, one of its richest crops died.

Marten Tiffin and I tried to join that world. We prepared a comedy act and wrote off to various variety managements, theatres and agents with fictitious details of experience and 'usual salary fifty pounds a week', but to no avail.

Marten and I decided to get digs together and, with the prospect of different girls at each port of call, we became a sort of Hope and Crosby act but Marten was happily married so I had a definite edge and he invariably was the Hope and I the Crosby.

Like Halifax.

We arrived late at this mecca of the north and found all the regular digs were full. Carrying heavy suitcases, we stood exhausted in a back street.

'That's it,' said Marten, 'I am not moving one more inch.'

'All right, let's try here,' I said, and ran up the steps of the nearest terraced house. I rang the bell and the door was opened by a young vision, remarkably upholstered.

'Hello, lads. What can I do for you?' Her strong northern dialect was dulcimer and clementine.

'Do you have any rooms?'

'Sorry, lads, we're full.'

Dejected and shattered we turned away.

The clatter of high heels on the pavement.

'Come on, lads, gi' me a hand wi' furniture. We'll fit thee in somehow.'

In quiet ecstasy we followed the heels into Illyria. Joyce Longbottom was her name, and Nellie Longbottom was her mother, laughing ecstatically at anything and everything, beating the piano and singing 'Rock a Bye my Baby to a Dixie Melody' until the ceiling shook. The house was cramped, but breathed strong and deep and brimming with life.

After my two daily shows Joyce and I would go off to the peace and safety of a darkened picture house and return to a knees-up with Nellie. Joyce would show me pictures in the family album of her brother Jack in the Merchant Navy. All the pictures were of shows on board ship with Jack wearing various long blonde wigs, with rouged cheeks and always in full drag. When the piano keys had been battered into submission and Nellie was snoring away and dreaming in her room of Al Jolson, I would creep into the parlour with Joyce where once more we rearranged the furniture.

From the rasp and the grit of Halifax the tour moved to the clean fresh air of Keswick in the Lake District where for thirty shillings for the week I had roses on my pillow, a bedroom to myself, four enormous meals a day including fish and chips and toast and brandy butter for tea – but no Longbottoms.

Back to London and the dole queue.

Unemployment was not rampant then but the labour exchanges always contained a high percentage of actors and actresses. The officials and cashiers, smug and bureaucratic, did their best to imply that any benefit was a grudging handout. Every claimant was an object of suspicion trying to hoodwink his or her benefactors by fiddling extra money and eager to avoid work. They coped with these queues of idlers using the patronising tones of prison warders, ticket collectors and inadequate schoolmasters.

As living and eating were essential this situation had to be accepted by those of us who spent most waking hours scrambling and searching for work. We retaliated by turning each labour exchange into a lively, drinkless cocktail party which 'unfortunately' we had to prepare to leave as we autographed one form and then joined another queue for the cashier. It was as if we were collecting our coats after the party.

The monotony of each day's quest for work could be broken by a coffee at the Arts Theatre and another in the afternoon at the S and F café, off Piccadilly. Regulars there included the drinking and high-living devil-may-care group of Bonar Colleano, Paul Carpenter and Patrick Doonan – alas, all now gone – the effervescent, talented actress, Joan Dowling, another who tragically died so young, Harry Fowler, Ken Tynan and Lionel Blair. We were a mixed bag, all skating on the perilous thin ice of the theatre and unconsciously part of a world which was about to fade and be replaced by another.

A new theatre was about to open in Pitlochry in the hills, in the heart of Scotland. I went to see Andrew Leigh, who was to direct the first season, at the offices of *Spotlight*, the actors' advertising manual, in Leicester Square.

The jovial, friendly little man, who had played so many of

Shakespeare's clowns, offered me parts including Darnley in *Mary of Scotland*, Malcolm in *Macbeth* and Simon in *Mary Rose*, at a salary of fifteen pounds a week. After deliberating for thirty seconds I graciously accepted the offer and did my best not to reveal that I would have swum the Channel three times to play the roles.

'Who is playing Mary Rose?' I asked.

'A little Scots girl from Africa,' he replied.

Six

The aged thespian spent the night with a whore. In the morning he stood in front of a mirror and adjusted his cravat as the whore, still spreadeagled, murmured from the bed, 'Well, darling, how about a couple of quid?'

The actor ran his hands through his silvery locks. 'My dear child, it would be a godsend.'

A large conspicuous hole had appeared in one of my shoes. I had arrived at the YMCA at Tottenham Court Road fifteen minutes early so I dropped into the nearest Dolcis where for thirty shillings my feet gleamed black and confident. But the shoeing had taken longer than anticipated, and when I reached the doorway to the rehearsal-room the cast were all assembled. A young girl with long flowing hair crossed the room, sat on a window-sill and I fell in love.

When rehearsal ended that day Rosemary Jean Kirkcaldy and I walked together to see if we could book seats for the Menotti opera *The Consul* with Patricia Neway. We were lucky. There were two seats going that very evening but we discovered that neither of us had any money. Then Rosemary produced some traveller's cheques and she took me to the theatre. Together we experienced the magic of a unique and wonderful show. Silently we left the theatre, took coffee together and I saw her home to her digs near Regent's Park. Silently we shared the emotions, touched off by the opera, saddened by the tragedy, elated by Neway and the music, and joined in spirit, heart and mind. Our joined hands unclasped when we reached her gate and there with a smile and a quiet goodnight we parted before the endless hours to the morrow.

The next day at rehearsal Rosemary told me that a solicitor friend had planned to take her to a couple of shows, but had been called away on a case and had left her with the tickets. It seemed the most natural thing in the world that we should use them.

One evening we were due to go our separate ways, Rosemary to meet friends, me to take another young actress to the theatre.

Before we parted we met Herbert Roland, who had also joined the company for a coffee and I then noticed that Rosemary was wearing a ring.

'What is that?' I asked.

'An engagement ring,' she said.

'You're joking!'

'I'm serious.'

The bottom dropped out of my world. I went numb, my mouth was dry and I left the table in silent, sulky anger.

I went to the theatre that evening deaf and blind to the play and the girl sitting next to me.

At rehearsal the following day the black mood prevailed and Rosemary told me that outside rehearsals we had better not see each other. The train journey to Pitlochry was tense as I chased and pestered and she retired deep into her silent self.

We stood midst the green hills by the theatre in the gleaming new tent and I begged her to walk with me. Reluctantly she walked by my side until we came to a stile in the open fields.

'Will you marry me?' I asked.

'A, I am engaged, and B, you're the last person I would want to marry.'

We returned to the tent, and then to Ascog, the house where, with other members of the company, we were both staying. Even our rooms were next to each other, but the division seemed total. However, in rehearsal the young lovers were easy to find. Gone were the tensions and restrictions that we felt in the real world and Rosemary became, quite beautifully, Barrie's lost fey childwife. Every day at least one letter would arrived from the fiancé, a wealthy young man, who was doing a hotelier course in Switzerland. At a distance I would watch jealously as Rosemary devoured his words until she would glance up and angrily catch sight of me. But gradually the play took us over and we began to walk together, long and often, to the Brown Trout and up the slopes of Ben Vrackie and sit silently by the mountain streams.

Eventually the horn sounded and the walls of Jericho tumbled down. When the season was well under way, one Sunday morning we went for a walk before lunch. On the spur of the moment we decided to hitch a lift to anywhere a car would take us. We expected to travel a few miles and be back in time for tea. Fate intervened. The car that stopped was going to Ullapool in the very north of Scotland, overlooking the Summer Isles. Because we had Monday free, as we were both out of the same play in the repertoire, we decided to go all the way. The approach to Ullapool was through rugged country. For mile after mile there was no sign of life. Not even a goat could be seen. We felt we were travelling away from the world, and then, suddenly, the small town appeared like Brigadoon and behind it the sea spread across the horizon.

For a day and a night we lived in a dream and the following afternoon we got a lift to Carrbridge on the way back to Pitlochry. There we spent an emotional night fraught with rejection, guilt and tears. On the last stage of our journey we sat in broody silence. When we got to the theatre the usual letters were waiting for Rosemary, plus one from her mother saying it was time she stopped frittering her life away playing games when there was a rich boyfriend to offer her security.

Rosemary stared at the letter in silence and then glanced up. 'Will you marry me?' she said.

We decided to marry in August but first Rosemary had the difficult experience of breaking off her engagement. She wrote to her fiancé in Switzerland and told him that she no longer loved him and wished to continue with her career. He flew over to reason with her and stayed at the nearby Green Park Hotel. Each morning we rose early and I would walk with her to the hotel where she would join him for breakfast and they would talk through the day. Determined not to hurt him she never mentioned me, but the evening came when he went to a performance of *Mary Rose*. We felt a weight had been taken off our shoulders. Now he would understand. When he saw the show he would sense the rapport between Rosemary and me, he could not miss the love in our eyes, he would know that we were one person. No more subterfuge would be necessary.

The following morning Rosemary approached her ex-fiancé tentatively, expecting him to kiss her gently on the cheek, smile bravely and say, 'Now I understand all – good luck to you both.'

But all seemed as usual.

'What did you think of *Mary Rose*?' asked Rosemary.

'It was all right – I suppose,' shrugged her boyfriend.

That evening he went to see *Susannah and the Elders*, in which Rosemary played a handmaiden and I was Susannah's lover. During the play I had one very quick change and so Andrew Leigh, the director, filled in the gap with a guard, played by that inimitable eccentric Graham Crowden, walking across the stage with Rosemary while Sibelius played in the background. Once they had reached stage centre they gave each other a peck on the lips and surreptitiously looked for the cue light which flicked on when I was ready, and then made their exits.

However. . .

That evening they sauntered centre stage, puckered their lips and looked for the cue light. But I had got my legs caught in the folds of my toga and was struggling to free myself. So the peck on the lips was forced to become a passionate kiss while I desperately kicked my garments out of trouble. Then I gave the thumbs up for the cue and they made their exit.

The next morning when Rosemary went to see her ex-fiancé at the Green Park Hotel he kissed her gently on the cheek, smiled bravely and said, 'Now I understand all – you are in love with that guard. Good luck to you both.'

The wedding took place on August 18th in a little church in Pitlochry and we had thirty-six hours for our honeymoon. For Rosemary it was a surprise honeymoon which we spent at Dalmunzie House high in the hills near the Spittal o' Glenshee.

Our first home was an old farmhouse on the third tee of the Pitlochry golf course and there we discovered the rich joy of each other's company and fitted together like the halves of a jigsaw puzzle. We shed our skins and were reborn. Our attitudes changed as we no longer searched within ourselves but through each other. Like young fawns we romped and played together, free and without cares.

On the last day of the season we set out for the train to London, ready to face the world. On the way to the station we stopped to visit a doctor who informed us that Rosemary was pregnant.

Muzz had prepared a bed-sitting room for us at Marloes Road. Rosemary had been offered a tour of the United States but now we settled down to an uncertain future. No work and a baby on the way. Muzz cleaned and polished and laughed, and with the help of the lodgers we fed. Eventually Rosemary and I managed to get into the repertory company at Salisbury, but by this time Rosemary was experiencing a lot of sickness with the unborn babe and had to drop out of playing Ophelia in *Hamlet*.

This *Hamlet* was directed by Val May, whose mentor was A. R. Whatmore, the giant of the provincial theatre. In the thirties, his company at the same Embassy Theatre where Tony Hawtrey now ruled had included Cecil Parker, Sybil Thorndike, Robert Donat, Donald Wolfit and Eric Portman. At Salisbury Watty was semi-retired, only directing the occasional play, but his authority, irascibility and humour were as strong as ever. When he left Salisbury

Rosemary and I took over his flat. And his protégé Val, long-legged and talented, carried on Watty's work. But *Hamlet* in two weeks was a big job for a young director. We were nowhere near ready when dress rehearsal arrived, and it carried on through the night and the following day. When we opened to the public we were bleary-eyed and exhausted. So tired were we that when I made my first entrance as Claudius, to a fanfare of trumpets, I swept in to the kneeling court, settled majestically on to a huge throne and said, 'Though yet of –' and dried. During the long silence the court remained nervously on their knees but no prompt came to save me from the corner. Eventually someone backstage ran round and found the stage manager, collapsed, fast asleep on the prompt book. Pushing him aside and hastily scanning the pages my saviour found the right place in the script. Placing one hand to his mouth he boomed out 'Hamlet!' I continued,

> Though yet of – Hamlet – our dear brother's death
> The Memory be green, and that it thus befitted . . .

And we went on to the end of the play.

The stage doorkeeper at the Salisbury Playhouse had never been to a talking picture show. The last stars he had seen on the silver screen were Charlie Chaplin and Mary Pickford. One week the local movie house was showing *The Eagle has Two Heads* with Eileen Herlie. As she had once been a member of the company I persuaded him to be adventurous and go and see it at its first performance on Monday afternoon. When he returned I asked him what he thought of her in the film.

'Not bad,' he replied. 'She didn't seem too sure but she'll be better by the end of the week!'

Rosemary continued to have a rough pregnancy so we found a cheap hotel just outside Salisbury where meals were provided. She began to get crazy yearnings for the most unlikely concoctions and her longings had to be satisfied. One night at about three a.m. her frustrated desire was for something quite simple – a piece of chicken. But how to get chicken at that hour in a quiet country hotel? There being no way that she could sleep without it, I eventually got out of bed and crept quietly through the corridors of the pitch black hotel, and slowly felt my way down to the kitchens, banging myself and several articles of furniture *en route*.

At last I reached my destination and, sure enough, hidden away in a small fridge was one leg of chicken. Proudly I made my perilous return and after what seemed hours I arrived back in the bedroom, turned on the light, and held aloft my victorious theft.

'*Voilà!*' I said grandly.

She stared at the chicken bone in silence, and then, 'I couldn't touch it now,' she said.

Just before Christmas we returned to London for the weekend. We had the house to ourselves. Muzz had gone to join her relatives in Birmingham and the lodgers were all away. We were due to return on the Monday because I had a performance of *Queen Elizabeth Slept Here*, but Rosemary was so ill she could not move and I had to leave her alone in the house with only a few cans of beans while I got the train back to Salisbury. And so we spent our first Christmas of married life.

I also became ill. I was suffering from piles and had to have regular injections. An operation was advised but there was no possible way that I could afford to plan a lengthy period of time without work. Twice during one matinée of *Queen Elizabeth Slept Here* I turned upstage while the audience were laughing and broke glass phials of ammonia which I held to my nose to avoid passing out.

Ironically the only person who was able to visit Rosemary in London over Christmas was my father, who had begun to appear on the fringe of our life. What I did not understand about him as a child gradually became clear in my teens. Born in Dublin to a fairly affluent family of bankers in Rathmires, by the time he was sixteen he got the maid into trouble and instead of going to Trinity College, he was making a bit on the side as a bookie's runner, so he was sent off to England as a remittance man. In London he stayed with his aunt Annie Winter where my mother worked as a maid, having come to the bright lights of London from her farming family in Worcestershire. Muzz became pregnant, but Dad was saved by the First World War. He joined the army, covering a great deal of territory not only as a soldier but also, part of the time, as a ship's purser.

When the war was over my brother Paddy was two years old. My parents married and my father became a journalist, taking a mistress and eventually spending most of his time with her at a flat in Randolph Road in Maida Vale. But Muzz remained faithful and accepted sadly his brief, unexpected returns. Five years after Paddy my sister Barbara was born and seven years after that, I appeared. As a journalist he became the country's leading writer on amateur soccer, but was always a frustrated serious writer. Thus, in the *News Chronicle*, he called himself Pangloss – after *Candide* – 'everything for the best in the best of all possible worlds'.

His uprooted existence and rich drinking love-life proved expensive, and when the Second World War broke out he, once again, leapt into the army and quickly became a major and moved from Dunkirk to Poona. When he divorced Muzz, it was to marry an eighteen-year-old, but by this time his old mistress, Maureen, was ill with tuberculosis and Dad, ever an honourable man, married her instead. Immediately he went to live with Jane, a waitress at the Press Club where he spent many of his working hours. Plump and Cockney, Jane was first his secretary, then his mistress and when Maureen died they moved into Randolph Road. But after his divorce from Muzz, Dad spent more time in our house than ever before. There was always an abyss between Dad and myself but he developed a strong affection for Rosemary and she for him; in a strange way she provided a connecting point between the two of us and gradually we got to know each other.

When our first child Melanie Jane was born, on May 16th, 1952, I was filming a second feature movie *The Ghost Ship* off the coast of Brighton. It had been a long difficult birth and I could not wait to finish filming and join Rosemary and experience the elation of seeing our first child. Rosemary or Pukky, as I have always called her, swiftly took to motherhood and we were now a family unit. But the long months of unemployment which followed now seemed even longer and the responsibility of providing for a family became all too apparent. Before Melanie was born I would try for work and shrug aside disappointment. Now it was essential to earn bread.

One day I heard of a non-singing role in the hugely successful Rodgers and Hammerstein show *South Pacific*, starring Mary Martin; an actor was leaving the cast and had to be replaced. Despite its lack of songs the role was quite good and the salary was sixty pounds a week – an enormous sum of money. I visited the agent Felix de Wolfe and asked him to send me along. He refused and said I was far too young, so I went home, cropped off most of my hair, put 6B pencil under my eyes and sneaked into the audition.

Every non-working American actor was up for the part and my heart sank when I saw the crowd of thespians backstage at the Drury Lane Theatre. I auditioned, received a cursory 'Thank you, leave your name and number' and went home. The following day the telephone rang and I was told that there would be a seat provided for me at the matinée, and I was to audition again in a few days. Once again with hair cropped and a few more strokes of 6B pencil, I joined a smaller group of actors backstage. Once again I received a telephone call. I was to do the fourth audition with three other actors and Mary Martin would make the final choice. Heart pounding I took the Number 9 bus to the theatre. Rosemary had left Melanie in the care of Muzz and came with me. I left her in a café in Covent Garden with a cup of tea. Silently she kissed me, checked the smudges of pencil beneath my eyes and I made my way to the stage door.

The four of us waited in a small room, full of squashed cigarette butts, as we paced up and down like expectant fathers. One by one we were called on stage and then asked to wait. Finally two of the actors were told 'Thank you very much – that will be all.' There were two of us left. Once again we were asked to do our piece. As I stepped from the wings on to the vast stage it seemed to grow bigger as I grew smaller. Sitting in the stalls was the wonderful, marvellous Mary Martin with a few figures clustering around her. I belted out my lines. There was a pause and then a muffled discussion. Mary Martin walked forward. 'Thank you so much for your help,' she said, 'but I am afraid we have decided to take the other fellow.' Silently I joined Pukky in the café. She said nothing. She knew. She smiled and we kissed and then silently walked to the bus stop to go home. Later Mary Martin wrote me a sweet letter saying how sorry she was but somebody always had to lose. I treasured it for years.

The gold was always at the end of the rainbow but every new prospect held intense excitement for us. I got into two pre-London tours. Neither got there. *Pagan in the Parlour* was a big blockbuster of a show under the management of Lord Vivian who had just taken over from C. B. Cochran. It was directed by James Whale whose previous production in England had been *Journey's End* in 1929. After that he had been offered a million dollar contract in Hollywood where he directed *Frankenstein, The Invisible Man, Showboat* and one of my favourite movies, *The Old Dark House*. This new show, *Pagan in the Parlour*, starred Hermione Baddeley as a cannibal without a word of English, who bounced around going 'ugga-wugga'. The other stars were Catherine Lacey and Moyna Macgill, the mother of Angela Lansbury and daughter of George, the politician. The lush settings were by Doris Zinkeisen and, after a six-week tour, it was planned to take the show to London and then New York. I played the comedy juvenile and Rosemary was understudying my girlfriend. In London we were to share a dressing-room. We would be in clover.

Despite opening to record business in Bath the play did not work out and we failed to reach the West End.

Not that the tour was uneventful. As Melanie was still only three months old we took a friend with us to act as nanny and instead of going to the usual theatrical digs we found a small private hotel in Bath situated in a charming Regency crescent. There were only two other guests, a travelling salesman and a ninety-year-old woman who looked like Ernest Thesiger in drag. The 'owner' was a brassy woman with peroxide hair who was out of place in the gentle old-world surroundings, and the staff was a maid who also acted as waitress. She was a trifle eccentric. Everything she said she repeated, and whenever one asked for tea it would arrive half in the cup and half in the saucer. When I foolishly asked her why she did this she said in her strong dialect, 'I don't spill it that way – I don't spill it that way.'

We accepted these minor eccentricities without demur but on our second day in the house we began to suspect that all was not as it should be when the old woman came up to us, opened her handbag, and said, 'Would you like to see my teeth?'

On the Wednesday we were in our bedroom at the top of the house when the ninety-year-old burst in and said she could not allow babies in the house because her mother was ill. Later that day Melanie was asleep in her pram on the porch outside the house, when the maid rushed into our room and said, 'I think you better go downstairs – you better go downstairs. The old lady's got the baby out of the pram – got the baby out of the pram!'

Like a flash I was down the stairs and in the street where Melanie was being held aloft by the dear old woman. After retrieving Melanie I had a difficult job getting the woman back in the house. Luckily her doctor appeared and after he had helped me get her back into her room he told me that he had tranquillised her and that she should have been locked in.

On Friday, at about three in the morning, I awoke suddenly. I sensed that there was someone in the room and switched on the light. The old woman was holding Melanie by the neck, trying to strangle her. Somehow she had climbed the stairs, opened our door and in the pitch darkness walked all the way around our bed,

93

without touching any of the baby impedimenta, and grabbed the sleeping child from her cot. Stark naked I jumped out of bed, grabbed Melanie, handed her to Pukk and held the old woman, who went rigid in my arms. It was like holding a skeleton and for a horrifying moment I thought that she was dead. I carried her down to a sitting-room on the floor below and put her on to a sofa. Then I hurriedly put on a dressing-gown while Pukk woke our baby-sitter and gave her the baby. We searched the house for the landlady and eventually I went into the street and rang the bell for her, but to no avail.

In the basement we found her – slumped fast asleep with her head on a table and beside her an empty whisky bottle. After reviving her and telling her what had happened, all she could drowsily say was, 'You should have locked the door.'

The following morning the travelling salesman, who knew nothing of the night's events, approached me and said that he was worried about the old woman.

'But she is locked in her room.'

'Oh no,' he said. 'She has just come to me and asked for a box of matches because she wants to set the house on fire.'

That did it. I told the landlady that the old woman was dangerous and must be sent to a home where she could cause no harm. This was promised and on the Saturday morning an ambulance arrived and the old lady departed, showing her false teeth to everyone as she left.

We were due to leave the next day but at least she would not harm anyone else.

The maid grinned when she heard this. 'Oh, she'll be back in a couple of days,' she said. 'She always comes back in a couple of days.'

The mystery of the house never became clear. Every room contained cameo brooches and paintings of a young girl which could have been the old woman in earlier days. Apparently her mother had always been an overbearing protective influence on her until she was killed in an air-raid and the daughter's mind became unhinged. Maybe if the house were hers and she died there the landlady might benefit. Maybe. We never knew.

The week of madness was completed the next morning when we caught the Sunday train back to London *en route* to our next date. The nearly empty train drew into Bath station. The rest of the company got into their reserved coach but as we were travelling *en famille* I opened a door further down the train. Sitting on one side was Stan Laurel and on the other side, Oliver Hardy. I did a double-take, quickly shut the door and we got into the next compartment. After a few minutes an actor I knew was passing down the corridor. He told me that he was stooging for Laurel and Hardy in their variety act and would we join them. We did so and had a great journey with my heroes who were just like caricatures of themselves. Ollie played with his tie and Stanley tapped his knees with his fingers. When we got out at Paddington the porters laughed and scratched their heads and Stanley did the same in return while Ollie adjusted his bowler.

As the weeks went by it became clear that *Pagan* would never reach London or New York. Hermione Baddeley grew frustrated saying nothing but 'ugga-wugga' and managed, at one performance, to get in a 'not bloody likely!' After one dreary matinée, as we took the curtain calls she stepped forward and told the audience that they should be ashamed of themselves for not laughing more.

'We work hard up here,' she said. 'The least you can do is to try and co-operate!' All the pensioners seated out front looked confused and stared blankly at each other, as we could hear Lord Vivian rushing angrily backstage, through the auditorium.

James Whale and Moyna Macgill soon returned sadly to Hollywood and the rest of us went back to the breadline.

The year 1953 started badly, but eventually I joined the company at the Theatre Royal, Windsor, and Pukky and I moved to a converted stable on a farm near Maidenhead. My salary was twenty-five pounds for each playing week but as the rehearsal period was two-weekly I was in every other play so, in fact, I earned twelve pounds ten shillings a week. Rosemary was expecting our second child and in the afternoons I ploughed fields to get extra money. I also sold a couple of paintings.

The three other juveniles in the company were Patrick McGoohan, William Franklyn, and William Millar with whom I usually shared a dressing-room as we always seemed to be in the same plays. He had obviously lived a very colourful existence, telling stories of working with Red Indians and surviving a shipwreck. In the play *Little Women* I wore a very large overcoat and one evening the famous film team, Frank Launder and Sidney Gilliat, came to the show. They were making a movie of the bestselling novel *Geordie* for Alexander Korda, with Sidney Gilliat directing. My large overcoat had impressed them because they invited me along to see them about playing Geordie, the big simple

Scot who became the Olympic shot-putting champion. After a couple of meetings I was optimistic of my chances, but I had to develop my muscles. Bill Millar was very helpful. He taught me exercises which reduced my chest expansion from five and half inches to two inches and I was soon walking around like Burt Lancaster. The day came when I thought the part was mine and Pukk and I decided that if the new baby was a boy we would call him Geordie. But without my knowledge Alex Korda was making his own investigations and the role went to Bill Travers. My big opportunity had slipped away.

From Maidenhead we moved up north to Chesterfield where I joined the local rep company directed by Chloe Gibson.

I had to go in advance because Pukk was back in Queen Charlotte's Hospital, having given birth to our son Paul Patrick, who leapt into the world with a great pair of lungs and an enormous appetite. Three weeks prior to the birth we had moved back to Marloes Road because Muzz had offered to look after Melanie while Rosemary was in hospital. The house was crowded with lodgers but we squeezed in somehow.

When her contractions began Rosemary was busy organising our trunk to be sent to the Civic Theatre in Chesterfield, because we had nowhere booked to stay. She insisted on carrying on until the pains grew intense and then we called the ambulance. Halfway between Marloes Road and Queen Charlotte's the pains stopped. Pukk was so embarrassed at raising a false alarm that she decided to pretend they were still going on. She bent low as I helped her from the ambulance, moaned, gave me a wink and whispered, 'I'll be back in the morning.'

That night I slept well, rose late and was in the middle of shaving when I decided to phone the hospital to find out what time I should collect her. A nurse answered my call. 'Your wife gave birth to a ten-pound boy a few minutes after you left last night,' she told me.

The following day I had to leave for Chesterfield, where I got digs, rehearsed and searched for a home for my family. Back in the hospital Pukk played for time and persuaded the doctor to allow her to remain there for a few more days.

On the outskirts of Chesterfield I found a sad, colourless stone mining cottage with no curtains, no linen, no light bulbs and no carpets on the cement floors. As luck would have it I had to return to London for a day's filming at the same time as Rosemary left Queen Charlotte's, where she got a cab to the station and with

Father as a boy, and my sketch of Mother

Me – aged eight or nine

Before I was born. My brother Paddy, and sister Barbie

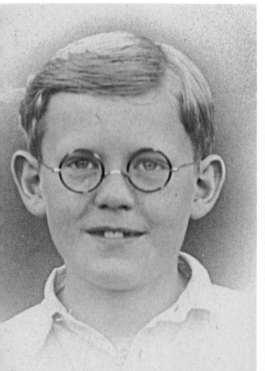

Young Rosemary; and, right, Pukk when I first knew her

Together in Pitlochry; and on stage in *Mary Rose*

In Nyasaland. Home
was called
Nachilonga. Centre:
with Friday at
Monkey Bay; and,
right, greeting the
magic bwana

In Cape Town. Disc jockey days – 'Springbok Radio for Brighter Broadcasting'; and with Moira Lister in *The Sleeping Prince*

At home in Oranjazecht; Melanie and Paul

Oxford days;
above, with
Rachel Roberts
and Alan Dobie in
Cards of Identity,
1958; and with Mai
Zetterling in
Darling, 1958

At the Old Vic; top left, in *Richard II*;
bottom left, in *Macbeth*; and, below,
with Judi Dench in *Twelfth Night*

Three Falstaffs: above left, with
Maggie Smith in *The Merry Wives of
Windsor*, 1960; in *Henry IV, Part I*,
1959, both at the Old Vic; and, right,
with Miriam Karlin in *Henry IV, Part
II*, for the Royal Shakespeare
Company at the Barbican, 1982

Scrofulovsky in *The Bedbug*, the Mermaid, 1961

Melanie and the new-born baby travelled by train to Chesterfield. We passed each other on the way. Chloe Gibson had arrived at the cottage at dawn to spring-clean the place and was there to welcome Rosemary and the babies. Meanwhile it turned out that I had gone on a wild goose chase as the filming had been cancelled. I did not get a penny – not even for the train fare.

The cottage was so cold it was like living in a fridge, and we were reduced to covering ourselves with newspapers at night because we were so short of blankets. After several months Chloe Gibson left the company and I left at the same time. The pantomime *Cinderella*, in which I had played Pong the broker's man, had been written and produced by a guest director, Frank Hauser, who had been up at Oxford with my sister. He was about to become artistic director of the Midland Theatre in Coventry and asked me to join the company. So early in 1954 I travelled with him on the train to the city that had been so badly bombed during the war. Poor Pukk and the two babes had to stay behind in Chesterfield until I found somewhere for us to live.

On the journey Frank told me who else was in the company. Gwen Watford, Kenneth Macintosh, Gillian Sterrett, John Ringham and an Irish actor, Stephen Boyd, who, as Frank described in some detail, had had a fascinating life. At the first rehearsal of my first play *Johnny Belinda* I met him. Stephen Boyd was none other than William Millar from Windsor whose background was as different as his name. When he saw me his embarrassment was obvious and our friendship never regained its former strength. In his eyes I belonged in another world – in another fantasy. That season his best performance by far was as Stanley Kowalski in Frank Hauser's splendid production of *A Streetcar Named Desire* in which I played Mitch. One evening he got so carried away in performance that he started knocking down the scenery, and we, the other actors, had to drag him off into the bathroom where I hit him across the back of his neck to subdue him. His photograph as Stanley was sent to Hollywood and from this he eventually starred, as the villain, in the epic *Ben Hur* with Charlton Heston.

The standard of the work in Coventry is high. Each play runs three weeks, two in Coventry and one on tour, so we enjoy the luxury of three weeks' rehearsal. Frank Hauser has a wicked sense of humour and is an interesting, stimulating director and the plays are a fine mixed bag.

But outside the theatre all is depression and frustration and now it is the estate agent's turn to be the bogeyman.

'Excuse me, do you have any accommodation for my wife, myself and two children?'

'Have you been resident here for three years?'

'Er – no.'

'Then it is impossible. You do realise that Coventry was the worst hit city in the war, sir? Half destroyed. We can only help residents, and they have a waiting list of ten thousand.'

Every morning, after an early breakfast in my digs, I start the round of estate agents. We rehearse at ten and break in the afternoon, when I continue my search. Occasionally I visit the lord mayor, a theatre fan, and he telephones various contacts, but to no avail.

Rosemary holds on to the cottage in Chesterfield for as long as she can but eventually she is pompously turned out by Chloe Gibson's successor, Gerard Glaister.

Mother's house in Marloes Road is full of lodgers so Rosemary takes Melanie and Paul from friend to friend, pushing their pram through the icy countryside until her hands freeze to the handle. Our only contact is by telephone which we limit to three minutes every other day, and one evening she calls me at the theatre to tell me that they are in Bournemouth. A small hotel for parents with young babies has just opened there and the young proprietors have taken pity on Rosemary. She and the kids can stay there in return for her working in the nursery. The long months go by. At last we can afford her travelling to Coventry with the children for one night and they sneak into my room.

Then, sadly, back to Bournemouth.

Rosemary's parents have arrived here on a business trip and her father is understandably concerned about his daughter's style of life.

Oh, God. What have I done? What have we come to? Where do we go? Is there a future? Three years of marriage. Just around the corner there is always – what? Success? Happiness? Protection? So many bloody corners. So many blind alleys. There has always been a hint of light at the end of the tunnel. But not now. Nothing. And finally my confidence has gone. During the past months I have cocooned myself from so many slings and arrows. Two actor friends and a director I knew committed suicide but like a blinkered horse I drove forward. The blinkers are off now and all I can see is an endless tightrope. Success that has always been there for the grasping was only a child's dream. Now that dream is broken I am married with two children and their own future ahead. Is the whole of life to be spent waiting for any form of employment, and when it comes will it mean further separation and little food or clothing for the children and possibly no roof over their heads? Three years ago Rosemary was carefree and talented and revelling in the magic of the theatre. Now all that she can do is help her children survive. Where has the joy of life gone for her? Our grinning masks are beginning to crack. My suit of ambitious optimism has become threadbare. Maybe – could it be possible? – maybe I am not good enough.

During the days we spent in Salisbury, Pukk and I used to scour the atlas dreaming of a holiday in France, but the dream never materialised. How we longed to travel. When we read *Venture to the Interior* by Laurens van der Post we found his description of Mlanje Mountain in Central Africa, as he called it the furthest point from civilisation in the world, rich, colourful and strangely magnetic – the antithesis of the concrete jungle of the theatre. Our regular evening phone call. Pukk sounds distraught. 'We can't go on like this. Maybe I should take the kids back to Africa for a while. Dad says he'll pay my fare.'

Hastily I break our rule and push another ninepence into the machine. The clanking of the coins sounds like our marriage breaking up.

'I'll come with you.'

The cheapest form of transport to Beira is on the SS *Umgeni*, an old cargo boat. It can carry twelve passengers but there is no guarantee how long the journey will take. Rosemary's father has offered to pay our passage to Beira, and the rail fare to Blantyre.

There are only three weeks before the *Umgeni* sails. Rosemary is in Bournemouth. I am in Coventry. There is much to prepare, to collect, to pack. Injections, vaccinations, decisions and farewells. Luckily I am only playing a small role in *Crime Passionel* and Frank Hauser has agreed to release me on May 14th in the middle of the run.

On the morning of the thirteenth I received a phone call at the theatre. 'Sorry to give you such bad news. Last night your father-in-law suffered a heart attack and died. Could you please break the news to your wife?' A day early I travel by train to Bournemouth and arrive at the Broughty Ferry Hotel late at night.

Pukk is sitting on her bed. Behind her are the two cots with our sleeping babes. Pukk's face lit up into a flowing, joyous smile. I take her on my knee, hold her tightly, break the news, and she sobs her heart out.

SEVEN

The blue sky is speckled with white foam, as the wash from the *Umgeni* leaps joyously in farewell to the English coast.

I stand at the stern and watch my world disappear. I am apprehensive but at the same time I can feel the tension of the past months evaporate as I relax into a euphoric, timeless stupor. The chaos of the last few days is over. Rosemary was at the funeral in Scotland while I stayed with my mother making last-minute preparations. Muzz was wonderful, working harder than ever and encouraging me to find myself on the other side of the world. She gave me confidence with her enthusiasm and her happy smile, and no sign of sadness.

On the scheduled day of departure, by magic my father had appeared and took us by taxi to Tilbury Docks. Once we had clambered aboard with our belongings he waved and marched off upright and humming into the distance. We were not allowed ashore again, even though the *Umgeni* remained in port for two days and nights, awaiting cargo for St Helena. On the third day the anchor was raised and we had slipped silently away, almost without our knowledge.

Day by day the weather improves and our whole world is the sea and the sun. We have grown accustomed to the steady chug of the engines, the occasional lowing of the bulls, the squeaking of the pigs and the other livestock, and the ripples of laughter from the passengers who stand in groups, arms folded for hour after hour. No pressures. No problems. I become a child again as the spray relentlessly disturbs the unchanging seascape and becomes itself part of the canvas.

> If all the world was paper,
> And all the sea was ink,
> If all the trees were bread and cheese,
> What would we have to drink?

What am I? A coward or an adventurer? Waste material or a caterpillar about to become a butterfly? What are our motives? Are they the same as the other passengers? Were the Pilgrim Fathers like us? Were they facing a brave new world or just looking desperately for any security without problems? The *Umgeni* is old and tired and is not meant to play host to human passengers but it is full of rusty character and each day our affection for it grows stronger, but, my God, the heat. We have the smallest cabin on the ship and it is situated next to the engine-room and the thumping engines and noisy fan drive us out on to the deck, where we sleep with the children under the stars.

The lascars* are friendly and always cheerful and full of fun, but once the other passengers become aware that we are actors, their eyes glaze with suspicion and they start to retreat. We visit Las Palmas, a dull barren island, and when we reach St Helena no one is allowed to go ashore because the ship's doctor thinks that Melanie and Paul may have German measles. Instead we sit on deck, aware of angry eyes, and the lapping of the waves blends with the gentle sound of Doris Day singing 'Secret Love' on our wind-up gramophone. Fortunately the German measles turns out to be heat rash. The days go by and the clear warm air lulls us into contented convalescence. Our nights on deck are always followed by a sleepy breakfast and then more sleep, read a little, play with the kids and then eat again.

'Oh, God, where is Melanie?' Panic. The ship is suddenly in an uproar. Pukk and I are cold and quiet with fear. We remember the story told us by the stewardess, of a young mother travelling with a five-year-old and a screaming baby. The mother lost patience. 'If you don't stop that row I'll throw you through the porthole.' She left the cabin and when she returned she found the cot empty. 'Don't worry, Mummy,' said the five-year-old, 'I've pushed her through the porthole.'

Melanie has been seen. She has crept outside a lifeboat and is balanced precariously on the edge, and there is no rail. Thank God, the water is like glass but any movement . . . How do we reach her? There is no room to crawl through.

We call her gently, she smiles but does not move. My hands are reaching under the lifeboat. After an eternity she crawls towards me, and is safe.

The weeks have gone by. There has been a tombola on board with everyone guessing when land would appear.

Suddenly there it is – surely the most beautiful sight in the world – Table Mountain from the sea.

* East Indian sailors.

When we go ashore the rich heavy scent from the giant flowers fills my nostrils and the red and gold and brown world stuns me and makes my heart beat faster.

A car is there to meet us. A brief tour, arranged by friends of Pukk's mother, while we are in dock. Sounds, smells, sights. All so strange. All so overwhelming. Our black driver is friendly and I ply him with questions about apartheid. I sense his compassion at my ignorance. 'Let me tell you a story,' he grins. 'A white girl here was a devoted fan of Nat King Cole and collected all his 78 rpm records. When his first long-playing disc arrived, with his picture on the cover, she saw that he was black, burst into tears and destroyed her entire collection.'

The drive is breathtaking. Colours are vivid, streets wide and clean, the music of Africa fills the rich and pungent air. But now the aroma is tinged with an acrid bitter smell.

Strange fruit.

At Port Elizabeth and East London there is the usual loading and unloading of cargo, but we have little money so we spend the days as well as the nights on board ship because we have no one to welcome us with a friendly driver. We pass these days alone with the lascars who keep us well fed and happy. In Durban we are in dock for a whole week but luckily a friend of Rosemary's father entertains us by day, and we return at night to the *Umgeni*. Melanie and Paul are fascinated by rides in rickshaws, pulled by Zulus in full regalia, and by snake charmers at the zoo with monkeys running wild.

We visit Umslangah Rocks where our world and mother, the sea, appears at its most beautiful. An enormous bright blue shimmering mass, calm and contented, and then exploding into a powerful cascade over the great white boulders. Hidden away behind we find a deserted hotel where you can sit in the open air and become part of this glorious panorama.

We see the lunch menu. We are tempted. We cannot resist. Our taste buds discover a new excitement as we tuck into chateaubriand stuffed with oysters. Magnificent and absurdly cheap. Maybe the price is a misprint. Maybe we shall finish washing up in the kitchen. But no. Exquisite satisfaction. Then Paul disgraces himself all over his chair and instead of washing dishes we end up cleaning the furniture.

On our last evening Pukk and I leave the children in care on the ship and visit the local Durban Theatre for a performance of *Arms and the Man*. After the play we meet the son of 'Sapper' who wrote

Bulldog Drummond. His name is Michael McNeile, who is in charge of the company. I tell him of my plans to try and get work near Mlanje Mountain in Nyasaland.

'Are you mad?' he says. 'Come and work for me here in the theatre.'

Rosemary and I both stiffen. My spine begins to tingle.

'Nice to meet you,' I say. 'Thanks for the drink.'

We run back to the ship.

Our final port of call is Laurenço Marques in Portuguese East Africa where the streets are even wider and whiter.

Pukk and I leave the kids in charge once more and decide to celebrate with our last few shillings at the Girasol nightclub where South American bands play in various lush tropical settings. We hold each other close and our bodies, now calm and relaxed, sway to the excitement of the future. The musicians play 'Quantalamera' and we ask them to play it again. We feel free.

After a voyage lasting seven weeks we disembark at Beira. Two letters are delivered to the ship. One is from Rosemary's mother with fifteen pounds to pay our fare to Blantyre. The other is from a firm in London to which I had applied for work near Mlanje Mountain. They had told me that there was nothing at present, but to let them know on which ship we were travelling in case anything turned up. The letter informs me that I should go for an interview in a few days' time in Blantyre. We make our way down the gangplank. We are going to miss this rusty old tub. We embrace our lascar friends and they give us a bottle of Scotch as a farewell present.

The train leaves Beira at noon and is due to arrive at Luchenza in the evening of the following day. It has a glorious old ramshackle steam engine and the coaches look as if the Marx Brothers have started to take them apart. The children's cots are put into a luggage van and, except for a couple of cases of personal effects, the rest of our belongings are locked away in bond at the other end of the train, which, eventually, chugs off through this wild and wonderful country.

During the day we stop at every village that emerges out of the dense jungle foliage and always the crude station platform is crowded with a mass of Africans selling their beads or begging beside the track. There are many lepers with long sticks and mangled frames with arms outstretched. The image has a dreamlike quality. Pukk once told me that she had seen part of a leper's finger fall off and I thought that she was exaggerating. Now I understand.

For the first time I hear the incredible sound of the heart of Africa. Insects, birds and animals scream their defiance and elation, and the cicadas rub their knees like washboards. Melanie and Paul take in the new sights and sounds with large eyes, and in silent awe. Night falls like a black curtain. The steward arrives with our boiled and filtered water and a mass of unfamiliar words pour from his lips. Rosemary is as surprised as I am when she answers in similar gibberish. Chinyange, the language of the country, has been hidden away since childhood but now returns effortlessly to her. The steward is delighted and exits happily, singing loudly.

As a young child I can remember the feeling of security and warmth and happiness I experienced when I hid beneath the sheets at the bottom of my parents' bed. If I wedged the sheets up with the pillows, I could make myself a tent. Lying under the mosquito net the feeling returns. Every few minutes the train clunks to an exhausted halt, and the air in the compartment buzzes with the sound of insects which swoop in through the ragged holes of the netted windows.

Oblivion.

At dawn I am awakened by a tickling sensation. An enormous praying mantis is doing its morning exercises across my chest.

Not for long.

We are stopped and searched by customs. We cross the Zambezi and the bridge seems to go to eternity. In fact it is four and a half miles long and below is the vast expanse of water dividing the continent. Then on and on into the green and brown steaming jungle until the train slows to a halt and the driver and fireman jump off and chop down trees because we have run out of fuel.

It is evening, just before nightfall, when the station at Luchenza comes into view. The platform is crowded with Rosemary's relatives, all, to her horror, dressed in black. Pukk is wearing a bright multicoloured cotton little outfit.

'Hello, Mum, did you have a good flight back? Darling, meet Granny – and Uncle John – and Catherine and Ken – and Robert and Betty.'

In two cars we travel the thirty-five miles to Blantyre. The family are warm and welcoming. Rosemary's grandmother is gentle, humorous and tough, the first white woman to settle in Nyasaland in 1896, travelling much of the way by machila, living through several uprisings and eventually opening Ryall's Hotel – the first hotel in the country.

Blantyre. A set for a western movie. At any moment I expect

John Wayne to appear out of the sunset. Most of the shops are run by Indians – from Calcutta not Arizona – who squat outside with their sewing machines, or fan themselves in the red dusty air. In the centre is Kirkcaldys, the store owned by Rosemary's father who was the town's mayor.

Guilt mixed with pleasure. These are the sensations I experience over the next few days. Pukk's parents' lovely house. Servants to care for the children. Permanent sunshine and the lazy sound of silence and contented crickets. Out of work I have been. By God, have I been, but always hopeful and always living frugally. Now I am without ambition, accepting security, and around me there are people paid little to take care of my every wish. And why? They are black and I am white.

The rusty fan in the office struggled to make its circular motion and squeaked intermittently with the effort. The tall slightly balding Englishman with a Ronald Colman moustache smiled benignly.

'I understand you want work near Mlanje?'

'That's right, sir.'

'Do you fancy being a tea planter?'

I thought of Somerset Maugham and Bette Davis. 'I do indeed, sir.'

'Well, it just so happens that we need a field assistant at Likongwe at the foot of the mountains, but I must warn you that there are two others who have applied for the job.'

My face dropped.

'However,' he smiled, 'as you have travelled so far you can have first choice, but you will have to make up your mind quickly. The salary is fifty pounds a month, plus a house, a nightwatchman and a garden boy. Any other servants you must provide yourself, but that won't cost you much. What do you say?'

The fan rasped to a temporary halt and gathered its strength for another journey.

'When could I start?'

'Right away.'

As the enthusiastic youngster left the office the benign man sat down with a sigh of relief. The fan was now moving quite smoothly. "Thank God we've filled that job," he thought. For three months his company had been trying to find a field assistant at Likongwe. It had proved an unlucky posting. The last fellow left after two weeks, the previous one had to leave when his wife got blackwater fever and the one before that broke his leg and had to be shipped home. It was a blessing when the youngster applied for a Mlanje job in London and as he and his family were travelling out anyway their passage was already paid. He looked at his watch and decided to have a drink before lunch. It could be a good day.

We packed the two trucks with provisions, a duck, some chickens and a giant Indian hunting dog for protection and, together with a cook and a houseboy, set out for Likanga tea estate in Likongwe. For seventy miles we travelled rough roads until the grey-blue mysterious mountain of Mlanje came into view. The trucks bumped along uneven tracks surrounded by jungle and dense brush. A tiny wooden newly-painted signpost with the words 'To the house of J. Ackland' came into view pointing along a concealed path through the jungle. Suddenly there was a clearing and in the middle stood Nachilonga bungalow. Covered with matting to keep out the sun it had a sheltered verandah which was called a *khonde* and was primitive and attractive. We quickly settled in and gradually got to know our new staff. Friday, the houseboy, had a great sense of humour, was intelligent, funny and full of gossip and was paid twelve shillings a month. There were days when his warm smile seemed more fixed than usual and he wore a tight band of wire around his forehead to cure a headache. If this failed he would cut his head with a knife to let out the blood and the pain.

'Cookie', who had four wives, was old and wise and solemn and in no time ruled the house but he was loved and respected by everyone. If Rosemary told him what we would like for dinner, he would always say, 'It is too late, Dona – I have cooked something else.' He was paid fifteen shillings monthly.

The M'londa had eyes like a leopard and appeared every evening at dusk when he would squat on the *khonde* and stare fixed and immobile as he hypnotised the world outside. He rarely spoke and was as much part of the jungle as the strong friendly blue gums that guarded the house. The garden boy spent the days slowly moving around the clearing on his knees and occasionally snipping away at this and that as he went about his ritual tasks.

Our two additions to the household were Effie and Dilly. Effie was Butterfly McQueen, likeable and a little mad, with as little knowledge of Chinyange as she had of English. She was the dhobi in charge of the family washing and also acted as a temporary nanny for the children. She claimed to be fifteen years old but, as she had two children aged five and three, this was doubtful. Every few days she would accuse the cook of raping her but nobody seemed very concerned, least of all Effie, and it was difficult to tell whether it was a complaint or a suggestion. She always wore the same dress which she took off and put on again thirty times a day. Cookie insisted on extra help in the kitchen and so Dilly was employed to wash up and do any odd jobs. Dilly was a Tigger among men and fell over himself in his effort to please. Whenever Rosemary or I appeared he would jerk to attention, give a massive grin and bawl, 'God save the Queen.' We soon discovered that this was not meant as patriotic ardour for Queen Elizabeth. It was a convention upheld over the years, because across the seas Queen Victoria was still believed to rule the world.

The battering heat of the day started early and by the afternoon became unbearable so I would start work at five in the morning. It was still dark at four fifteen when Friday woke us with tea which we sipped cosily in the privacy of our mosquito net. Melanie and Paul slept with the legs of their cots standing in tins of paraffin to stop the ants crawling up. A few years previously, only a few miles away, a young mother had left her baby in a cot and a line of ants had got inside and choked the child.

The only other whites in the area were the manager of the estate, Leslie Shepperson and his wife Dorrie, the first field assistant, Richard Awdrey and his wife Jocelyn and the factory manager, Cliff Spencer and his wife Elsie. The factory was a large wooden shed.

The Sheppersons were always in bed by six in the evening and were great believers in homoeopathic medicines. They lived in a house with the most stunning panoramic sight of the mountain and the valleys below, but, as they were both very short-sighted and yet determined to conquer weakness with willpower, they never wore spectacles and never saw the view. One day Shepperson was driving a truck, with me beside him, when he squinted through the windscreen and said, 'Is that Richard Awdrey on his motor-bike?' Before I had time to reply Shepperson had driven into a herd of cattle. The poor man also suffered from gastroenteritis and sent off for some pills advertised in his homoeopathic magazine, but he was so short-sighted he sent off for pills for constipation by mistake and finished up in the loo for three days.

After three years in the tropics it was compulsory to return to a temperate climate for three months for health reasons, so the Sheppersons would get the slowest ship that they could find, sail to England, step on shore, walk to another ship and go straight back again. Leslie Shepperson would sit silently for long periods and it was always difficult to know which way his thoughts were heading.

On one occasion, after a long and broody silence he stared quizzically at me, and said: 'You were in the theatre, I believe?'

'Yes, I was.'

Another short silence and then he spoke again. 'So was I.'

I could not conceal my surprise. 'You were in the theatre, sir?'

'Yes, I was – in Oxford – but after five minutes I got claustro-phobia and had to come out.'

The Spencers lived on a diet of lettuce extract. Cliff Spencer spent his time in his shed, bare from the waist up except for a sweat rag which was never washed and hung permanently around his neck. And he always wore two hats. Literally. He spoke in a jargon which would have stopped Biggles in his tracks and he referred to money as 'ukeri dukeri' and pound notes as 'quidlets'. As he was responsible for all financial dealings it is not surprising that he was never taken seriously.

Jocelyn and Richard Awdrey were a charming couple with a twinkling sense of humour and brought a touch of sanity into the newcomers' bizarre world.

On my first working day I was taken to the edge of a field by Peter, an interpreter. It was shortly after dawn and a cool grey mist was rising from the sweet-smelling earth. In the distance the mountain was black, covered with a blanket of cloud and still asleep. But, in the centre of the field, a mass of workers were already hacking away at the tea branches with their pangas or machetes. It was my responsibility as overseer to make sure that they worked well and consistently. I stepped into the field and the interpreter followed.

'No,' I said. 'You stay here.'

Peter hesitated. 'Bwana, perhaps I should come with you.'

'Don't worry, I can manage.'

Peter shook his head but stayed on the path. All eyes were turned towards me as I strode towards them and I made my first mistake. I was wearing shorts and the tea branches tore my legs as I walked, and little patches of blood appeared from numerous scratches. I gritted my teeth and moved without hesitating towards the quizzical faces. Shepperson had given me a pep talk telling me that the workers would take advantage of my lack of experience. I must show strength and confidence and never weaken. I had learned a few useful tea-planting Chinyange phrases. '*Mpazi wankukoo*' – the claws of a chicken. If the tea branches grew inwards they were like chicken claws and had to be hacked. '*Chotzenchingwi*' meant cut the string.

I could cope.

There was silence when I reached the group. As if frozen in time, their pangas stopped in mid-movement, the men stared at me with casual interest. The silence was broken by a huge African who stepped towards me and lifted his massive arm which was bleeding from a cut, and in deep bass tones said, 'Hospital.'

"What delayed you," I thought, and then said sternly, 'Hospital! A little cut like that! *Chotzenchingwi.*'

The African's eyes narrowed. 'Hospital,' he said, and his voice was louder.

'*Chotzenchingwi,*' I said, and my voice was softer.

'Hospital,' said the African, and the knuckles on the hand that held the panga turned white with pressure.

All eyes waited for the outcome.

I looked to the solitary figure standing on the path in the distance. 'Peter!'

The interpreter ran towards me. 'Yes, Bwana, can I help?'

'You certainly can. This fellow has a small cut and he wants to go to hospital.'

Peter shook his head sadly. 'Bwana,' he sighed, 'the hospital is that hut at that end of the field. He wishes to put on an Elastoplast.'

'Well, he should have said,' I mumbled. 'All right, hospital.' I looked fiercely at the group. '*Mpazi wankukoo,*' I said firmly. Then I swung on my heels and fell into a six-foot ditch. When I looked up there were a dozen grinning faces peering down at me. I hesitated. I grinned back. Many outstretched arms hauled me up and brushed me down. I walked happily back home to bathe my scratched, bruised and battered body.

Once I had learned the fundamental rule that the tea should have two leaves and a bud, and as Chinyange became more familiar to my ears, the job became fairly simple but by mid-morning, when the sun's powerful rays dominated everything, the work became arduous and tiring.

The most constructive time spent was in the cool morning air and I would return home for breakfast at eight o'clock and devour an enormous meal of tinned sausages, fried potatoes and several eggs. The basic ingredient for most meals was chicken, small scraggy creatures, which could be bought from locals for sixpence. There were few vegetables – chemanga, carrots, rice and sweet potatoes. Two avocado trees beside the bungalow bore fruit, and, eventually, some banana palms were discovered in the bush. There was no meat and supplies of canned food soon ran out, but Cookie could always create meals of delicacy and magic. He was proud of his desserts, banana fritters and surprise puddings – various fruits whisked up into frothy egg whites. There were a few cows on the estate which I milked and kept the cream for the calves. We had a supply of gin at six shillings a bottle – whisky at nine shillings was too expensive – and a couple of large skins of cheap Portuguese wine.

By mid-afternoon it was too hot to work so I would return home and spray 'Flit' at the white ants which were permanently attacking the house. They would crowd through the holes in the wall and fall in heaps with their legs kicking in the last moments of life. But the stream of insects never ceased and this great Gulliver became obsessed with keeping them at bay and I kept squirting until they ran out of troops.

'Sad news, Bwana,' said Friday, as he handed Rosemary and me our early morning tea. He led us into the spare room. The bed had been lifted three feet above ground level and was resting on great mounds of earth and thousands of ants raced in seething circles of victory.

With the darkness came the weird music of the jungle. Strange screeching sounds from a thousand birds. The clatter of cicadas was magnified at night, and blended with the hooting owls, whose silhouettes were caught in the light from the *khonde*, and the whining hyenas greasing their way around the bungalow. Occasionally there was the cracking of twigs as unknown creatures passed through the bush, and if we walked through the clearing after dark we took a torch to avoid the frogs, toads and lizards that jumped and scuttled across the cracked scorched earth, while bats silently swooped from tree to tree.

Long after we had retired beneath our net there began the sound of the tom-toms. It started gently and then gradually grew into a crescendo as the festivities in the villages became more excited. Always they played with the same regular beat, and, in time, we found that our hearts pumped in unison with the drums. But one night there was a sudden silence, and then the tom-toms changed their rhythm. Instantly we were awake and we lay in the dark confused and frightened.

But if this experience proved strange, it was minor compared to what happened some nights later.

I was in the centre of sleep. The layers slipped away, one by one, until I balanced on the edge of consciousness. I became aware of the sheet that covered me, the pillow that embraced me and the warmth and the touch of my loved one's arm. I was lying face downwards, and so was she. I was sweating. A strange cold sweat. My heartbeat was loud and fast. I knew it was night but the room glowed. A white light. My heart seemed to stop beating. There was something in the room, outside the mosquito net, at the bottom of the bed. I wanted to turn my head. I could not move. My body was heavy. The room was hushed, soundless and very cold. Icy. My eyes could only turn to Pukk. She too was awake. Her eyes, facing me, were confused. Awestruck.

Neither of us moved, neither of us breathed. I knew that we were both experiencing the same emotions. Fear. Joy. Elation. And something else. An emotion so rich, content and full, that it was beyond understanding, and whatever or whoever stood at the foot of the bed was the awesome reason for it all. We knew that we were, at that moment in time, complete. We were floating in space. Pukk breathed the words, 'What's happened? Have we died?' I could not answer. The light faded. The air grew warmer. Silently we gazed into each other's eyes. We held each other tightly.

The next morning we spoke tentatively of the previous night's experience. A precious gossamer so delicate that we felt it could disintegrate unless we treated it with reverence and gentle care. But that elusive butterfly of a moment created a bond between us, strong and secure, and our lives were never quite the same again.

EIGHT

As the weeks went by the new pattern of our lives took shape. The expected rainfall did not come and the heat and the humidity grew stronger. Each morning before work I would help the houseboys pour water over the thatching that covered the bungalow, but by midday the temperature inside was one hundred and eight degrees, and the tea fields were like a giant sauna. There was little contact from the outside world. Newspapers were three months old and there were only rumours of the Suez crisis and Mau Mau uprisings to the north in Kenya. Our change in lifestyle was made only too apparent when every few weeks letters from camp theatrical friends arrived by runner through the bush.

The relationship between us and the black workers in the bungalow was good, and mutual humour and fun strengthened the bond. But our diverse cultures still left a gap that was difficult to bridge, and the blacks' strong tribal instinct dominated our lives, whether they were Yow, Angoni or Zulu. For a man or woman to be cut off from their village was as painful as cutting off a limb. In 1949 there had been a great drought and Rosemary's brother-in-law, Ken Robinson, had the job of allocating maize to the villagers. When the healthy men and the unmarried women – the *namwalis* – kept coming back for extra rations he became very angry. Nor could he understand why. There was usually great concern and affection for the very young and the very old.

What was so different in time of crisis? Years later he got the answer. He mentioned this to a black friend who was a member of the government. The friend smiled. 'Of course the virile and the healthy would seek extra rations. The very young and the very old would give them theirs willingly. You see, with us it is imperative that the tribe should continue at all cost. The very old have already played their part and the very young can be replaced. The future of the village depends on the people most likely to survive.' Then the friend said farewell, climbed into his government car and went off to his village for the weekend.

There were other dissimilarities. Here is a story, based on personal experience, that I wrote at the time we spent in Nachilonga.

*

The sun beat down like a boxer's glove. The Englishman, weary after eight hours' onslaught, tramped heavily through the African tea fields. His head throbbed with every step, but to him it sounded like the heartbeat of the sun. The rains had broken but the heat remained, heavy with humidity. The invisible mosquitoes made music in the air, and created burning discord. He walked like a jockey, legs wide apart, because the heat made sweat, the sweat made the salt, and the salt grated harshly against the redness of his skin. He stumbled over the uneven ground, between the green sea of tea bushes, and made his way towards the path. Two giant snails moved silently, an inch from his descending boot, and his stomach turned over at the thought of crushing one. Like stepping on an egg.

As he reached the path a lizard ran between his legs and then stopped, with an unnatural extended paw, halfway up a small tree. Its beating heart convulsed its tiny frame while its eyes revolved like a roulette wheel. The path was hard under his feet and his shoes crunched against the loose laterite. He became conscious of his rambling daydreams, and this sudden material awareness was so startling that he lost track of preceding thought and, try as he may, he was unable to lose himself in any fresh meditation. His mind became a vacuum and he was only conscious of walking in limbo, so that each familiar landmark took an age to reach and pass. His eyes ached behind his moisture-covered sunglasses and he pressed his fingers hard against his eyeballs to relieve the pain. When he lowered his hand and the mist cleared he became conscious of a grin surrounded by a face. A native was walking towards him, pushing a bicycle. A pair of boots was slung over the handlebars.

'Morni, Bwana.'

'Morni, morni.'

The native stopped and removed his hat.

This action irritated the Englishman. No native ever approached, or even passed within yards, without removing his hat and the accepted deference never failed to embarrass him. He felt guilty and half-inclined to remove his own. Instead, he sublimated his disgust at the originators of white supremacy, by attacking the innocent grin confronting him. His weariness only accentuated his annoyance as the native swung his hat round in a full circle, and nearly fell over his bicycle. The beaming smile remained.

'Well, what is it?'

Without a word the African handed him a neatly folded piece of paper. The white man scanned it impatiently.

'Please, sir,' it said, 'the man standing before you, Ninepence Katemango, is a good man and an honest man and is a seeker of work at your factory. He is a seeker as a clerk and his home is in your district. He is a good worker and a good man and has many times had the position of clerk. Thank you, sir, Ninepence Katemango.'

'So you want a job as a clerk, eh?'

'Yes, sir.'

'Well, you had better see the manager – but I don't think we have a vacancy.'

'Sorry, sir – I do not understand.'

A cow fly stung the Englishman behind his ear, and he swung at it wildly with his hand. He pointed above the hills of tea. 'Tomorrow morning go over there to the factory. Ask the M'londa for the manager and give him this letter. Do you understand?'

The native nodded but the grin remained. 'Yes, sir, I understand well. But I have been at the factory today and the day before but did not see the manager.'

'Well, he has been there all today and all yesterday, so I don't know how you missed him.'

'I do not know the manager and what he looks like.'

'He is white like me, and as there are only three other white men here it is not too difficult.'

'But, excuse me, sir, I do not know who to ask.'

'I've told you, ask the M'londa.'

'It is very difficult, sir.'

'For God's sake.' The Englishman removed his hat, wiped the sweat from the leather rim, and replaced it. 'Look, do you see that path? Go along it for a mile or so and you will see the manager's house. Give the note to a houseboy and wait for the Bwana N'Kulu.'

The native paused. 'I would not go to the house of the Bwana N'Kulu because of the dogs.'

'But the manager has no dogs.'

'Excuse me, sir, but there are dogs there, and I would be afraid that they would bite me.'

The Englishman grew impatient. 'Look here, old boy. I've just told you that there are no dogs there!'

'Pardon me, sir, but there are big dogs and I should not like to be bitten.' His grin remained, but he made a faint click with his teeth at the thought.

'Don't you understand? The manager has no dogs! I have a dog – a great big dog – but the manager does not like dogs. He has a cat because his Dona likes cats, which catch the rats, but they both hate dogs, so they do not have a dog!'

The native frowned but his grin remained. 'Excuse me, sir. I had better not go to the house. They are bad dogs and I am afraid.'

The white man loosened his shirt which clung tenaciously to his skin. His temples throbbed and he looked for some shade. There was none but his look had only been abstract in an effort to control his blood pressure which had become dangerously high. For some seconds he watched, fixedly, as the native idly swung his boots over and under the handlebars and then sharply shifted his gaze.

'Look here, I don't give a hoot whether you see the manager or not but I'll give you five shillings if there are dogs at the manager's house.'

'Ah, yes, sir, but five shillings would not help me when I have had bad bites from the dogs.'

The Englishman lost control. 'Are you deaf! I've told you there are no dogs. Do you understand? THERE ARE NO BLOODY DOGS!"

'Yes, sir.' The native saw that the Englishman was disturbed and his grin grew less and showed pity.

The Englishman stepped a pace backwards and wagged his finger. 'I shall give you ten shillings if you see any dogs.' His voice came from his stomach and emerged strangely distorted through gritted teeth.

The native shook his head sadly. 'But the dogs would bite me.'

The Englishman's words came slow and separate. 'I shall give you fifty pounds if there are dogs. Surely it would be worthwhile to be bitten for fifty pounds?'

The native paused. The grin was now the grin of a man who shuts his eyes with sadness. 'I think, Bwana, that, perhaps, I should see the Bwana N'Kulu at the factory tomorrow. Perhaps.'

The white man removed his sunglasses and wiped the sweat from his eyes. 'Come with me,' he said thickly.

They walked together beside the tea and then moved in silent procession along a jungle track. They looked slightly ridiculous, the tall caucasian and the squat negro pushing the bicycle, because the white man was determined that they should walk side by side, which confused the native who was concentrating on remaining a yard behind. First the white man would stop, and then the native, until their journey became something of a relay race. Once they had passed through the trees there was nothing to be seen but tea fields and a small hut on the edge of the clearing. The Englishman stopped outside, and said, 'Wait here.'

Three clerks stood to attention as soon as he stepped inside but, for once, this did not embarrass him. He spoke to one of them. 'Salkiri,' he said quickly. 'Outside there is a boy who will not go to the house of the Bwana N'Kulu because he says that the dogs will bite him.'

'But the Bwana N'Kulu has no dogs, Bwana.'

'I know that the Bwana N'Kulu has no dogs. Will you tell the man outside that the Bwana N'Kulu has no dogs?'

'But how can the dogs bite him when the Bwana N'Kulu has no dogs?'

The Englishman's voice grew faint and lacked conviction. 'Never mind. Just tell him that the Bwana N'Kulu has no dogs, will you?'

Salkiri shook his head and clicked his teeth but he shuffled outside with the white man.

The path was clear. The countryside was deserted.

Salkiri looked quizzically at the white man. 'Which man, Bwana?'

'Damn!' said the white man. 'Damn! Damn! Damn!'

The sun beat down.

I was writing by the light of an oil lamp when I heard a strange rustling sound, which grew in volume as a huge swarm of flying ants flew in through the open windows and covered me and blackened the house. Scamp, our Indian hunting dog, rushed around with open mouth and devoured them, and the houseboys grabbed all the lamps in the bungalow, put them on the *khonde* and filled basins with water, which were soon piled high with a wet sticky mass of insects. Later they fried them and ate them. My shirt was heavy with trapped insects which I scooped out by the handful. The rest of the evening Pukk and I spent in fluttering darkness, hidden in the safety of a mosquito net.

By dawn the insects had gone but the floor of the bungalow was covered with a carpet of wings.

Scamp was an affectionate creature and we were very upset when he disappeared, as we thought that he had been taken by a leopard. However, three days later there was a scratching noise on the *khonde*. We ran out and found him collapsed on the cement floor. All four pads of his feet were hanging loose as if they had been cut with knives. Gently we lifted him on to the sofa and Pukk covered his paws with Dettol, pressed the pads back on, and tenderly swathed him with bandages. He stayed there for several days, took food and water from a hand-held dish, made no effort to move, and then, fully recovered, took the bandages off with his teeth, jumped down and went on with life.

Snakes were everywhere. Most were harmless and even the poisonous varieties would only attack if trodden on. Many times in the tea fields I would push a branch aside to find it soft, cold and clammy against my skin. The black mamba, however, was vicious and deadly and had been known to kill by spitting venom into the eyes. Two of these creatures were nesting in the eaves of the nursery, so we had to move Melanie and Paul into our bedroom. Every evening as we lay beneath our net we were woken by the swishing sound of a mamba taking his evening slide around the bed. One night Rosemary's patience snapped. She pulled up the net, grabbed my shoes and flung them at the snake, which shot under the bed. Eventually I leapt mightily across the room, barefooted, and rushed out to the M'londa for assistance. We returned together with large sticks, but the mamba escaped and continued its nightly excursions.

I decided to seek help from the witch doctor. Housing the workers on the estate was my responsibility. Every house was made of wattle and daub, covered with elephant grass, and cost six shillings to build. Every few days I would be summoned to one of the hastily constructed dwellings and, invariably, I would find a family sitting outside their hut, together with chickens, maize and any possessions. The ants had been at work and had built a mound of solid earth which filled the home. It was only natural that the witch doctor should be called in. He would throw salt around the mud hut, stare gravely at me, shake his head, and say, 'Build another house.' 'Build another house,' said I, and, lo, it was done. The witch doctor was shown the home of the mambas in the eaves of the nursery, and was asked if he could magic them away. He nodded and disappeared for three days. When he returned he brought with him the root of a tree which he stuck into the opening in the roof, beneath the matting. And, lo, oh wise one, it came to pass that the mambas were forced to flee. But it came to pass that our entire family and all the household were nearly forced to flee, also. The power and the pungency of the heavy camphor-like smell was overwhelming.

Then, when the air was clear again, other snakes arrived. During one bad period the houseboys averaged killing a snake every other day. We were visited by a compulsory pest remover team who cleared the bungalow for several hours while it was filled with a poisonous vapour. Two puff adders and another mamba were killed that day but, alas, so were all the friendly little lizards which ate the insects, and had become pets.

One morning I was walking through the tea fields when I felt a sharp pain in my left hand. My arm recoiled automatically and a spider fell and disappeared into a bush. Within a few minutes the hand had swollen to twice its size. Fortunately Nachilonga was close by so I ran home and showed Cookie my swollen paw. Without hesitating, Cookie dragged me into the kitchen and thrust the tumescent extremity into the boiling water in the copper. A fleeting moment of excruciating pain, then numbness and the pain had gone. In time the outer layer of skin came off but Cookie's swift action had been successful and my hand was back to its normal size.

The tea fields of Likongwe stretched for miles, and, no matter how hard I tried, I could only cover a limited area on two legs. One morning a beaming Leslie Shepperson sent for me and produced a brand new motorcycle which had just arrived from across the seas. For two hours he explained, very slowly and in great detail, how to start the machine. Just as I thought that I would die of boredom, listening to the repetitious instructions, Shepperson was called away and asked Richard Awdrey to take over, but on no account was I to move the bike.

'How much has he told you?' asked Number One, when the boss had disappeared.

'Everything,' I grinned, 'at least eighty times. I'm off.' I opened up the throttle and the bike moved forwards along the path.

'Steady on,' shouted Awdrey. 'Don't go too far.'

'Not to worry – I'm okay,' yelled Mr Toad, as I felt the power between my legs and the elation of the wind rushing through my hair. I knew what to do. I would ride once around the field and stop when I reached Awdrey again. Stop?

'Oh my God,' I thought. 'I don't know how to stop.' For all his precision, Shepperson had not reached that point in his instructions. My face paled beneath the hot sun as I clutched desperately at the handlebars. Every time I pressed anything the bike seemed to go even faster. I looked back. The distant figure of Richard Awdrey could be seen leaping and gesticulating, but there was no question of circling the field now. I knew that I must just go straight onward until I stopped. On and on along the narrow path. The tea fields came to an end and I was sandwiched between heavy bush on either side. The hairs bristled on the back of my neck when I saw the stream ahead with only two planks of wood joining one bank to the other. My eyes became pinpoints and I drove along the tightrope but the wheel of the runaway bike went straight along one plank and I had reached the other side. How would I find my way back? I must keep an eye on the mountain and use it like a compass. I glanced around. There was no mountain to be seen. Minutes later I passed a sign in Portuguese and I realised that I was in Portuguese East Africa. Maybe I would run out of petrol. No, it had just been filled. Another sign. 'Beware of elephants crossing.' That could be a solution. The bush grew deeper and luckily I found myself going up a steep hill. I bounced the handle-bars and was able to come to a bumpy halt.

Now what?

I was miles from anywhere. There was nothing for it but to try and go back the way I came. I turned the bike, kick-started, and jolted forwards. I still had no idea how to work the brake. Once again I held my breath as I negotiated the shaking plank across the stream. In the distance I could see a car approaching. Richard Awdrey was driving and Leslie Shepperson's head was protruding from a side window, looking for wreckage and a body on the path. Awdrey slowed when he caught sight of the bike rushing towards him.

'Stop!' yelled Shepperson.

'Sorry – can't,' I replied, as I manipulated my iron horse around the car and whizzed on my way.

Mount Mlanje was smiling down at me, and Likanga well in view, when I found another hill and drew once more to a halt. I switched off the engine and waited.

Eventually the car appeared and a weary sweating Shepperson climbed out. Pain and despair showed on his craggy features. He paused intermittently and then turned to Richard Awdrey, who was grinning faintly beside him. 'Awdrey,' he said, 'I want you to ride Ackland's motorbike back to his house. He can come with me in the car. After I have dropped him, we shall all go our ways for a much-needed lunch, and then at two o'clock we shall meet at his house and we can continue with the instructions, which are obviously incomplete. On no account is he to be allowed near the motorbike until we meet again.'

Over lunch I told Rosemary of the morning's adventures, and when we had finished I took her outside to see the unbroken mass of horsepower where Awdrey had left it standing, regal and gleaming, by the bungalow. I sat astride it proudly.

'Isn't it beautiful?'

'Yes,' said Pukk.

'I know how to stop it now. Let me show you.'

'No,' said Pukk.

'I'll go just a few yards.'

'No,' said Pukk. 'Wait for the others.'

'Don't fuss,' I said. And I opened up the throttle, released the clutch, the bike leapt forward and crashed into a tree.

And not just a tree. It was the only tree that stood, solitary and proud, in a vast area of space. Cookie and Friday ran forward and helped me, bloody and considerably bowed, to an upright position, and helped me inside. When Shepperson and Awdrey arrived at two o'clock they found a field assistant swathed in bandages, and a mass of twisted metal that had once been a motorbike.

It was ten weeks before the machine was repaired and returned and at last I was able to race happily around the estate. I only had one other accident. Every week I paid the natives their *posho* (wages). This involved a great number of coins which I delivered to the *posho* hut, in sacks, balanced precariously in front of me, on my handlebars. I was crossing another plank bridging another stream when the wheel caught a stone, and I was flung through the air. This time the bike was unmarked but my world became a thousand stars, and when I recovered consciousness I was surrounded by dozens of Africans who had collected all the bags of money and any loose coins. Not a penny was missing.

Rosemary's brother-in-law was called 'The Bull'. So Friday informed the young couple. 'But he lives over a hundred miles away. How do they know this?' 'We know, Bwana – we have the word.' No more needed to be said. The tom-toms could be accurately relied upon for news and gossip. The natives believed that life should be painted in the air musically. Not written in dull ink on uniform pieces of dull parchment. Every white man was pictured with a name. The second field assistant was known as 'the Magic Bwana'.

It came about, so. If there was an overflow of paid workers, they would be allocated unnecessary little chores to fill up the time. Occasionally I would lead a group of young children through stagnant water infected with bilharzia,* while the kids cut away

* Tiny flatworms which enter the pores of the skin and eat away the liver and the kidneys.

the overhanging foliage at the side of the bank. After a while I would take them into the bush, where they squatted down, and I showed them simple tricks with matches and a handkerchief. From that time forth, I was known as 'the Magic Bwana'.

One day I discovered Gilbert. A tiny scarecrow of a boy, aged about ten or eleven, he was working with a group of hefty workers who were throwing bails of tea to each other. The heavy sacks were each bigger than the energetic, emaciated child. So I took Gilbert back to Nachilonga where Pukk gave him a job in the house. The boy was cheerful, funny and very intelligent and he learned English quickly so he was given the job of looking after the two babies. The unfamiliar world of the West seemed miraculous to him. The wind-up gramophone made his eyes grow like saucers, and when we told him that in England there were houses with many floors on top of each other he would gaze in amazement. 'I'a-i!' he would shriek, and clap his hands with excitement. 'You are joking with me!'

He became part of the family.

There were no baboons on the estate.

Two years before, the tea fields had been overrun by the creatures, and so all the white planters, for miles around, travelled to Likanga to kill them off. When most of the baboons were gathered together in one field they were huddled in a mass in the middle of the field and the hunters raised their guns. As they did so a large baboon scooped up her child, and held it above her head. This way she approached the hunters, and slowly walked in a large circle, holding her infant for all to see. One by one the hunters lowered their rifles, and silently left the field. The next day the baboons had vanished and, from that time on, not one was seen again.

All the white planters had guns – except for the Acklands. One weekend Pukk, Gilbert, the two babies and I were driven to visit Pukk's sister, Catherine, and her husband, Ken, on their tobacco plantation at Magomero, one hundred and twenty miles away. Also visiting were Pukk's brother, Robert, and his wife, Betty.

Ken and Robert took their guns and suggested that I went with them for a drive. After a few miles we left the truck in open country, and walked. A bird flew high above us. Robert raised his rifle, fired and missed.

"Now they will ask me to shoot," I thought. "They are testing me." But the sky was clear. We walked on but luckily there was no sign of life. Eventually we reached a stream. A flat rock protruded from the water. The two old hands placed three white pebbles on the rock and then led me some distance away. Looking back, three tiny splashes of white could be seen glinting in the fading sunlight. One old hand sighted his Winchester and fired. A pause. He fired again. Another pause. He fired a third time. The smoke cleared. The pebbles remained intact. The other old hand followed suit. After the third shot there were only two splashes of white gleaming on the rock. I was offered a .22 rifle.

'You have a go.'

"This is it," I thought. "At least it is not a bird." It was time to be Gary Cooper. 'Hand me a Winchester', I said coolly, and just refrained from adding 'in a dirty glass'. Slowly I sighted the heavy gun. During my short time in the army I had discovered that I could shoot accurately, but that was years ago, and it had been a very short time in the army. I squeezed the trigger very gently and fired. But the power of the heavy Winchester took me by surprise. My shoulder jerked back with the blast, my trigger finger pulled a second time convulsively and caused a further explosion. The two old hands and the newcomer stared silently as two white pebbles shot into the air. The grey flat rock was empty. Not a word was spoken. Not another shot was fired. Two men picked up their guns and led the way back to the truck, while the third followed looking, I hoped, quite unconcerned.

The rains were three months late when the storm broke. During the last few days the heat had been intolerable. The air had become heavier, and the ground was taut and dry, as if it was about to explode. In fact, it had cracked badly with earth tremors, which rumbled and shook our jungle world, and left gaping chasms in the dusty red land.

In the middle of the night we were jolted awake by a deafening clap of thunder which shook the bungalow to its foundations, and for the next two hours we lay huddled together, as the skies opened, and Nachilonga was blinded by flashes of white lightning, and shattered by pulverising explosions. Frankenstein's monster could have been brought to life that night. We felt that we were descending to hell on a flickering neon sign. There was no sound from the cots but we did not have the courage to emerge from beneath the mosquito net to see if Melanie and Paul were awake or not. Eventually the storm subsided, but in two hours nearly five inches of rain had fallen.

Several natives were killed in the deluge, struck by lightning as they tried to shelter beneath the trees. When we stepped out on to

123

the rain-soaked land we found that most of the outbuildings had been destroyed, and all the chickens drowned. During the day the steam rose up, and by mid-afternoon the earth was once more scorched hard and the chasms gaped wider than ever.

Friday had become a good friend and confidant. One morning he spoke quietly to me.

'Bwana, tonight there is great excitement in the village – a big celebration. It is a very important initiation ceremony. Our chief's daughter is to be circumcised, and there will be much rejoicing. Would the Bwana like to see?'

I could not believe my ears. 'This is a great honour, Friday, but how? I thought it was forbidden.'

'If the Bwana comes with me and my friend, we will show you where to hide in the bush. We shall stay with you and, if you remain quiet, there will be no trouble.'

I found it difficult to contain my excitement. It was unknown for any white man to have been present at an initiation ceremony. I had heard tales of intense, elated hysteria, culminating in the subject and the participants falling into deep trancelike states, and doing impossible things with knives. I could hardly wait for the night to come.

But by the early afternoon in the tea fields I found it impossible to move. The constant friction from my motorcycle had brought about a severe recurrence of piles, from which I had suffered for the past few years. That night, instead of watching the ceremony of knives, I watched the lower part of my anatomy being shaved by an African, with an open razor, as I was prepared for an operation, ninety miles away in Zomba Hospital.

Three days after the operation, Rosemary was driven by truck to stay at her sister's house at Magomero, which was only forty-five miles from the hospital. She was accompanied by Friday, Gilbert and the two babies. A few miles from the house they stopped by an aged African who was working by a tobacco field.

'Is this the way to the house of the Robinsons?'

'It is truly,' the old man replied. 'Are you the Dona of the Magic Bwana?'

'I am.'

'But he is in the hospital at Zomba.'

'That is right,' she said. 'But how do you know of the Magic Bwana?'

The aged one showed his teeth in a smile. 'We have the word.'

The drums had passed their message through a hundred miles of dense bush country.

It was several days after the operation before she was able to visit me. I stayed in hospital for three weeks. There were five others in the ward which was always bright and cheerful. Through the matted windows the view, of the green plateau and the world beyond, was breathtaking. There was always laughter in the ward and the patients' spirits remained high to the end, but a few weeks later three of them were dead.

Lake Nyasa covered fifteen thousand square miles. It was three hundred miles long and fifty miles wide. It was three hundred feet above sea-level and at one point had a depth of three thousand feet. It had tides, like the sea, which swept over the sand, and the foliage of the surrounding jungle glistened with tiny specks of foam. The natives called it Malawi – shimmering water.

It was to the lake at Monkey Bay that I went to convalesce, together with Pukk, Friday, Gilbert and the two children. We ate the chambo that swam in the waters, and we rested beneath the cool palms. Occasionally Pukk, Gilbert and I would pluck up enough courage to swim also, while Friday watched carefully for any sign of crocodiles. Hippo could also be unreliable creatures, especially if they were in calf. When she was a child Pukk's canoe had been overturned by a nervous mother.

After a week of bliss we returned to Nachilonga and the tea fields.

A few nights later we were awakened by the M'londa. He was no longer impassive. His eyes gleamed with excitement.

'Bwana, Bwana, come quickly! The cisywe are coming! We must make fire.'

We ran outside, collected hot ash from the kitchens and by the light of the lamps, scattered it in a circle around the bungalow. Then we added twigs and small pieces of wood which smouldered with sparks of yellow fire. Assisted by the garden boy and others from the compound, after two hours the circle was completed. There was still no sign of the threatening army of ants.

'How do you know that the cisywe are coming?' I asked.

'Listen, Bwana.' The M'londa lay down and placed his ear to the ground.

I did likewise. I could hear a rumbling sound.

'What do we do now?'

'Sleep, Bwana. I will feed the fire.'

I obeyed and returned to bed. At dawn Pukk and I looked out

beyond the *khonde* where the ground seemed to be alive. An endless line of ants was heading straight for the house, devouring everything in their path. The line was not wide but it was thick with the tiny creatures as they clambered over and along each other. When they reached the hot ash, defeated and confused, they scattered in all directions as far as the eye could see.

For two days no one could leave the bungalow while the cisywe frantically darted everywhere in muddled disarray as they tried to form another line. On the second day there was the sound of a car approaching the clearing. We all rushed on to the *khonde* and waved frantically at the man who was stepping from his car. But it was too late. As his feet touched the ground the ants were on him, and with an anguished yell he leapt back into his car and drove off. Pukk and I stared sadly at each other. It was our first visit from a stranger. We never discovered who he was. By the third day the cisywe had remobilised their forces and marched off in a different direction.

'It looks safe now.'

'No, Bwana,' said the M'londa. 'We must wait one more day.'

A few hours later baby Paul managed to squeeze through a hole and toddle into the clearing. With one bound I was over the gate, grabbed the child, and threw him to Effie, who watched with wide eyes as I flung off my trousers, which were crawling with the eager cisywe. As if by command they aimed straight for my testicles and bit in unison. I yelled furiously. Friday rushed to prepare a bath.

By the next day the ants had gone except for a few stragglers running in confused circles.

The native was found lying behind the mud hut. He was a pathetic sight, his body mutilated by leprosy. It was possible that he had once been tall and strong, with that natural, proud dignity inherent in his ancestry. But the disease had infiltrated deep for many years, and all that was left of the once-powerful frame was seventy pounds of ravaged skin and bone. He had been hidden away from the outside world by his family in fear that he would be sent to hospital. It was widely accepted that hospital was the place that people went to die, and so the ill must be concealed from prying eyes. I told Leslie Shepperson of my discovery. We wrapped the tiny creature in sackcloth, which we sewed together with string around his shaking, feverish body. Gently we lifted him, like a baby, and drove him to the nearest hospital.

The next day he died. He died from meningitis, not leprosy. But the natives were not surprised. He had gone to the hospital. He had to die.

We decided to return to England.

It was not a healthy environment for the children – we said. The climate caused the pupils of their babies' eyes to dilate with an unnatural glow – we said. And there was always risk. One day Melanie pushed Paul aside as he was about to pick up a large scorpion. 'Naughty Paul,' she gurgled, as she squashed the insect with her foot. Separated from the rest of itself, the tail continued to wag dangerously.

And there was another reason.

Insecure as it was, we felt drawn back to theatre life. The jungle had taught us much. It had changed our lives. Ambition had been replaced by determination. Survival seemed more important than success, which no longer was the ultimate goal. Our real world of make-believe had been replaced by a dream, but now we had picked ourselves up from the canvas with a different perspective on life and were ready to continue the fight.

We tried to analyse our own mental outlook.

'If you stand at the top of a mountain and look down, the people below look like ants, and you are all-powerful. But you also know that you are as small as they are, and, ergo, they are as large as you are. When one is able to accept both these facts, simultaneously, life can be much easier. Take life seriously and at the same time laugh at yourself, and you can harness fate a little.'

As a child I had read Hendrick van Loon's *The Story of Mankind*. It had a preface with a moral which had always stayed, tucked away in my mind. It went something like this:

'Far away in the land of Nvorjord there stands a rock. It is two hundred miles wide, and two hundred miles high. Once every thousand years a little bird comes to sharpen its beak on this rock. When the rock has thus been worn away, a single day of eternity will have gone by.'

Maybe our mountain was the rock of Nvorjord.

One evening, after work, Pukk and I drove thirty miles to see a movie. Every few months the local planters hired a film, which they showed, with an ancient projector, on the side of a large shed in the middle of the bush. There was one performance only. As we travelled to Cholo in the fading light, our truck ran over a huge python, which stretched the width of the road. Quickly I reversed, in order to finish the job. For the second time the heavy vehicle ran over the squashed python. Before we could go forward again, the 'dead' monster pulled its vast length into the heavy grass and disappeared.

The movie was *Torch Song* with Joan Crawford, saccharine and schmaltz, eating her heart out for blind pianist Michael Wilding. Maybe he was only shutting his eyes to the banality of the dialogue and the histrionics of his leading lady. The tea planters sat fascinated and serious, and they frowned in disapproval when Pukk and I exploded with uncontrollable laughter. It was the vision of Miss Crawford covered with sequins and singing a sexy number, blacked up like Al Jolson, that caused our hilarity. We looked at each other with wet eyes. The movie was quite dreadful. But it was our life. It was home.

We wanted to return by the east coast, and stop off in Zanzibar. But how? We had saved a little money, but not enough for the fare back to England. Pukk wrote a letter to Brian Brooke who ran a repertory theatre in Cape Town. She had known him when she was at university. He wrote back, and offered her a temporary job with the company. He could not make any promises regarding myself but would try and fit me in somewhere.

We had a jumble sale. Tea-chests were packed with books and clothes, and would cost a fortune to send, so we decided to get rid of them. Cookie and Friday organised the sale solemnly and with great enthusiasm. No article cost more than threepence. Most items were a penny. The natives came from miles around and bought everything. The women acquired Pukk's hats, which they perched precariously on their heads; and Pukk's shoes which dangled from the toes of their large feet; and Pukk's dresses, which Cookie had laid out neatly on the grass, or hung on wooden clothes-horses; and Pukk's brassières, which some of the women put on back to front, with cups protruding from their shoulder blades. Their breasts were weighted down with clay and dried by the sun to stretch them, so that they could feed their babies, who lived permanently on their mothers' backs. When some of the women turned their breasts into Swiss rolls and tried to stuff them into the bras, Cookie, Friday and Gilbert collapsed on the ground, with tears rolling down their cheeks, as the breasts shot out like great sausages.

There was excitement until the end.

On our last morning in the jungle, Pukk and I were eating breakfast, when we heard a great commotion outside the *khonde*. One of Cookie's wives was sitting, with Effie, doing last-minute mending on a sewing machine, when a huge eagle swooped down, captured a chicken in its beak, and started to fly off. But the chicken screeched, the women screamed, the eagle dropped the demented creature, and, in panic, flew into the room where we were eating, brushed both our heads with its enormous wing span, and crashed through a high window, removing the entire pane of glass. Despite the impact, the giant bird could be seen in the distance, flying into the bush. Only at the last moment, as it was about to disappear from view, was it seen to falter.

The train travelled through the night towards the coast.

Gilbert sat with the two children asleep against his legs. On his lap was Paul's pillow, which he had used to protect the baby from the jolting movements of the train. He looked shiny, clean and smart in the sailor's outfit that the Dona had worn as a young teenager. Silently he stared at us. The moment that we had been dreading drew near.

We had spent much time discussing the possibility of adopting Gilbert. He was, indeed, part of the family, but could he exist in such a different world? A world that he could not, even vaguely, conceive? How would he cope with the rigid apartheid of South Africa? Or the polite patronising hypocrisy of the English? After much deliberation and prevarication, we decided not to take the risk.

He was all that remained, now, of our jungle life. Friday, Cookie, Effie and Dilly had scattered in various directions. Scamp had gone to another planter and, sadly, was quickly taken by a leopard. Only the M'londa remained, isolated and impassive, still staring, cross-legged, at a world that he alone understood.

The train shuddered to a stop in the middle of the jungle. It was the nearest point to Gilbert's village, or so he said, but there was not even a platform. The cicadas created their usual discord in the darkness.

Gently, the small boy handed us the sleeping babies. His eyes were lowered now. Then, suddenly, he grabbed Paul's small white pillow, and, clutching it tightly, he ran off – a tiny figure in a bright white suit vanishing into the blackness.

NINE

Last night in my dreams faces floated around me, my son, my mother, my father, my brother, together with friends and those who only appeared on the perimeter of our lives. The faces were alive but not the people. Today I am sitting in our flat in Covent Garden with the windows open and I can just hear the faint sound of a choir rehearsing in the Royal Opera House opposite. It is thirty years since the small boy in the sailor suit ran off into the bush. On reflection it seems that the time I spent in Africa was the end of my adolescence. The dictionary describes adolescence as a period of growing up, but to what? Does maturity mean that we cease to develop? If we are no longer floundering confused, lost and searching, have we really found our way? Or have we merely shut our eyes and blindly followed the herd? Have we become part of a set pattern? Whatever the answer my adolescence was over; either a cog slipped into place and I found myself, or a padlock was bolted and I began to rust.

We stopped off in South Africa for a few weeks and stayed two and a half years. Two of those years were spent in Cape Town which was then the most cosmopolitan part of that beautiful country, which was run by the fearful, the blinkered and the prejudiced. We lived in a 1930 Hollywood set of a house in Oranjazecht on the slopes of Table Mountain and then in a flat on the sea-front. We found security. My approach to the theatre had changed. The jungle had evaporated that gnawing ambition. I returned to acting because it was what I knew best, it was my profession, my trade and I suppose my vocation. Because we were able to afford a black or coloured nanny, Pukk and I were able to work together in the theatre, and on the radio I became a disc jockey and Pukk and I presented the *Bovril Family Show* which included tape-recordings of Melanie and Paul. As the work poured in I stretched out and swallowed it like water after a desert. I was on the run sixteen hours a day, Sundays included, rehearsing and playing in the theatre and doing nine broadcasts a week, including six shows for which I wrote, presented, chose records and interviewed visiting guest stars. For each of my shows I was paid five pounds per week, but it was security.

My greed for work surfaced one afternoon when I rushed in the middle of one broadcast to do a *Woman's Hour* which always ended with the words, 'And this is Joss Ackland saying goodbye until next week at the same time.' As the red light went on I rushed through the doors to the live studio and read the script which had been thrust into my hands. The words came out automatically, but all went well until I heard myself speak the words, 'And this is Joss Ackland saying how sorry I am that this is,' my voice rose in horror to a squeak, 'the last in the series.' Thirty shillings a week down the drain.

Eventually the pressure caught up, I lost nearly twenty pounds in weight in two weeks and I had to give up my regular theatre work with the Brian Brooke Company and only did occasional selected plays. My two favourites were for the director Leonard Schacht, *The Diary of Anne Frank* and *The Crucible*, that beautiful play by Arthur Miller which was made even more memorable on the first night when I walked on the stage and said, 'I have three children.' Rosemary, always eager to help me in my approach, had given birth to our third child, Antonia (Toni), in the Salvation Army Hospital one hour earlier. Pukk and our doctor friend Hymie Shrand both had tickets for the first night and fought it out together. He won. Working with Pukk in *The Diary of Anne Frank* was an extraordinarily moving experience and every night the audience walked out mute and not one person ever clapped.

One afternoon during the run, Rosemary had taken Melanie, Paul and Toni to visit a friend and I was alone in our sea-front flat. Suddenly I felt an agonising pain in my stomach and collapsed. I crawled to the telephone and called Rosemary. She contacted Dr Shrand who examined me and advised me not to do the play. It would be quite simple because I was contracted to do *The Sleeping Prince* in Johannesburg, and another actor was ready and waiting to take over my role of Otto Frank, but vanity would not allow me to miss a performance and Rosemary and Hymie drove me to the theatre. The first act went by in a blur as I kept going off backstage where buckets were strategically placed for me to be sick. The interval was extended by fifteen minutes as a surgeon prodded and pummelled me. This made me feel even worse, but I managed to get through the play and at the end I stood alone on the stage and the father's last speech was not only mentally agonising but also physically, as he recollected the fate of his family. The curtain fell and I fell with it and had to be carried in full make-up on a stretcher through the auditorium. When I reached the hospital I had to have an immediate operation as my appendix had burst. The next day I read in the newspaper that I was doing as well as could be expected. I'd been trained to believe that the show must go on. In a hospital bed, with a wife and three children waiting at home I had a new thought. Why?

After a year in South Africa we still lacked enough money to return to England, but we could afford to pay for my mother to join us for a holiday. When we met her off the ship she seemed vaguely lost. Her usually buoyant personality was subdued and she seemed older. I feared she might be ill, the joyous laugh had gone and she had lost a great deal of weight. Apart from our trip to Ireland she had not been out of England in her sixty-two years. Although we had no car and I was therefore unable to show her much of the countryside, Muzz played with Melanie and Paul and enjoyed the sea and the sun.

I have not attempted to describe this strong, proud, understanding lady who had endured so much without complaint, while troubles bounced off her round frame, who accepted all the setbacks of life with peasant wisdom and courage. If I have not gone into detail describing those close to me, it is because they are too close to observe dispassionately. The bond that binds us also blinds us and it is that phenomenon, family relationship, that heightens all the other senses so that we see without seeing and touch without touching. As for my wife, the dream-girl whose beauty filled my fantasies and desires, strong, gentle and tenacious, she not only helped me to survive but drove me onwards with her determination, while her deep love for me and the children has always been a safety ledge for us to cling to, making us one. When Muzz returned to England I wondered if I would ever see her again . . .

Pukk and I were no longer afraid of the future. We had food and drink, gone were insecurity and uncertainty and our bodies were warm. In fact in our new relaxed state our bodies grew increasingly hot and we spent our free evenings locked in each other's arms while the romantic songs of the fifties poured off the record player and Toni slept in her carry-cot on top of the table. The popular music was taking a different form. Elvis Presley replaced Pat Boone and groups appeared on the scene. The Mills Brothers, the Ink Spots, the Andrews Sisters, even the Merry Macs had all had their day but they were rarities in a world of solo singers. Now young musicians worked mainly in groups and The Kinks, Gerry and the Pacemakers, Herman and the Hermits replaced Julie London, Katherine Grayson and Johnny Ray. There were exceptions, of course; it was during the fifties that Ella Fitzgerald, Frank Sinatra and Nat King Cole reached their peak and Judy Garland skated between disaster and magic.

The movies of the fifties had become a wasteland; the Americans produced large-scale epics with grey plots in glorious garish Technicolor and slow coy romantic comedies that had no connection with reality. Only a few moments of magic broke through. *High Noon, On the Waterfront, Twelve Angry Men* and the occasional musical, *Seven Brides for Seven Brothers, Singing in the Rain* and *A Star is Born.* Marlon Brando had magnetism and the new age of frustrated teenagers identified with James Dean. In England there were tepid films about alligators, mermaids and doctors, where James Robertson Justice parodied a fading class.

Bodies relaxed and became free as we discovered rock 'n' roll. The waltz, the foxtrot, the quickstep, cinema organs and Victor Sylvester vanished as if they had never existed, as for the first time it was not the twenty-year-olds who set the rules and created fashion – it was the teenagers. But in South Africa these revolutionary cries of youth drifted across like echoes from another world.

Our other theatrical base was Johannesburg where my first play was Terence Rattigan's *The Sleeping Prince*, in which I partnered Moira Lister, a local girl who had become a big success in England. In order to start rehearsals in time after my appendix operation I went by plane, so Rosemary followed in our first car, a Volkswagen. She drove off the same day she passed her driving test, a fifteen hundred-mile trip, with three very young children and, to help with the children, a girl who had just come out of a mental home after having a nervous breakdown. It was a traumatic journey, but they arrived safe and well after two days on the road. We lived at Sleepy Hollow, a hotel with separate rondavels, thirteen miles from the city, where Melanie and Paul played in the long grass while Pukk and I read by Toni's cot and listened to Sibelius and Bach and Eartha Kitt and Sarah Vaughan. I also continued with my radio work. *The Sleeping Prince* was presented by a group of wealthy amateurs, well-meaning and generous but without very much idea about professional theatre. In the play I spend much of the time trying to seduce Moira and during the course of each performance we were seen to consume two bottles of vodka, four bottles of champagne and a bucket of caviare. Reluctantly we had to explain that it would be a little difficult for us to drink sixteen bottles of vodka and thirty-two bottles of champagne a week and remember all the lines. We kept the caviare.

In the play I wore a black wig and eyelashes and made myself a straight putty nose. With considerable preparation, elegant costumes and good lighting I managed to look quite dishy. After the second performance I had taken off all my make-up and sixty schoolgirls came backstage to see me. As they entered the dressing-room one by one their faces fell. By the time I had seen sixty faces disintegrate my confidence was completely shattered. Ever after I kept my make-up on every time the show finished, just in case.

On another occasion a woman came backstage, flung open Moira Lister's door and said brightly, 'Very good, Miss Lister, but tell me, are those your own teeth?'

Our second trip to Johannesburg was for me to play in Noël Coward's *South Sea Bubble* with Dulcie Gray, which we had done very successfully in Cape Town. This time Pukk and I drove up with the children and Mrs Barros, who had been acting as the children's nanny. Mrs Barros was a French-speaking, bright, intelligent, seventy-three-year-old from the Seychelles, who had become a good friend. *En route* we stopped for the night at a motel in a small dorp. When we asked for rooms we were told that there was a room for us but that Mrs Barros would have to sleep outside in the courtyard. It was bitterly cold, the night temperature near freezing. Pukk and I had come across some absurd examples of apartheid but really! When we asked for food for Mrs Barros we were advised that when we had finished our dinner we should give what was left on our plates to the kaffir. There was an extra bed in our room and we smuggled in Mrs Barros and she slept contentedly through the night. Later we learned that the punishment for sleeping in the same room as a black was twenty years in prison.

In *South Sea Bubble*, a light-hearted romp, I had to black up to play the extrovert South Seas islander Hali Alani. In one scene I played the drums, got drunk and tried to seduce the very English Dulcie Gray. In Cape Town this scene had been hilarious and the audience cried with laughter; however, when we opened at Johannesburg to an audience of diamonds and starched shirts, we played this scene to shocked and silent horror. There was much censorship. I even had trouble with my radio shows and when I finished one programme with the words, 'Happy Christmas to every colour, race and creed' I was questioned and the words erased from the tape. There were moments of ironical comedy in this world of confused politics. One day for no apparent reason our

Johannesburg flat was visited by young Afrikaans police who examined our shelves and confiscated one book.

It was *Black Beauty* by Anna Sewell.

When Rosemary had been at university in Cape Town in the forties she spent her spare time teaching drama in District Six, the poor quarter inhabited by the black servants of the white city dwellers. Together with coloured students Pukk had directed *A Midsummer Night's Dream* with an all-black District Six cast, and by calling it a University of Cape Town production they received permission to perform for two nights at the City Hall. The all-white audience were astonished to see Shakespeare performed by black actors and it was a great success. Pukk was invited to the farm of Dr Malan, the South African President. It was after he succeeded General Smuts that the policies of apartheid were introduced. During the afternoon Rosemary walked with him in the gardens and very quietly and politely he informed her that she was undermining the prestige of the Europeans and would have to surrender her passport. So Pukk was unable to return to Blantyre for the holidays.

Later, when she applied for a job escorting white schoolchildren back to their homes in Rhodesia, she received a temporary pass. Once she had delivered the children safely in Salisbury she took the train to Blantyre where she applied successfully for her British passport. There were further complications when she went to England in 1949 and decided to visit Vienna, stopping *en route* in Paris. As she was to pass through the Eastern bloc she had acquired a special visa. One morning she was noisily awoken from her Paris bed by three gendarmes and taken to the Palais de Justice. Because of student riots it was a spiky time in Paris and Pukk's passport, with an Eastern bloc visa, coupled with her inability to speak French, caused grave suspicion. Unfortunately the British Consul was away for Easter. For three days and nights she remained behind Palais de Justice bars until she was released and put on a plane back to England – she has yet to visit Vienna.

In the English summer of 1957 we heard that Muzz had suffered a bad haemorrhage and was in hospital. Pukk and I had already decided that it would be expedient to return to England; it was a question of action or apathy and the bad news only hastened our departure. The world of red tape forced me to go on ahead while Rosemary was left to fight out the battle over Toni's birth certificate and passport. We had not anticipated how hasty my retreat would be and the gangplank had been raised a few feet from the quayside when I leapt aboard and my luggage and cases of records were flung up over the side by hysterical Africans and caught by laughing lascars. Pukk was left with the three children, and weeks of frustration and confusion, as she wiped the slate clean of our African world and fought her way through the bureaucratic web to join me at Marloes Road. For five months Muzz was ill with cancer of the brain, her personality completely changed, but after several operations she seemed to make a miraculous recovery, and was walking around the hospital ready to leave when she suffered another haemorrhage. Early the next morning the hospital phoned me to say that she had died in her sleep. I remember a sensation of calm and concern, almost relief. I returned to bed, held Pukk tightly and we went straight to sleep, then rose and ate a hearty breakfast . . .

We had been out of England for three years. Would it be difficult to find our place in our old world and how would our old acquaintances react?

We need not have worried. No one had noticed we'd been away.

And it was not our old world. In the theatre with *Look Back in Anger*, french windows had become obsolete pieces of scenery, to be replaced by the kitchen sink. Many young rivals had been swept away by the new tide as BBC elocution was replaced by gritty regional dialect. The new drama was a searching cry as the young shed their skins and sought a different direction. Rattigan and Fry and N. C. Hunter left their houses as the young mice, Osborne, Pinter and Wesker, nibbled at the floorboards. This was the world I had been waiting for. I had been an unwanted guest and had drifted away from an unwelcoming shore but now slipped in on the new tide.

We moved from Marloes Road as we could not afford to buy the house and got a mortgage on a semi-detached in Madrid Road, Barnes, just over Hammersmith Bridge.

After a few scrappy jobs – doing a live fifteen-minute commercial magazine for television in which I raised the sales of St Ivel cheeses with a slip of the tongue when I said there was sex in every packet, playing a villain in a four-part television serial and Tony Perelli for a week in *On the Spot* at Wimbledon – I rejoined Frank Hauser who was now very successfully running the Oxford Playhouse. It was as though the last three years had been a dream.

Each production ran for two or three weeks, often followed by a short tour to Brighton and Cambridge. In the company were Rachel Roberts, Christopher Hancock, Alan Dobie, Annie Walford and Edgar Wreford and the plays included *Under Milk Wood* by Dylan Thomas, *Cards of Identity* by Nigel Dennis, *Henry IV* by Pirandello, *Darling* by Roussin and *Life with Father* by Howard Lindsay and Russel Crouse. For the latter play Pukk joined the company as my future daughter-in-law. I was the determined-to-be firm and Victorian father whose large family wrapped me around their little finger. When Melanie and Paul were aged six and five and came to see the play they could not understand why everyone was laughing. They thought it was just like home.

One of my sons was played by a young man who seemed hopelessly lost behind the footlights and was obviously not part of the theatre scene. His name was Alan Ayckbourn. Rachel Roberts and Alan Dobie were married; she was warm, Welsh and extrovert with a great relish for life, he was taciturn and gritty, still and silent. They seemed well matched but there were moments of lunacy. One day before a matinée of *Cards of Identity* I was going to buy some wood; Rachel said she would come with me, Alan wanted her to do something else. In the middle of Oxford High Street they began to bicker, the row suddenly turned into an explosion and Rachel ran back to the theatre pursued by Alan. I went on to buy my wood. Back at the Playhouse Rachel locked herself in the lavatory and flushed away her wedding ring. Alan stormed out. By the time the matinée was due to begin he had not returned. The stage management asked Rachel where he was. 'Don't ask me,' she said sweetly, in her low Welsh purr. 'He's nothing to do with me in the theatre.'

Cards of Identity was a difficult piece, deliberately confusing the audience by legerdemain. Rachel and I played a scheming married couple and Alan was our son, but we all kept changing identity by putting on different disguises. That afternoon when Alan finally arrived, the curtain went up fifteen minutes late, and the row between them continued on stage and was only concealed from the audience by the complications and plot of the character. But despite the eruption her rich ebullience and his quiet strength seemed to be the perfect complement, and it was a shock when the partnership disintegrated. Rosemary and I next got to know her after she was married to Rex Harrison and her personality had quite changed. Whether it was the different chemistry or the new style of life, she was insecure and confused and hitting the hard stuff, and when she died tragically she was not the same warm, compassionate girl, but someone lost and crying for help.

When I saw Mai Zetterling in the Swedish film *Frenzy* in the late forties and she reached out her hand to remove the light bulb and seduce the young schoolboy, she seduced me in my cinema seat. The only other creature who disturbed me sexually on celluloid was Françoise Arnoul who could manage to upset me even in long shot. Mai joined the company to appear in *Darling* and when, at our first meeting in the play, she walked up to me and gave me a passionate two-minute kiss, I was a little nervous. I had no conception that the day would come when Pukk and I would wake up in bed and find Mai lying on top of us with a camera. But more of that anon. We had hopes that H. M. Tennent would present *Darling* in the West End but, as so often happens in this profession of dangling carrots, it proved to be false optimism. In Pirandello's *Henry IV* with Edgar Wreford as Henry, I thought I was miscast as the slim, sophisticated, effete Belcredi. I was probably right because Michael Benthall came to see the play and asked me to be Sir Toby Belch in *Twelfth Night* for the Old Vic's American tour. He had obviously forgotten my disastrous season in Stratford. Accompanying Michael Benthall was Philip Pearman, the theatrical agent with perhaps the best reputation in London. He offered to represent me. As I had tried many times to see him, and always in vain, I leapt at the chance. But the American tour was a different matter. It was to be the most extensive tour of the States ever made by an English company and it would mean six months away from the family. Pukk was due to give birth to child number four on the day the tour began. It was an agonising decision. We had gone through rough times in our seven years of marriage and the worst had been when we were separated. But it was a good opportunity and Pukk insisted that I take it. I could not help feeling guilty of chauvinism. She had given up her chance to tour the States to marry me, but now situations were reversed it was another matter. The contract was signed.

The season at the Oxford Playhouse was coming to an end. *Hamlet of Stepney Green* by Bernard Kops had been successful and was to play for a few weeks at the Lyric Theatre in Hammersmith, but first we did a short, but exotic tour of *A Midsummer Night's Dream* and I gave my Bottom not only in Cambridge, but Geneva, Bloemendaal and Venice. In this latter magical city we played on the island of San Giorgio and the audience came by gondola. But the Italians are unusual theatre-goers and a continuous stream of people walked in and out during the show. The press did not make it any easier by jumping on to the stage and clicking away with their flashlight cameras while they actually stood amongst the actors. When I voiced my disapproval they looked confused and hurt.

The majority of Americans, Germans and English are bad travellers, they are incapable of blending in the new surroundings and can only cope by travelling in groups. Americans invariably become caricatures of themselves, insecurely clutching desperately at their identity by talking in strident tones as if the rest of the world were both deaf and invisible. Foreign countries and traditions are treated as cute little curios to be collected and placed on the mantelpiece or shown on home movies. The German priority abroad is to come first: first on the beach, first on the ski-slope and first in the food queue, as they push and shove with monotonous vulgarity. The English travel defensively and become more insulated than ever. The centuries of concealed patriotism leap to the surface as they disapprove of food and climate and do not understand why things are not the same as they are back home where everyone speaks a sensible language. There is a story of an English colonel who ordered a meal in Paris.

'I'm sorry,' said the waiter, 'I do not understand – you're a foreigner.'

'Don't be a bloody fool,' roared the colonel, 'I'm not a foreigner, I'm an Englishman.'

English actors are no exception and I was surprised on this delightful little tour that there was so much discontent. I loved the new sounds, smells, appetites and ambience and jumped from the high board without inhibition. Like approaching a role in the theatre or film it is only by going all the way into the heart and soul of the country that you experience its true pleasures and delights. *Vive la différence!* I determined then that Pukk and I would see the world.

Back in London rehearsals started for the transfer of *The Hamlet of Stepney Green* when I was taken ill with a high temperature and driven to St George's Hospital where I was kept for a week. Naturally I had to leave the show. When I returned home I collapsed again. Back in St George's, after tests from the Hospital of Tropical Diseases, it was discovered that I was riddled with malaria. As it was four years since I had left the tropics this caused some confusion. Eventually the doctors decided that I must have been bitten by a renegade mosquito in Venice. But whatever it was I had it bad, and it was only after a final bout, when my temperature was one hundred and six degrees for eight hours while several nurses sat on top of my shaking body and held my flailing arms, that I was cured.

Two days later I started rehearsing as Toby Belch in *Twelfth Night* which the Old Vic were performing at the Edinburgh Festival before we left for the States. I had lost so much weight I looked more like Andrew Aguecheek. It was a fun company, a medley of crazy, interesting characters; but it was still a company. When a group of actors and actresses work together in close proximity for a length of time they become a family and invariably turn into a mutual admiration society, and any newcomer is regarded with tolerant mistrust. But with the wicked, wise and understanding Michael Benthall in charge I put on my blinkers, drove forward and we formed a new team.

TEN

Our plane landed in New York and the company went directly to
the train for the famous, three-day, coast-to-coast journey. New
York to Chicago and then westward-ho through the Rocky Mountains to San Francisco. There could be no more exciting way to
travel: your compartment became your apartment and the observation car your balcony, as state after state drifted past. The
ever-changing scenery was superb and for three days and two
nights the company was charged with excitement. And each state
had its own drinking laws which provided certain complications
en route. In one state you could drink what you pleased, in another
you could only drink a ghastly concoction called 'Near Beer' and
in a third alcohol was not allowed to be sold. If you ordered
vodka on the rocks you were given a glass with ice in it. The vodka
you had to supply yourself. All this at the same bar with the same
bartender.

San Francisco is one of the world's great cities and in the fifties
it vibrated with energy and colourful characters, but I could not
anticipate how swiftly I should be plunged into its swirling caul-
dron. After getting off the train I found a small, cheap hotel before
going off to see a bad production of a musical version of *Grand
Hotel* with Paul Muni. I then took a cab to Nob Hill, paid the
driver off and walked slowly along a deserted street. There was a
high brick wall with a small door through which the faint sound
of music could be heard. Inside I paid a one dollar entrance fee,
bought a beer at the bar for another dollar and sat at one of the
few tables in the not over-large room and looked up at the group
playing on the small stage. It was Louis Armstrong and his tympany
five. Before I could recover from the shock, in walked Frank
Sinatra and Peter Lawford who sat at the next table.

From this extraordinary beginning in a new country my next six
months were formed as I was involved with the world of jazz across
the States. I lived by night and slept by day, often only waking in
time to get off to the theatre for the evening show. I got to know
Kid Ory, Sarah Vaughan, Miles Davis and Count Basie; Ernestine
Anderson and Joe Williams became friends. The great Billie

Holiday was going through a bad time; she would trip over her microphone and shout 'Fuck' and slur her songs but still the magic was there. One night she tugged my arm and pulled me over to the manager of the club at which she was appearing and asked for a hundred-dollar advance on her next salary. 'Sorry, Billie,' he said. 'You close on Saturday.' That was in San Francisco. A few months later when I was in New York I picked up a newspaper and learned that she had died in poverty in a hospital.

The jazz world was exciting, but the Mafia had dug deep into its defences and were obviously much in control. Guns were out on one occasion in East St Louis. Everywhere there was an element of danger, as I experienced in the early hours of one morning when another actor, Jimmy Mellor, and I found ourselves in a rough street on the outskirts of Chicago.

Earlier we had attended one of the numerous receptions held to welcome the Old Vic and, still dressed in tuxedoes, we must have looked pretty incongruous. Somehow we got separated and I walked the deserted street listening for the sound of footsteps and glancing in every sleazy bar because Jimmy was fond of the occasional drink. Suddenly the street was no longer deserted as a large group of figures emerged from the shadows in the all-black neighbourhood. In seconds I was surrounded by a gang and the leader moved up very close. 'What are you doing here, boy?'

'I'm looking for my friend,' I replied.

'You shouldn't be here, boy,' and a dozen blades flicked into action. 'I think we should take a walk.'

They huddled round me and slowly we moved down the street. I started gagging desperately and the leader gave me a sympathetic smile. He was the controlling element in this situation but his side-kick kept pointing to the other dark tenement and saying, 'I think we should take him up to the office.'

'Are you kidding?' I grinned, hiding my fear. I suspected that once up there I would never come down.

The leader laughed. 'All right, boy, you can call this your lucky day.' He waved his hand and a local cab screeched from nowhere. 'Now get in the cab, boy, and don't ever come here again.'

'But what about my friend?'

'Fuck your friend. Now disappear!'

I clambered into the cab and the driver drove off. 'Okay, where to?' he asked. We turned a corner and the lights of an all-night bar drifted across the street.

'I must find my friend,' I said. 'Could you wait for a moment outside that bar while I have a look?'

'Are you kidding, you heard what they said.'

'I'll give you five dollars.'

He glanced round. 'Okay, but make it fast.'

I leapt from the cab and left the door open. Then I pushed through the swing doors and made my way through the dim interior. Crumpled figures leant idly along the long bar. As I entered the room familiar figures assembled outside in the street. The gang had returned and were nonchalantly waiting my return. I glanced at everyone at the bar. No sign of Jimmy but everyone appeared to be either high on drugs or low on alcohol. As I reached the end of the room I turned as one huge fellow mumbled to anyone who happened to be listening, 'Let's take this honky' and followed me. I felt like Baron Münchhausen in between the Lion and the Crocodile and slowly made my way towards the exit with the big man at my heels and the gang quietly waiting behind the doors. Then I caught sight of Jimmy. He was slumped over the bar with a glass of brandy in one hand and an arm around a girl who was sitting with her pimp who had a very unfriendly expression on his face. We were in trouble. I leant forward. 'Jimmy,' I said, 'it's time to go.'

He raised glazed eyes. 'Piss off, old boy, I'm fine.'

'Jimmy,' I repeated quietly, 'we really do have to move fast.'

He smiled and waved his hand in farewell. I was stymied. Luckily the matter was brought to a head. The big man behind me flicked out a switch-blade. Jimmy gulped, threw back his brandy and leapt from his bar stool. I pushed him through the swing doors, past the startled gang who closed in as we leapt into the waiting cab.

'Go!' I yelled, and the confused driver pressed the accelerator and we shot away to safety.

The following day I happened to be lunching with a lawyer friend whom I had known in England. He was accompanied by several colleagues. When I told them of our adventure and where it happened, they were amazed. 'Do you know how lucky you are? Nobody goes there at night, not even if you're black. There are so many murders on that street they don't even mention it in the newspapers.'

Before our first performance in San Francisco – the first of the tour – the usual telegrams waited at the stage door. One of them said, 'Congratulations, it's a girl.' It would be six months before I would hold our new baby in my arms. Pukk decided to call her Penelope because as in the Greek legend she was waiting patiently across the sea.

The tour was a great success and played to packed houses throughout the States. John Neville played Hamlet and Laurence Harvey Henry V and a more diverse pair of leading men would be hard to find. John Neville was a popular, natural leader, always joking with the company and a regular theatre man. Laurence Harvey was the product of the lunatic world of the cinema, possessing charisma, but little experience on the boards. He was also incapable of making an after-dinner speech without saying the wrong thing. In each town and city we played he would gather all his energy for each first night and have no voice for the rest of the run. He was ambitious, full of guile and had the air of an arrogant dandy. But a small uncertain boy hid behind the mask. He was not popular with the company, but I never heard him utter a malicious word about anyone. Life was a fantasy which had gone on since childhood and I suspect his one fear was of waking up and facing reality. His insecurity showed in some infuriating ways. He was incapable of sitting down in a restaurant without sending the food back, sometimes before it reached the table, and he always carried his own cold Chablis with him, as he drank nothing else. But his innocent assurance on stage paid off, and the American critics loved him. He certainly had style. When I met him once in London he arrived on a moped driven by a chauffeur in a peak cap.

From San Francisco we travelled south to Los Angeles. Hollywood in the late fifties was bizarre and unlike anywhere else in the world. The Old Vic's success meant we were desirable guests and for two weeks we lived in a world of the phoney, the glamorous and the absurd. At one party where Reginald Gardiner wore evening dress and tennis shoes and Jayne Mansfield wore hardly anything, champagne poured ceaselessly from a vast fountain. This looked great but ruined the wine which grew flatter every second of its circular tour. José Ferrer invited the company to his home where liveried footmen served champagne by the pool, while Ferrer spent the day playing tennis on his court with, naturally, two of the world's best players to help his backhand. That evening his wife, the enchanting Rosemary Clooney, broke away from the party to give birth to another child and swell her large family. On my way to the house in the morning I was given a lift but insisted on walking the last few blocks. Within seconds a police car drew up alongside and I was surrounded by cops who demanded to know who I was and where I was going. After checking me over they said, 'Sorry, fella, but nobody walks the streets around here, understood?'

Another encounter with the police was more amusing. I think it was Boston, and John Neville, Judi Dench, Richard Wordsworth, Laurence Harvey and I were on our way from a restaurant in the early hours of the morning when we discovered a lavatory bowl with a chain attached, left unattended in the middle of the pavement on a street corner. Deciding it might come in useful, John, Larry and I carried it through the streets with Judi and Richard trailing behind. When a police car slowed and approached us Judi, in very Yorkshire voice, yelled out, 'Officers, stop those men, they've stolen that lavatory.'

After a brief explanation the confused cops grinned and said, 'Carry on, if you want it, it's yours.' So we took it and delivered it to Douglas Morris, the company manager, wrapped in pink tissue paper. When he awoke the next morning there was an extra loo standing in the centre of his living-room.

From the sweltering sun of Los Angeles and a freak heatwave we flew to Montreal where the temperature was well below zero and the icy winds froze our ears and little icicles formed from tears of pain. But if the climate varied so dramatically, the endless receptions were always the same. After a show, when the adrenalin is high, actors are always ravenous, but the effort to acknowledge the same platitudes that poured out in every city and town as we crossed America gradually began to wilt. Finally I thought of a game to relieve the tedium, three phrases which would come out on every occasion, 'Typical', 'Well that's show business' and 'Sex mad'. These became stock phrases which satisfied any question or comment and we went on using them until the crowd drifted away and we could scoff the food and wine in peace.

We spent Christmas in New York and from the record shop on the corner, by the Broadway Theater where we played, the schmaltzy Chipmunk song which was top of the pops sounded out non-stop, twenty-four hours a day.

I had a happy reunion, meeting up with my sister-in-law Zena and her second husband Ken. No longer was I the kid brother. We became friends. We opened *Henry V* on Christmas Day and as not many shows open on Christmas Day I remember it well, in particular because apart from the roles of the Archbishop of Canterbury, MacMorris and the Duke of Burgundy, I also took over the part

145

of Bourbon-Orleans for the first time because Harold Innocent was ill. The papers, however, were on strike. When they finally did come out they all loved everything about the production, except the *New York Times* which thought Judi Dench was saccharine sweet and Joss Ackland was considerably overworked.

The first night of *Twelfth Night* also stays in my memory: when I walked on for my first entrance as Toby Belch I took a swig of non-existent wine from the bottle, but, unfortunately, in transit the bottle had fallen and my mouth was full of shattered glass. There's also a story that I was seen approaching the stage for my first entrance clutching a tissue containing two eyebrows, a moustache and false beard, all covered in spirit gum which I pressed on to my face with one swift movement, but I swear this is a myth.

The Broadway Theater was opposite the home of jazz, Birdland, which sadly no longer exists. Joe Williams was singing with Count Basie and his orchestra and he would watch Shakespeare from the wings at the Broadway and after the show I would join him at Birdland until the early hours of the morning. He was obviously a great hit with the ladies because they were always sending him surreptitious notes to which he had little handwritten replies ready saying, 'Not now, baby, maybe later.'

It was there that I met Cognac. She was a voluptuous, flamboyant Creole, who was a rarity in the late fifties, even at Birdland, because her breasts hung unconcealed over the top of her dress. She preferred the company of girls. One day, with a touch of devilry, I took her and her companion to a smart reception for the Old Vic which was a very snooty affair. I enlisted another actor to escort the girls. On the way to pick them up I told him they were very attractive, but not to get excited. 'Don't worry about me,' he said. However, when we arrived at their flat, the door was opened by Cognac's friend. She too was a young Creole, a mixture of Ava Gardner and Lena Horne, who wore a pink chiffon negligé and carried a copy of *Forever Amber*. My friend's jaw dropped and he remained silent and confused from that moment on. The two beauties did cause a certain amount of consternation at the reception because there is no snob like an American snob. I also recall with delight another member of our company, the young and pink Barbara Leigh-Hunt, talking animatedly with my two new friends and getting pinker and pinker with innocent confusion. I bumped into Michael Benthall as he was leaving; he shook his finger at me and then gave an enormous grin.

On one occasion I arrived at Birdland at about four a.m. to meet

Joe Williams and go back with him to listen to some records. He was not there, the club was almost deserted and the Count and the band were packing up their instruments. Suddenly two men appeared. They were both white, one of them looking like chalk with flaming red hair, and as one of the staff approached they hit him and then threw him against the wall. I started to move forward, but Joe the drummer grabbed my arm and said, 'Cool it.'

'But they hit him,' I said.

'Never mind, cool it, they're hoods.'

The Count stepped forward. 'What's the trouble, boys?' he asked calmly.

'Trouble, I'll tell you the trouble. We want to see the guy who runs this joint.'

I did not know it then but Birdland was run by one of twin brothers. 'He's not here,' said the Count.

'Well, you tell him we want to see him and we'll be back,' and the two thugs pushed the chair and table over and stormed out.

The following day when I saw Joe I asked him what the trouble was. 'Trouble,' said Joe without expression, 'there was no trouble.'

A week later I was in Washington when I picked up a newspaper and saw that the previous night in Birdland in New York two white men, one with red hair, had walked into the club while Sarah Vaughan was singing and stabbed the twin brother of the owner of the club, and walked out leaving the dying man on the floor. As far as I know the killers were never discovered.

Washington was a clean attractive city and there I met many funny, intelligent, generous people, but the fear of the Soviet Union found its way into most conversations and like most young countries America had a precocious vanity. I still remember a postcard of the capital which said, 'The beautiful building has been seen by millions of Americans and also by people of less fortunate lands.' Standing in at a mixed reception of politicians and actors for Laurence Harvey who was ill, I joined the Old Vic's Barbara Jefford and two leading politicians to welcome the guests. One of them was tall and stooped, with a fixed grin and a clammy hand and he uttered the same insincere platitudes to every arrival. When I heard later that this character was running for Vice-President I could not take it seriously. By the time he became President and the Nixon administration began, I hired a straitjacket and decided to join Blanche Dubois.

When the tour of America was over I was not finished with the Old Vic. After only a few weeks in England I flew to Moscow,

Leningrad and then Warsaw where we performed *Macbeth* and *Saint Joan* and *The Importance of Being Earnest*. At the final dress rehearsal of *Macbeth* Paul Rodgers and William Russell were in the middle of the fight between Macbeth and Macduff when, as their huge broadswords clashed, one sword broke in two and the blade flew into the stalls and became embedded in the centre of a seat in one of the front rows. At the next performance Khrushchev and his party would have been seated there.

Before we went a member of the Foreign Office gave us a pep talk advising us to behave with decorum in Russia, to be on our guard and to be aware that we would all be under perpetual observation. Luckily when he had finished Paul Rodgers leapt up and advised us to take no notice. 'If we are to be ambassadors,' he said, 'let us go with open arms in friendship.' Moscow had a powerful pungent smell of beechwood. The people were warm and friendly and only the maddening bureaucracy spoilt the atmosphere. The fear of the Russians in the States was matched by the fear of the Americans in the Soviet Union.

Some years later I recalled one young Russian's reply when I said, 'Well, surely you think that Kennedy is working for peaceful co-existence.'

'Oh, yes,' he said, 'but if he goes too far they will destroy him.'

Warsaw was a revelation and was still independent of Russian influence. The people were poor but in the evenings made magic out of nothing. The women were elegant and danced with joy into the night. Since the war the city itself had been rebuilt, brick by brick, and copied from the detailed paintings of one of the Canaletto family.

Back in London the dreaded labour exchange was avoided when Michael Benthall asked me to join his new Old Vic company at the Old Vic itself. We could pay the rent and Pukk, the children and I could be together.

Eleven

The sudden solitude of a crowded desert – in a thick smoke, many creatures moving without direction – for no direction moves anywhere but round and round in that vapour. Without purpose and without principle of conduct, while the slow stain sinks deeper into the skin – tainting the flesh and discolouring the bone.

T. S. ELIOT

After the bomb fell on Hiroshima there was a revolution. The world could end at any moment. Until that moment there had always been a definite future – if not for yourself, for your children, or your children's children. Behind each corner there was the possibility of something different. But by the sixties the new adolescents felt cheated. They gently closed the door on God, and looked elsewhere for compensation. Forget tomorrow – live for today. They sought an escape. They found it in drugs.

Our family was growing and spreading. In 1963 Melanie was ten, Paul was nine, Toni six, Penny four, and now there was also Samantha. Five different personalities developing, and all leaping with life. Before Samantha was born Rosemary had gone through another pregnancy, but lost the baby, a boy, four months before he was due to be born. After losing the baby we tried for another, without success. Eventually Pukk went to the fertility clinic where she was told that her tubes were blocked, and to telephone the clinic to make an appointment ten days after her next period. On that day they sorted her out and told her that, if she wanted to conceive, she would have to have intercourse within twenty-four hours. Unfortunately I was working in Scotland, so she took the night train up to Glasgow where we met and raced off to Pitlochry where we lay by a stream in the woods and Samantha was conceived. At the time I had grown a red beard. Samantha is our only child with red hair.

Our life at last had a rhythm and for the first time in England we experienced a sort of security. I was now known in the trade as a 'working actor'. No longer clutching at survival I was part of the acting establishment fringe. I had become lucky. The dice had fallen well, but I knew that with the next throw a gaping abyss might appear. In the acting profession that can always happen – to anyone. I had worked with the Old Vic for three and a half years and in the London company Michael Benthall had assembled a group of unknowns to form a different pattern. Maggie Smith, John Moffat, Alec McCowen, Stephen Moore, Judi Dench, John Woodvine and myself. From the ballet Moyra Fraser and from the cinema George Baker, Donald Houston and John Justin. All good players. Who better to play tennis with?

When Michael Benthall was edged out the company disbanded, but to this day the young group still meet from time to time and little has changed. After the Old Vic I went to play Scrofulovsky in *The Bedbug* at the Mermaid Theatre. I had seen Mayakovsky's satire performed brilliantly in Moscow, and had longed to do the play. So when Bernard Miles phoned to offer me the role I leapt at the opportunity. But the company at the Mermaid did not have quite the same spark and Bernard took over one of the roles at the last minute. He was also directing the play with his wife, Josephine, but as I had various ideas which I stole from the Russian production, and, as Bernard was having to learn his role in a hurry, an element of confusion prevailed. This led to Bernard writing in the programme that the play was directed by Giles Fletcher, a deep-sea diver whose grandfather had been hanged for sheep-stealing.

The play opened to mixed reviews but two or three critics gave high praise to the new young director – Giles Fletcher. Two days later Bernard gave a press conference and announced that it had been a 'bit of fun' and Giles Fletcher did not exist. The hoax did not go down too well with the press and the Sunday reviews got their revenge. Harold Hobson, in the *Sunday Times*, said that as we did not see fit to give a curtain call, he was not going to write a review which might be our pride and joy. As the play ended with me locked in a cage after running into the auditorium, and my keepers telling the audience not to worry but to leave the theatre as quickly and quietly as possible, a curtain call would have been a little out of place. Hobson then proceeded to write a two-page review, in the *Boston Herald* in America, saying it was one of the most exciting theatrical experiences in years.

A few days after *The Bedbug* opened Bernard said, 'Why is this play not working?'

'Confused direction and bad casting,' I replied.

For ten minutes Bernard did not speak to me. His sly and cheeky face creased into a sullen scowl. Then after a long tense silence he mumbled, 'Bad casting, eh! Why don't you come and do it.'

For the next two and a half years, at a salary of fifty pounds a week, I joined him as associate director. For six days a week, from nine in the morning until eleven at night, I cast plays, helped choose them, acted in them and even directed. Bernard could be infuriating, inconoclastic and stubborn, a mixture of naïve child and scheming prankster, brilliant and foolish, kindly and cruel. But it was these very contradictions that, against all odds and heavy opposition, had enabled him to build the Mermaid in the heart of the City and produce a throbbing exciting theatre in a cultural wasteland.

For the first time I became involved in the problems on the other side of the footlights. The excitement of casting a part could be as thrilling as it was for an actor or actress to get the role they wanted. Again luck plays an important part in the proceedings. Thespians all hate to audition – to compete with other nervous, often desperate, creatures, by reading a few lines at sight on an empty stage in front of unseen strangers, in a darkened auditorium. But to this day, no one has come up with a better solution. If it is any consolation, when someone is chosen to play a part it does not mean that they are better than their competitors. They just happen to possess the qualities that the unseen strangers happen to be looking for on that particular day. The next morning they could wake up with quite different ideas. And they are probably wrong about what they are looking for anyway. My advice to any actor or actress is try not to get depressed at not succeeding at auditions. Raise two unseen fingers at the unseen faces, and plough on.

There were times when I became a trifle over-ambitious with casting. When we did *Schweik in the Second World War* I approached Charles Chaplin to play Schweik and Spike Milligan, Peter Sellers and Harry Secombe to play Goebbels, Hitler and Goering. It might have been managed with the latter three, because they would only have appeared on screen, but it was impossible to get them together at the same time. As for Chaplin – he wrote me a sweet little letter saying, 'Thanks for the offer but it has been forty years since I have set foot on the boards and I would be too nervous.'

The two and a half years at the Mermaid were tough but rewarding. At one stage four consecutive shows transferred to the West End: *All in Good Time* and *Alfie* by Bill Naughton, *The Bed*

Sitting Room by Spike Milligan and John Antrobus and the musical *Virtue in Danger*, and the first three were all successes.

But Bernard could be devious. I was going to direct *All in Good Time* and asked Eric Portman and Marjorie Rhodes to play the leading roles. Eric wept when he read the play, and said that he would love to do it. I told him the dates and he could just manage to fit it in.

One Sunday Bernard and Josephine asked Rosemary and me to join Erna and Bill Naughton for lunch at their home in St George's Square, Victoria. When we reached dessert Bernard said, 'I think we should open *All in Good Time* a week earlier.'

'Not possible,' I said. 'Eric Portman won't be free.'

Bernard's eyes gleamed. 'Well, we'll have to get someone else.'

'But he will be wonderful – we could not get anyone better.'

'No one is irreplaceable,' said Bernard. 'I could always do it.'

I took a deep breath. 'But I don't think you're right for the role,' I said.

'Well then,' said Bernard, 'one of us will have to go, won't we?'

The play opened a week early, Bernard and Marjorie Rhodes played the leads and Josephine directed. Two days before the play opened I asked Bernard, 'How old is this character you're playing?'

'Fifty-five,' said Bernard.

'And how old are you?'

'Fifty-five,' said Bernard.

'Then why are you putting on a rough voice and playing it with a stoop?'

Bernard glared.

Shortly afterwards, at a press photo-call, Bernard was on stage and I was sitting at the back of the empty hall. In front of dozens of bemused press photographers Bernard roared at me, 'That was a bloody stupid thing to say to me just before we open. I know the character of this man.' The press slowly made their exit. After the play opened Bernard grinned at me one day and said, 'Good note that, one of the best I've ever had.'

It was a deeply moving, funny play and Bernard got the *Evening Standard* Award as Actor of the Year.

Bill Naughton's other play *Alfie* was also a great success. Donald McWhinnie was directing and for the title role I suggested John Neville, Bernard Cribbins and a new young Cockney actor Michael Caine. It was generally agreed that such an enormous role needed an experienced leading man who could carry major parts with ease. John Neville, who I think has always been a better character actor than straight man, took the part by the scruff of the neck and made it breathe with life. I think now it would have been beyond the capabilities of the young Michael Caine who eventually got his break in the movie where he played the role superbly. The play also had a strong, relatively unknown, supporting cast including Margaret Courtenay, Gemma Jones and Glenda Jackson.

Thanks to Bernard and Josephine the Mermaid always had that greatest of theatrical qualities – danger. Each production had to cross a high wire and live dangerously. Occasionally the result was disaster, but the aims were always exciting and sometimes a new boundary was broken and the public flocked in to experience unknown territory. Without danger the theatre is dead. Behind the scenes at the Mermaid successes and failures were constantly being juggled by such diverse creatures as the brilliant inspired lunatic Spike Milligan and the anarchical John Antrobus, the live-wire Frank Dunlop, the cheerful Patrick Ide, trying to keep finances in order, and always Bernard trying to stir the conservative City dignitaries into generous theatrical life.

Bernard decided to revive the Mermaid's first show and first success: the Henry Fielding-Lionel Bart musical *Lock Up Your Daughters*. The show had been directed originally by Peter Coe with Hy Hazell and Richard Wordsworth as Justice and Mrs Squeezum, who had both given enchanting performances. For the revival we got Hy to play her old role and I asked Dickie Wordsworth, whose future plans made him unavailable for the run, to direct. Bernard played Squeezum. I felt there was no point in reviving the show unless it was transferred to a West End theatre, but Bernard was very protective of the piece and wanted to hold on to it like a child in a close-knit family. I also knew that the possibility of a West End contract would attract a stronger cast, as obviously the salaries would escalate. Once again the audiences flocked in and Binkie Beaumont offered us Her Majesty's Theatre with the proviso that once we played to less than six thousand pounds per week the show would come off. This was typical of his guile because he had four different shows on the road and he could not decide which one to bring in. Rather than keep the theatre dark he thought that as *Lock Up* had played for so long when it opened originally it would drop below the six thousand pounds figure and he would have time to make his final choice. But this time the gamble did not come off. *Lock Up Your Daughters* stayed at Her Majesty's for a year and a half.

For the first six months I played the young drunkard Sotmore,

Bernard played Squeezum for three months and I directed that lovely eccentric George Colouris in the role, which he also played for three months. Neither Bernard nor George found the rapier-like eccentricity that Dickie Wordsworth had given the character. Then I took over and played the role for six months and was the worst of the lot.

After the show had run a year I left to play Galileo at the Mermaid with Bernard directing. The play was performed twice nightly, was complex, ran for three hours and the role of Galileo was enormous. The two shows were so close together that I hardly had time to wash the white out of my hair from the ending of the first performance before I was opening the second, washing my wet hair on stage before the audience as the young Galileo.

The play had only been on a few days when my family's lives changed.

At home our electricity was cut off. When Rosemary rang the Electricity Board, she was told that the cheque she had sent had bounced. She went to see our bank manager: 'Why did you return the cheque?'

'Because you would have been overdrawn by twenty-three pounds.'

'But we have five children, I'm five months pregnant and you allow our electricity to be cut off because we shall be overdrawn by twenty-three pounds!'

'I'm sorry,' said the bank manager, 'but you have no security.'

'We have a house, for God's sake.'

'That is not security. Your house could burn down at any time.'

Rosemary's temper snapped. She took a wild swing at him with her handbag. 'And you could drop dead at any time,' she said and swept from the office.

The next day our house burnt down. A week later the manager dropped dead in his office . . .

On June 24th, 1963, I was tired after two performances of *Galileo*. I had said I would go to a party with the *Alfie* company in the West End to celebrate the seventieth birthday of Jerry Verno who was a member of the company. I decided to go straight home. But there was a message for me at the stage door – 'Don't forget Jerry's birthday.' Someone offered me a lift and I dropped in, the party was just getting under way and I left at twelve. 'Why are you going so early?' asked John Neville.

As it was after midnight I changed taxis at Hammersmith to avoid paying double fare and arrived at Madrid Road at twelve forty-five. The street was full of people, half-dressed, the dark sky was lit up by a strange unnatural light and I was aware of glistening torsos. As I paid the driver people rushed towards me and flashlights exploded in my face. There was a powerful sickly smell, there were fire engines; someone pushed through the crowd, Dr Brown, who was always helping with the children's illnesses, and put his hand on my arm. He seemed to speak slowly, everything was in slow motion, sounds, movement, thoughts. 'Don't worry,' he said, 'they're all right. The children are with neighbours, Rosemary and Paul are in hospital but they're all right.'

I felt odd, unemotional, acutely aware and yet floating. I looked up at our house and it was not there. Just a mass of smouldering wood and bricks, and that smell, that bloody awful smell. The taxi driver was staring too and his hand was still held out unconsciously for the tip. After that clear concise moment my memory catches only vague shadowy recollections. I was in a hospital and Rosemary was there on a stretcher, her face and hands burnt and blistered, her hair like straggly charred wire and again there was that pungent smell. She saw me and gave me that warm open smile that has lifted me so many times.

'Do you know what the matron said?' she murmured. 'She said she did not want that burnt herring here.' Paul, meanwhile, was over-bright with shock; he had a few minor cuts but was kept in overnight. Then I was back at Madrid Road with the children confused and wide-eyed. They slept on neighbours' chairs and couches and I lay next to them and held their hands. There was little sleep for any of us that night, just confused numbness and at dawn I stood in the rubble of what had been our house. I had no sense of loss, only desolation and relief. We had nothing left, but Rosemary, Melanie, Paul, Toni, Penny and Sammy were all alive – that was all that mattered. In a few hours I had learned that material possessions meant nothing. They were only things, life was all and it had been a very near thing, a matter of minutes.

Gradually I discovered what had happened. The evening before, the family had all gone to bed early because Rosemary had thought I would be going on to the party, and soon after midnight Paul was woken by his bed-wetting alarm. Always hypersensitive, he would worry because at the age of nine he still pee'd his bed. Drowsily, as he made his way to the loo, he heard a low heavy rumbling noise and a faint mist filled the air. He went into his mother's bedroom, and with difficulty woke her. Rosemary took baby Samantha in her arms, woke Melanie aged ten and, still drowsy from the fumes, they made their way downstairs. Rosemary opened the front door, handed Samantha to Melanie, told her to keep away from the house. Smoke was filtering out from under the door to the sitting-room. Pukk opened the door and there was a tremendous explosion. Glass shattered everywhere, in seconds the house became an inferno.

Rosemary, her hair burning, ran through the sheet of fire that had raced up and engulfed the stairs, her only thought being to reach the other children. People came in from the street, but could not get through the flames. Upstairs the four bedrooms were divided by a landing with two bedrooms on either side: Toni and Penelope's room, and Paul's room on one side; Melanie's room and Pukk and my room with a cot for Samantha on the other. Penelope was unconscious behind the door of her room and Pukk took a while to find her. Then she carried Penny and Toni across the landing into our bedroom above the street.

In the front garden several neighbours and bystanders were calling out for Rosemary to jump. She threw the unconscious Penny down to outstretched hands twenty feet below, and the four-year-old was safely caught, but Toni aged seven was not so easy. Conscious and crying she was naturally reluctant to make the long leap and clutched her mother desperately, then she too was thrown and caught by the people below. 'Now jump,' they called. But Pukk thought Paul was still in his room; she ran back to try and cross the landing to reach his room but the landing was by now a mass of flames. Hard as she tried she could not fight through, then her mind went blank with despair while the cries went on below: 'Jump! Jump!' It was only instinct that drove her back to the bedroom and she leapt from the window, but by this time the fire was so intense and the smoke so thick no one could see her and with her child inside her she plummeted to the ground and lost consciousness. Despite her injuries neighbours had to pull her away from the house because the lead from the pipes had melted and was dripping beside her.

By a miracle Paul was safe. When the house exploded and the flames rushed to the top floor he was in his room. Luckily there was scaffolding down the back of the house. We had had an attic built which had just been completed and the following night some of the children would have been sleeping there. But on this night, thank God, they had slept in their old rooms. Paul climbed down the scaffolding to safety and then, when he realised the rest of the family was still inside, the nine-year-old broke into the rear kitchen window, cutting his leg, and tried to get up the stairs. Then neighbours pulled him out of the rear window, carried the naked boy around to the front of the house, where his mother lay. By now Pukk was semi-conscious and convinced that Paul was dead. Even when neighbours showed him to her she could not believe it. She thought that she was dreaming. Fifteen minutes later the house had gone.

The next few days were a haze. Rosemary was on the danger list; everyone assumed she would lose her baby immediately, as she was five months pregnant. She refused any pain-killing drugs. When they were forced on her she poured them into a flower bowl by her bed. The next morning the flowers had wilted. She had no feeling from the waist down: she had broken her back, an L1 fracture. The doctors thought that she would never walk again, and her burns were very bad.

One day Diane Lasselle, who lived in Madrid Road, called on Rosemary in Putney Hospital. 'I've been sent to heal you,' she said. 'May I lay hands on you?'

'If you like, but I'm afraid I don't believe in faith healing.'

'It doesn't matter.'

And for several days she sat by Rosemary's bed for hours at a time with her hands nicely resting on the covers. Before Pukk had left Putney Hospital four months later, there was not one trace of any scar anywhere and somehow she kept the baby.

The day after the fire my first action was to buy seven tooth-brushes. Fellow actors and the people of Barnes were wonderful. For the first few days neighbours provided beds for the children and I slept with baby Samantha at the home of Edna and Lloyd Mills, who lived next door to our ruined house. It was their son Robert who had caught the children from the windows. Then Maureen Mitchell, whom I had never met, lent me her house in Barnes and we had a home packed with piles of children's clothing supplied by helping hands. Joseph O'Connor, Barbara and Alfred Burke, Margaret and Tony Sharp, Timothy and Sheila Bateson, actors all, providing strong arms of support. Marks and Spencer's sent a trunk of children's clothing. The first thing to arrive on the morning after the fire was a cheque for fifty pounds from Peter Finch. Some dolls for the children were sent by Jean Simmons. I had never met either of them but ironically years later they both became friends.

For all the generosity it was a strange encounter that restored my sanity. The children were sent by the Actors' Charitable Trust to a place by the sea. Only one-year-old Samantha stayed with me, but eventually I was forced to take her to join her brother and sisters. The musicians Eileen and David Parkhouse drove us, and I shall never forget her confused tears as I left to return to London.

I was now alone in a borrowed house. One day there was a ring at the bell. 'Sorry to trouble you,' said a woman I did not know, 'but I've had such a job finding you. I've just come from your old home and I had to ask neighbours where you were. I'm the mother of your daughter Melanie's friend. A few weeks ago she came to play with Melanie and left a pair of black tights in your house. Are they all right?'

I looked blankly at her. 'I'm sorry,' I said, 'but I'm afraid we lost everything. There was nothing left.'

The woman frowned. 'I knew it,' she grumbled. 'I told her to bring them home.' And she stamped her foot in anger.

I did not know whether to laugh, or to hit her. I did neither. 'I'm so sorry,' I said, 'things are a bit confused at the moment, but when I get sorted out I shall get you a pair.'

'Oh, that's very sweet of you,' she said and left.

I was back to the real world. And I was still playing Galileo and did not miss a performance. The rhythm of life is a powerful thing. The night after the fire was the most difficult. Rosemary on the danger list, the children scattered and I was tired and high with confusion. But I needed a very large brandy to get into the role. Bernard was furious about the fire, it was upsetting the flow of organisation at the theatre. Three days later he took me into his office. 'Do you know we're going to do *The Possessed* by Dostoevsky and Julius Gellner is going to direct? Well, he's had a minor operation. After the show each night could you go and stay with him at his house in the country and as he doesn't know any actors could you cast the play for him?'

'Are you serious?' I asked. 'Rosemary is dangerously ill, it's psychologically important that I see her as much as I can through the day.'

'Julius has been ill too, you know,' said Bernard. 'It's psychologically important that you should see him too.'

I called him a very short word and walked out. But I ended up casting the play in London.

Pukk was in Putney Hospital for four months. By September I had got a flat in the no-man's-land of Roehampton. It was very expensive, but at last the family were all together. Then Pukk was allowed out of hospital for the occasional weekend. In October she was sent to Stoke Mandeville. With the L1 fracture it was not expected that she would walk again but less than four months after the accident she could stand with the aid of a cage. In November she was allowed home for a few days. On the 23rd of that month I was at the Mermaid when the news came that President Kennedy had been assassinated. I was glued to the television when Rosemary phoned. 'Have you heard the news?' she said. 'Kennedy has been – ouch!' There was a moment's silence and then she spoke again. 'I think the baby's about to arrive.'

Our sixth child was born a few hours later at Queen Charlotte's Hospital. There was naturally quite a little concern about the birth, not only because of the jump from the window but also because of the paralysis. Pukk had little control of her muscles. However, on November 23rd Kirsty leapt from the womb effortlessly. For six weeks Pukk was allowed to breast-feed her at home.

Home was now in Kitson Road in Barnes. I'd put some money down on the house when our insurance eventually reluctantly came through. We had insured the Madrid Road house for four thousand pounds when we moved there, but of course it had increased in value since then and the contents were not covered at all, but at least we had the four thousand pounds. The family was all together for Christmas and there was a great feeling of security to have Pukk home, because, immobile as she was, she was still our anchor and our strength. A Swiss girl, Eliane, joined us to help with Kirsty and six weeks after the birth the breast was replaced by the bottle and Pukk returned to Stoke Mandeville.

Ludwig Guttman, who ran Stoke Mandeville, was a hard task-master, and a great man, who positively bullied his patients into discovering their full potential and conquering their disabilities. If someone had only six months to live Guttman would say, 'You have six months of rich wonderful life, now live it.' Sadly he could not always succeed. In the next bed to Rosemary a young woman, who had been in a car crash in South Africa, could not accept her disability. Her husband would sit and hold her hand and make sympathetic cooing sounds but she had no fight in her. Two weeks later she died because she did not have the will to live.

Margot Fonteyn's husband, Roberto Arias, was flown in from South America with Margot by his side. He still had bullets inside him and his temperature was so high that Guttman had literally to keep him in ice. The reporters were everywhere. 'This man must not die,' said Guttman. He didn't. Malcolm Sargent's secretary was brought in after rushing to her employer in a car and crashing. She broke her neck, a C3 break. In time she was able to type by blowing through a pipette and the power of each breath determined a different letter. Below her neck she could not move one muscle. Strangely enough, the people who could not accept their injuries were often the ones who had brought it on themselves attempting suicide.

Guttman was thrilled with Rosemary. After concentrated physiotherapy and sheer determination she was able to walk. She had achieved the impossible. In May 1964 she was released from hospital for a time. She could only move by wearing heavy callipers on her legs. All those months in hospital had institutionalised Pukk. She was shy and apprehensive at being with the children, so after coming out of Stoke Mandeville we went first for a quiet meal in the West End at Little Wheeler's in Duke of York Street and then to the movies before returning home when the children were asleep.

Two days later I took Pukk off to Venice where she was forced to walk everywhere. I felt guilty about being cruel, but I was determined that Pukk would get back to normal again. The magic of the old city cast its inevitable spell and we decided to send for ten-year-old Paul to come and join us. Paul was a weekly boarder at Highgate School as a junior. Before the fire he had longed to go there, and after the shock of that appalling experience we thought it vital that his wish come true. But the school was on the other side of London and he felt lonely for the family; he flew out alone in time for the last few days of our holiday.

When we returned Pukk settled into our little community of Kitson Road and once again became a guiding light. The fire had caused confusion in our fairly organised lives, but Pukk had given birth to our sixth child and against all the odds could walk and we were all alive. Even our cat, Ladyday, who had disappeared after the fire, had been found two weeks later sitting in the rubble where her chair had always been. It was not until 1982 that Ladyday finally died aged twenty-four.

Pukk's concern for the family had given her the determination to conquer her injuries and like a determined terrier fought her way back to normality. I felt that I too had to start again. I did not stay long at the Mermaid; I had to spend more time with the children and seeing Pukk. At the Mermaid I was dangerously close to a breakdown. Eager to grab any extra work I strained too far. At one time, apart from preparing other shows, I was rehearsing Long John Silver and Blind Pew in *Treasure Island* in the morning, rehearsing as Falstaff in *Henry IV*, Parts I and II, for a broadcast

Galileo, Mermaid, 1963

After the fire, 1963

All together again – in
Kitson Road

In the *Kipling* television series,
1964

Jorrocks, 1967. Above:
making up, watched by
some of the family; and,
left, the finished article

Ravenswood

Early Ravenswood: with Toni, Penny, Sammy, Kirsty, Toby and Paul

Dad joins us for a light meal! Clockwise from left: Sammy, Toby, Melanie, Pukk, Me, Dad, Kirsty, Toni and Penny

Towards the end of our time at Ravenswood: Penny, Sammy and Kirsty

A pair of Mortimers: above, with Glynis Johns in *Come as You Are*; and left, with Glenda Jackson in *Collaborators*

A couple of Bergmans: above,
with Jean Simmons, in *Little
Night Music*, Stephen
Sondheim's musical inspired
by Ingmar Bergman's *Smiles of
a Summer Night*; and on
television in *The Lie*.

Another Bergman: with Ingrid in *Captain Brassbound's Conversion*, 1971

in the afternoon and playing the suicidal introvert Kirilov in *The Possessed* in the evenings.

We approached *The Possessed* with some trepidation: I had brought together a number of performers who were known to be temperamental, but, apart from Sonia Dresdel who never looked once at Ina de la Haye when she was alone on stage with her, and the glorious moment when Ernest Milton chased Ina de la Haye down to the stage with an axe, all was peace and quiet. Miss de la Haye behaved in such a monstrous manner that everyone else was open-mouthed. Even the volatile Kenneth Griffiths was at a loss for words. In the large company only Ina had a dressing-room to herself. One day she asked Jane Griffiths, who was giving a lovely performance, 'Tell me, my dear, why are you playing this role?'

'Because I think it's such a fine play,' said Jane.

Ina smiled benignly and wagged her little finger, 'No, my dear, that is not true. If you truly loved the play you would know how wrong you are in the part.'

Finally Bernard Miles could resist it no longer. He sent Ina a letter from a fictitious fan, telling her 'how superb she was in the play and how she alone understood Dostoevsky while the rest of the cast floundered in their roles'. The entire company knew about the letter and waited. Sure enough Madame de la Haye knocked on every dressing-room door and read the letter in detail to each straight-faced member of the cast.

Gradually I broke away from theatre work and concentrated on TV, although I still had a few months more at the Mermaid in a late-night bawdy review called *The Buxom Muse*. Thanks to Shaun Sutton, who was now working in drama for the BBC, I played Stephenson, the link character roughly based on Kipling, in the Kipling series, and we recorded twenty-six episodes in six months. Most evenings were free, but the pressure was still there. We rehearsed each episode over a period of two weeks and recorded every weekend, so I was always rehearsing two episodes at the same time, one in the morning and one in the afternoon. This could lead to confusion. One afternoon I rushed from one rehearsal to the next. In a makeshift tent Gary Bond was playing a subaltern who was breathing his last. I rushed over to him, sat on his bed, held his hand and he expired in my arms. The director Donald McWhinnie came over, embraced me and said, 'That was beautiful, quite beautiful.' Then he paused. 'There is only one problem, you're not actually in the scene.'

Gradually we returned to normal. Gradually we found our feet.

Gradually the bruises disappeared. Somehow with the insurance we managed to buy our house in Kitson Road. There were now eight of us in the family, the nurse Eliane had returned to Switzerland and Signe, a happy, plump, friendly Norwegian took her place. And my father was around. After the fire he materialised like the Cheshire cat and proved a great chum to Rosemary. Maureen, who had been his great love for years, had died in her flat in Randolph Road in Maida Vale, and Dad, who had been staying in Woolwich with Jane, a waitress at the Press Club, moved in permanently with the devoted warm-hearted Cockney.

Jane's weakness was her honesty. When making a telephone call, if the pips went and she was not cut off, she would say, 'Fair's fair,' and put the phone down. One day when she arrived back at Woolwich she discovered that she had paid a penny less than she should have for her railway ticket, so she walked all the way back to the station to return the extra penny. If we invited her to lunch she insisted on bringing her own food, but she was devoted to Dad and she treated him like the baby she had never had. Eventually this had fatal consequences, but of that anon.

Over the next few years I made several hundred TV appearances: plays, series and serials, mostly for the BBC. The most hazardous piece turned out to be *The Further Adventures of the Musketeers*, an adaptation of *Twenty Years After* by Alexandre Dumas. It was done as a thirteen-part series and in the role of d'Artagnan I succeeded in being thrown from my horse four times, spraining an ankle running after my horse, and being bitten by a Dobermann pinscher. This particular dog took a leap at me when I was fighting and grabbed my arm between his teeth: the only way that a skilled swordsman like myself could be captured. My sleeve concealed a leather gauntlet that the dog was meant to grasp with his teeth and release when his trainer commanded it. Unfortunately the massive dog was not only short-sighted so that he missed the gauntlet completely, he was also very slow-witted. When the trainer bellowed, 'Drop it', he took what seemed like minutes before the signal reached his brain. Blood was therefore drawn and I was whisked off for an anti-tetanus injection.

Another scene nearly ended in disaster. The other musketeers and myself were trying to save King Charles of England. We were trapped in a room, and I held the door and told them to escape out of the window while I played for time. They leapt from the window on to a waiting mattress and I suddenly pulled open the door and the wicked Roundheads fell into the room. Then I grasped one fellow, threw him over a table, grabbed another by the arm, whirled him around and in the mirror saw the chief villain Mordant about to shoot me in the back with his long heavy pistol. So I whirled around again, the Roundhead took the bullet, I threw him at Mordant, jumped out of the window on to the mattress and then hid behind a piece of scenery.

All went well except for the end. The actor playing Mordant was a method actor and his one object during the scene was to kill d'Artagnan. After I escaped he had to run to the window and look furious and frustrated. But he saw me out of range of the camera hidden behind the piece of scenery, so he flung his long heavy pistol which hit me hard on the shins, and I yelled a short sharp expletive.

'Cut,' shouted the director.

'Oh my God, I'm sorry,' said the actor and he was crying quite loudly. 'I don't know what came over me.'

'Never mind,' I said through gritted teeth, 'let's do it again.'

We set up. On action the musketeers, Jeremy Young, Brian Blessed and John Woodvine, jumped through the window. I pulled open the door, the Roundheads fell into the room, I grasped one man, threw him over a table, grabbed another by the arm, whirled him around, looked in the mirror, saw Mordant about to shoot me and I whirled round again. But this time the actor playing Mordant was a bag of nerves. He was too close to me and the pistol was pointing straight at my eye. He fired and I saw a red explosion, then pain, then everything went black. I was blind and remained blind for five minutes. Then I could see mistily, hazily. I was taken off to Hammersmith Hospital with Mordant weeping and begging the world to forgive him. I arrived at the hospital still wearing my sword and leathers and a small false beard, hanging casually from my chin. A queue of bemused faces turned in my direction as I was taken into casualty. We explained that we were in the middle of recording and the doctor said I could continue but would have to go to Moorfields Eye Hospital in the morning.

By the time I had returned my face had swollen up badly; we had already shot the exterior following scene of us riding fast through the woods and the next interior was inside a hut. Jeremy Young as Athos had to put in the line, 'D'Artagnan, your eye!'

''Tis nothing,' I said, ''twas the blast of Mordant's gun!'

The following morning at Moorfields they told me I had to have an immediate operation. I had to be conscious so that I could move my eyeballs at their command, so I was given a local anaesthetic by injection. This kept me happy and I felt nothing. I kept thinking it was a movie, faces in close-up staring at me and muttering 'Forceps, scalpel, scissors' blowing through green face-masks. 'I just can't get hold of it,' said the surgeon. 'Ah there it is, give me the bucket.' 'The bucket?' I gulped. They put three stitches into the eyeball and I was sent back to the ward. The pistol had been overloaded and a piece of the charge had gone into the eye. I missed blindness in that eye by one centimetre. I was told that I would have to remain in hospital for ten days, but rehearsals had already started for the next episode and I explained that I would have to return. I remember saying petulantly, 'If you don't let me go I won't finish reading your book for the blind.' So the next day I was back at rehearsal.

I felt fine except that my right arm was beginning to itch; by the next day the irritation was so bad that before rehearsal I went to Kingston Hospital for a check-up. Within minutes I was surrounded by nearly every doctor in the place. 'This is amazing,' one said. 'It must be a million to one chance!'

'What's amazing?' I asked nervously.

Then I was told that the injection I had been given must have been done by a dirty needle. I had gangrene. They put a tube into my arm and sucked out the poison, then I went back to rehearsal, but for the next eight months every day I had to have my arm irrigated. Even when we went on holiday Pukk had to insert a tube to draw out the uninvited pus. Today there is still a hole in my muscle. When the serial was over I received a letter from the BBC which said, 'We understand that you have been a brave little soldier and on the understanding, of course, that we accept no responsibility for anything that may have occurred we would like you to accept this cheque for fifty pounds.' Actors know the BBC as Auntie – always protective.

In 1966 I returned to the theatre to play Professor Gilbert Medlin in *The Professor* at the Royal Court. Although well directed by Robin Midgeley the piece did not work. Starting off as a light comedy, it ended with me presenting the lovely Japanese actress Yoko Tani with a box containing her lover's tongue which I had persuaded him to cut off. The transition was too much for the audience to accept.

Half a Sixpence had been a big success for its writer Beverly Cross and composer and lyricist David Heneker. Their new show was called *Jorrocks*, based on *Handley Cross* by John Surtees, to be directed by Colin Graham and presented by Donald Albery at the New Theatre. I was asked to play the title part, the lovable Cockney hunting enthusiast. I'd known Beverly since he and Maggie Smith had first got together but I'd never met the warm-hearted David Heneker, who turned out to be a true gentle man, admired and loved by all who knew him. Shortly before rehearsals were due to begin, Donald Albery and Colin Graham, who had spent a long time preparing the show, had an argument and Colin walked out. The new director was Val May. Rehearsals were intense as we worked to find a shape. New numbers went in and others thrown out. The hard-working cast included Thelma Ruby as my wife, Paul Eddington, Michael Malnick and, my neighbour, Willoughby Goddard were the villains, Cheryl Kennedy my niece Belinda and Bernard Lloyd played Charlie Stobbs.

Before opening in London we played a season at Wimbledon and the changes continued. There was little dancing in the piece, but we succeeded in having eight choreographers before we were through. The pressure escalated. One evening David handed me the score of a six-minute number for my trial which involved us all dancing over most of the tables and chairs in the courtroom. It was a very complicated piece in which I had to come in perpetually on the half-beat as we sang contrapuntally. As I cannot read a note of music, learning is not easy. I can only work by rhythm and repetition. Somehow we performed it at the Wimbledon Theatre the following night. The conductor Kenneth Alwynne was almost leaping on to the stage in his eagerness to keep us in time to the music. But the number was good and the next few nights were spent in improving it and moulding it into the show. It is strange how many hit numbers only appear in musicals at the last minute. 'Flash Bang Wallop' by the same writers was a late entry in *Half a Sixpence*, and in another musical I did years later, *A Little Night Music* by Stephen Sondheim, the show had been on the road for weeks and was just about to open on Broadway when Sondheim put in a little song called 'Send in the Clowns'.

When *Jorrocks* finished at Wimbledon there were three days before we opened cold at the New Theatre. In other words there were no previews, but I was worn out after three months' intense rehearsal and playing eight performances a week, and my heavy rough Cockney voice packed up. A specialist told me the only cure was not to utter a sound for three days. This meant my understudy having to play the dress rehearsal at the New Theatre. This did not stop Donald Albery from phoning me incessantly at home. I would write some short expletives down on a piece of paper and a grinning Rosemary would read what I had written to him through the mouthpiece. The dress rehearsal was in the afternoon and we opened to the press that night.

Thirty minutes before the show, already encased in my enormous padding, I opened my mouth and, thank God, a sound emerged. Then the overture began and the curtain went up. In the theatre when actors say the reviews were mixed, it usually means that the reviews were bad, but for *Jorrocks* the reviews were truly mixed: a few critics were half-hearted in their appreciation but many loved the piece as did the audiences. One young man saw the show thirty-nine times and each time he came he would buy up the entire front row and two of the boxes. What *Jorrocks* had in abundance was an extraordinary enthusiasm and zest for life. The energy required was enormous, everyone worked their hearts out and as Jorrocks I used to sweat so much I had to change the padding which covered my whole body in the interval. During the show I would drink half a dozen bottles of lager and swallow a salt pill otherwise my energy would go, through dehydration. And we went on improving the show.

One evening after playing at the New Theatre for several nights I was disturbed during the first act by whispering from one of the boxes. I asked the company director to get it stopped, but the noise got louder and my irritation grew. During the interval I rang Donald Albery from my dressing-room telephone and asked him what was going on.

'Don't worry,' he said. 'It is George Balanchine from the New York City Ballet.'

'I don't care who it is. If he's still making that row in the second act I won't go on.'

Eventually Donald agreed to keep him quiet on condition I lunched with Balanchine the next day.

When the great man entered the restaurant in St Martin's Lane, he swept up to me with a Russian bear-hug and his dark brown voice boomed, 'I thought last night you were going to jump from the stage and hit me. I apologise but let me explain. I have flown here from New York to sue Donald Albery and Donald has suggested that while I'm waiting I do his choreography!'

So much money had been spent on the preparation of *Jorrocks* that we had to play to almost full houses – even at every matinée – to make a profit. The title did not help. Many people thought it was an expletive, others did not want to see a show which praised blood sports.

The main concern of the show was *joie de vivre*, and also to ridicule snobbery and hypocrisy. Ironically I was invited as a guest to hunt with the hounds all over England and I had politely to refuse by saying that the manager would not allow me to ride while the show was on. I could not tell them the real reason was that I am anti blood sport. That would have confused everyone. The last night was quite extraordinary. The curtain call went on for half an hour as we repeated many of the numbers in the show and when we sang the last song, a fantasy sequence of Jorrocks in heaven,

> tell me who will have his name
> in the hall of fame
> a hundred years from now?

the whole audience stood and sang 'John Jorrocks, John Jorrocks' and then joined in with us. The stage disappeared under a mass of flowers which were flung from all parts of the theatre.

Very sad. Very moving. Very exhilarating.

TWELVE

In the sixties America was still the number one power in the Western world – but Liverpool was the hub of the universe. Music, art, poetry leapt from the city where the Beatles had broken the shell, and drew the world's attention like a magnet. The city puffed out its chest with confidence and vitality. This energy spread throughout the rest of the country and feelings were high. The young matured early and led the field. But the balance of old and young moved in unity and there was still romance in the air. For a period people really cared for each other and courtesy and respect were a natural part of life. Wealth, however, was possessed by few and it was not only economical, but also fashionable to live in small compact dwellings. Castles in out-of-the-way places could be bought for a few hundred pounds, because the upkeep was so high.

Our home in Kitson Road was bursting at the seams. After the accident Rosemary was told that she would not be able to have another child. She thought differently. In June 1966 our second son effortlessly dropped into life and we now had seven children. Someone suggested that for an actor to have seven offspring was equivalent to a three-year-old horse carrying sixteen stone in the Grand National. But at the time the fences did not seem too high. Fitting nine of us into a four-bedroom house was a different matter. We had dreams of getting something larger and we used to play games looking at estate agents' boards and literature, and sometimes at actual houses.

I was rehearsing a play for television at Kingston Boys' Club. It was the first of three plays I did, written by William Trevor. By this time we owned a car, and one day I drove back to Barnes by way of Kingston Hill. I had details of a house there. I thought that I might have a quick glance. After persuading a neighbour to let me borrow a key, I went inside – and fell in love. It was huge – about twenty rooms, with a minstrel gallery, fourteenth-century double doors leading to a thirty-five-square-foot drawing-room, and a magical secluded garden. I did not stay long enough to take more than a quick glance. I jumped into the car and drove back to Barnes where Pukk was washing up.

'Come quickly,' I said.

'I'm busy.'

'Never mind. Trust me – come!'

We drove back to the house. I opened the door, and Pukk also was bewitched.

The asking price was twenty-four thousand pounds, plus four thousand five hundred for the curtains and carpets. Our Kitson Road house was worth nine thousand pounds and we had no capital. The owner was Edgar Coles, who lived in the country. We found his telephone number and called him.

'Could we come and see you regarding buying Ravenswood House?'

'Sorry, but we are not anxious to sell any more.'

'We have seven children,' I said.

'Come to tea tomorrow,' said Mr Coles.

Edgar Coles and his wife were charming and anxious to help. They said that God meant us to have Ravenswood. Eventually, by getting a double mortgage, and Edgar and Mrs Coles lending us money, we bought it for seventeen thousand five hundred pounds, curtains and carpets included. For sixteen years we lived inside the friendly, welcoming home where the children spent an idyllic time growing up. We thought we would live there happily ever after.

And life indeed was rich and full. The huge house was surprisingly easy to run and Pukk was perpetually on the move, organising, planning and coping as she helped seven eager young creatures form their characters and personalities. As for not walking again, she was constantly active, and apart from a slight limp she conquered her paralysis and concealed it from the world.

After local primary schools Melanie went to Farlington where she boarded. Paul was still at Highgate, the next four girls all went to Putney High School and Toby went to junior school at Rokeby, in Wimbledon. Local transport was difficult, so Pukk also spent a great deal of the day as a chauffeur. But by late afternoon the house was full of lively children, each with their own nook and cranny in that crazy maze of a house; there was tea on the patio, ferocious games of badminton in the garden, and feeding the hens, before the children settled down to homework.

And I was working hard. To keep the house I had to make sure that I was continuously employed. I could not afford to be choosy, and played every part on television that came my way, although I managed not to stay too long in anything. Being an actor on television is a butterfly existence – you are remembered for a day after the transmission and that is it. Very few people can remember the titles of any three TV plays that they have seen. Television is watched casually, as a background to life. When you go to the theatre or the cinema you make an effort, you pay, and you concentrate. On the other hand, if an actor or actress stays too long in a series they become identified as the character they play and it is difficult to throw off the image. Apart from *Kipling*, the longest series I ever did were *Z Cars* for five and a half months, as Inspector Todd, and some years later *The Crezz* by Clive Exton, which lasted six months. I think the latter was ahead of its time because it mixed farce and tragedy. Though essentially about middle-class Londoners, the scripts had charm and wit and a very good cast.

The individual plays were more rewarding. The most satisfying included *Access to the Children*, by William Trevor, in which my marriage broke up; *The Bankrupt*, by David Mercer, in which I had a mental breakdown; *The Lie*, by Ingmar Bergman, in which I had a mental breakdown and dressed as a woman; and in the *Country Matters* series, *Crippled Bloom*, in which I shot myself. Somehow, on television I was always disintegrating. When I played Jerry Westerby in *Tinker Tailor Soldier Spy* I was looking forward to the adaptation of the next John le Carré book, *The Honourable Schoolboy*, because I think it is his best and Jerry Westerby, the 'honourable schoolboy' – only a pencil sketch in *Tinker Tailor* – is a full rich painting, a wonderful, complicated character with that attractive combination of weakness and strength. But the action of the book switches from country to country and the BBC thought it too expensive, so they skipped it and went to the next book, *Smiley's People*.

Friends told us that, when we moved to Ravenswood, we had taken on too much, and would not stay there longer than six months. But we had been lucky, television work had come in steadily and I was kept happily on the run. There was only one problem which we thought time would resolve. Young Paul was very unsettled. Unhappy at senior school at Highgate, he became more and more restless. Always ebullient and full of life he began to suffer great depressions. Every so often he would turn up at home after playing truant from school. His housemaster was very sympathetic and was almost daily on the phone making suggestions and asking advice. But Paul's distress increased and he begged to leave. Eventually we gave in and tried to find another school.

Purely by chance Frith Banbury, who was casting *Dear Octopus* for the West End, rang and said he was looking for a young boy for the play.

At a loss which direction to take with Paul, we allowed him to try for the role. Maybe a few months in the world of the theatre would help him to find his feet. He got the part, and went off on tour with the company. Pukk and I saw the play in Oxford and were thrilled with Paul's performance, which was truthful with natural charm. Puffed with pride we went backstage after the show, only to find a policeman in his dressing-room. Apparently Paul had been throwing fireworks out of the window.

Two weeks before the play was due to open in London the company manager telephoned to say that Paul had been dropped from the show. He had been rude to Cicely Courtneidge and had yawned during Richard Todd's speech. When I explained that Paul had been under psychoanalysis because of his emotional confusion at school, the company manager said maybe they had been too hasty. But by this time Paul was on his way back home on the train and the damage had been done. He then went off to stay with a family in France but somehow managed to end up in Morocco and return home without a passport. Eventually he went to Finchden Manor, which was recommended as a school for bright boys whose emotions and intellect did not balance. Paul appeared to be happy there but it was about this time someone offered him drugs, and if there was one thing that Paul could not resist – it was temptation. Sadly, he would always try anything. But at that time we had no idea – not even when Paul's best friend at Finchden died from an overdose. We were innocent and unenlightened; drugs were not part of our world.

By the time the penny did drop Paul had become two people – the Jekyll-and-Hyde syndrome – the warm, loving, over-enthusiastic, generous person that he really was and the next day deceitful, suffering and monstrous. It was as if good and evil were completely divided. Gradually this anguish came to dominate all our lives. The other children became both fearful and protective. We dreaded his arrival, and missed him when he was not there. One day, while trying to reason with him, I lost consciousness. In retrospect I think this must have been a form of flight from the inability to cope. Paul also was searching for escape from himself and would go anywhere. He wanted to go to Australia. I spoke to Googie Withers and John McCallum, who said they would help him with a job in their theatre, but as fate would have it, on the day Paul arrived in

Australia, Thames Television did a *This is Your Life* on Googie Withers and flew John McCallum to London for the show, so Paul moved north and ended up with a hippy community in the rain-forest near Cairns.

At Ravenswood, in the middle of one night, the telephone rang. Paul was stranded in a desert. He was suffering withdrawal symptoms and was very low. The operator interrupted the call and said, 'I can hear this is an emergency. I am not charging for the call – so relax.'

We arranged for Paul to be picked up by private plane and organised his flight back to England. At that time we had a small house in Cornwall at Treyarnon Bay near Padstow, which we had bought from Sir Malcolm Arnold: a dream cottage with a stream and a rustic bridge and a separate studio where Arnold had spent his time composing. Paul felt he could make a new start from here. But the drugs moved to Cornwall and Paul was lost. On the beach he met a girl, Sue, who was in the same scene. She had a very young baby and they moved in with Paul. Her family came from Bolton, and it was from this town, some time later, that I received a phone call from a hospital nurse.

'I'm sorry to have to tell you that your son is unconscious and not likely to recover. Could you come and see him?'

In a daze Pukk and I collected Toni from Putney High School and took the train to Bolton. Paul lay without moving for three days. As they sat at his bedside, Toni, aged fifteen, said to her mother, 'Mummy, I don't know whether he should come round or not.' And she idolised her brother. Paul was then eighteen. He had taken an injection of mandrax and cider. After three days his eyes opened and he jumped out of bed.

We took him to Cornwall to recuperate and even resorted to removing wires from the telephone so that he would not be tempted to contact his old friends. Somehow he got together with Sue again and they married hippy-style. They went out to Australia with the baby. There she gave birth to Paul's child, but they got caught up in the floods in Darwin and the new baby was nearly drowned.

When they returned home, with the help of John Harris of the Life for the World Organisation, Paul and Sue went off to the L'Abri Fellowship in Switzerland for treatment. It worked for her and for a time it worked for Paul. Their relationship eventually broke up. Paul met Irene, who was a stabilising influence and full of love and affection, and they had a son. Paul tried many forms of work – as a sheep herder, a builder, with cattle, stage managing

– anything that came his way. Always he leapt in with enthusiasm and worked twice as hard as necessary, and always he would get depressed when his enthusiasm was not returned by his co-workers. But gradually he overpowered his craving for drugs.

THIRTEEN

In the late sixties every day was a new surprise. It was as if we had climbed another rung in life and reached a new exciting world. After the fire I began to take more risks because I realised that life was so valuable it was important to try and climb the peaks instead of clinging to the safety ledge. I still found time to romp with the children, to play badminton with them and bath them, but I was steadily increasing my pace, and time with the family became even more precious. And the itch had started. I began to miss the theatre. After *Jorrocks* I felt I should stick to television for some time – the world of movies showed no interest.

Over the years the balance of love and hate I have for the theatre has gradually swung towards the latter. Apart from the repetition of eight shows a week, the piece always controls my life. I am not good at donning a role as I set foot on a stage and tossing it aside as I leave the stage door. Something of the role that I play becomes part of me and I sacrifice part of myself to the character. From the moment I wake in the morning life is dominated by the performance that looms over me that night. The days seem longer, yet sadly life goes by quicker. When I want to remember the date of a past event I do not look at a calendar – I think of the play I was in at the time. Every time I finish in a play I swear that it will be the last. I will never go through that agony again. But playing in the theatre for me is like breathing. If I want to live . . . I have to do it.

But always there is that wretched repetition and the search for the unobtainable and the extraordinary when the audience understand without being told. In movies you do things once and you are on to something else but saying the same lines over and over again is inclined to put everything out of proportion. Small irritations become major problems and actors revert to childish behaviour as their emotions get out of hand. The discipline required is colossal and as I think back now over various plays I have done it is the unusual that invariably provides the memories. Here are a few.

1968: Hotel in Amsterdam by John Osborne – Royal Court, New and Duke of York's theatres

In this play the angry young man began to get angry with his servants. It was a piece with virtually no plot but full of rich, exciting dialogue. Paul Scofield, Judy Parfitt, David Burke, Isobel Dean, Susan Engel and I sat and waffled – but the waffle sparkled. It was a very static piece and we kept the bubbles in the air by having fun amongst ourselves.

Back to back with the New (now the Albery) was the Wyndham's Theatre: a passage runs underneath the courtyard joining the two theatres. At the Wyndham's Kate O'Mara was playing in *The Italian Girl*.

During our play Paul and I were left alone on stage; he walked back to the French windows and stared out, and then joined me on the couch as we looked silently into space. One night Paul walked over to the french windows and stared. The delectable Kate was standing just offstage, naked except for her long Italian eyelashes, and holding a cardboard sign saying, 'Is there anything I can do to help?' Paul went on staring – then he walked back to the couch and joined me. Together we looked out silently – but that night the silence was a beat longer.

The title did cause complications. One day an American couple went to the box-office asking if they could book a room for the night.

It was indeed a charming small hotel – with just the right clientele. A happy experience.

When I left the stage door after the show all was not so happy. Our son Paul was going through a bad period. On many occasions I would leave the theatre and search for him in the streets of Soho, or Pukk would be called from home at Ravenswood to pick him up at Bow Street Police Station.

1970: Come As You Are by John Mortimer – New and Strand theatres

Glynis Johns, Denholm Elliott, Pauline Collins and I were in four one-act plays about different parts of London. A very exciting cast. Allan Davis, the director, had a lot on his plate, as he was also presenting the piece with Alexander Cohen, and when one play was dropped and replaced by another, rehearsals became a bit chaotic.

One day Glynis and I were working on a scene when Allan came up to speak to us. Without thinking, I said, 'Sorry, Allan – not now, we are rehearsing.'

'Sorry,' said Allan, and left.

Allan was not the most tactful of creatures. In the last play – 'Marble Arch' – I played a Scots porter. Two days before we opened Allan said to me, 'Do you know Simon Lack, the actor?'

'No,' I said.

'Perhaps you should meet him,' said Allan. 'He's a Scot – he might be able to help you with your dialect!'

Two days before we opened in Edinburgh the show was nowhere near ready. I phoned John Mortimer in the middle of the night and asked him to come and help. He did. At the dress rehearsal on the Monday afternoon, the revolve, which was instrumental in leading the audience from one play to another, did not work. But there was no time for repairs. A few hours later we opened.

At the end of the first play, 'Mill Hill', Glynis was left onstage in her lover's fantasy Elizabethan costume, talking to me offstage in the bathroom while I, as her elegant dentist husband, chatted excitedly as I supposedly was also getting into Elizabethan rig. In fact, I was standing in an East End pub set, putting on my publican costume for the next play, 'Bermondsey'. The lights lowered, and thank God the Mill Hill set rolled away and the revolve revolved. When the lights went up on the next play the audience saw me standing in the Bermondsey pub talking to Glynis offstage as she was changing into the publican's wife. Our nerves were on high gear as we skated through the first half.

In the interval, with two plays to go, Allan came back to my dressing-room and gave me a note. It was so outrageous that I have had a mental block ever since as to what he said. But whatever it was, it heightened my sense of panic – and we still had two changes to go. Somehow we got through the show and the reception was very good.

Denholm's dressing-room was next door to mine, and after the play his cousin dropped backstage to see him. The first thing we heard was John Mortimer and Alex Cohen arguing in the hall, because Alex wanted to extend the pre-London tour from three weeks to seven weeks to get the show settled. Then the usually cool and collected John Mortimer went into Denholm's dressing-room and within seconds of heated dialogue he had grabbed Allan Davis by the lapels and pushed him against the wall. Denholm's embarrassed cousin fled for safety to my room. I was unaware of the brouhaha that had been going on. A moment later Allan appeared in my doorway, rubbed his hands together and said, 'Well, that went all right then, didn't it?' I snapped. Whatever Allan had said in the interval had built up in my mind, and this innocuous remark burst the bubble. I also grabbed him by the jacket and heaved him down the hall. Denholm's cousin, who had never been backstage before, looked goggle-eyed. 'I never dreamt it would be like this,' he said. 'Why the audience bother to go to the front of a theatre I can't imagine!'

The company all met up later for a meal and a lot of drinks. By two a.m. Allan had not appeared and I suggested to John we telephone him at his hotel.

'We shall leave notes everywhere,' said John.

At three a.m. Allan appeared. 'May I come in?' he said.

We all embraced heartily.

For seven weeks we toured England. Alan Bridges was brought in as an extra pair of eyes and we rehearsed eagerly through the days and performed in the evenings. Glynis, Denholm and Pauline, all very individual and talented, were a joy to work with. The second play, 'Bermondsey', was a very delicate, moving piece in which I was married to Glynis, having it off on the side with Pauline, but was forced to reveal that my great love was Denholm. I believe it was the first time on the West End stage that two men kissed passionately.

At the first rehearsal we had looked warily at each other.

'All right,' said Denholm, 'let's plunge in at the deep end.'

We opened at the New and the play was a big success with audience and critics. We were well away.

But . . .

After a few weeks in the West End the adorable Glynis, one of the few film actresses in the world who can fill a stage with their presence, started to get a trifle neurotic. Immediately prior to our first meeting she had been in hospital and had to plunge into rehearsals without a break. Throughout this preparation and the seven weeks on tour, with yet more work on the play during the day, and then the high opening weeks in London as *Come As You Are* received the plaudits of success, she attacked her four roles with the tenacity and resolution of a real pro and overcame all pain and anxiety. Then her adored mother fell ill. Glynis got her father to bring her over from South Africa where she stayed in Glynis's flat, but her mother was dying. Finally the strain was too much and Glynis had a breakdown and was unable to cope. She became so insecure that she would telephone me at least ten times a day.

The record was eighteen times, and that was through the night as well.

For two or three weeks the show became a nightmare. Pauline Collins had left because she had been contracted to do another show, and Celia Bannerman had taken over. Denholm became more introvert than ever and hid within his shell, and it was me whom Glynis clutched at for security. Nearly every night, ten minutes before the show, she would leave the theatre and I would have to run after her down St Martin's Lane and haul her back. Then I would have to coddle her and cuddle her to make her go on stage. I have even slapped her and pushed her into her make-up chair. Many times she did not make it to the theatre at all. She had a stand-by and an understudy. If the theatre knew before the half hour that Glynis was not going to play, the stand-by played her role; if it was after the half hour was called, the understudy played. Sometimes she would drop out during the show. When the first play finished I would be talking to her offstage, I would be transported in on the Bermondsey set and someone quite different would come in and kiss me. The worst night was when Glynis could hardly manage to get a line out and Denholm and I had to take over. As the curtain came down at the end of the first half Denholm slammed down the piano lid and said, 'That is the last time I appear on any stage with you, babe.'

The show ran thirty minutes over that night, and I was late in getting to the BBC for a programme in which I spoke of the great unity in the cast.

When I arrived home at Ravenswood, Pukk looked amazed. 'My God, look at your hair!'

I did. My hair had gone white at the sides.

After two or three weeks Glynis was back to normal – her breakdown was over. Once more she was a joy to play alongside.

1971: Captain Brassbound's Conversion by George Bernard Shaw – Cambridge Theatre

One afternoon at Ravenswood, Frith Banbury rang and asked me if I would like to play Captain Brassbound opposite Ingrid Bergman's Lady Cicely. 'Yes,' I said.

Binkie Beaumont was presenting the show for H. M. Tennent and he asked me to dinner at his home in Lord North Street to join Frith and himself and meet Ingrid and Kenneth Williams, who was to play my mate Drinkwater.

The statuesque Swedish beauty rose to greet me. 'Thank goodness you are taller than I am,' she said. 'My only other leading men taller than me were Gary Cooper and Gregory Peck.'

A good opening for that small boy who had sat enraptured watching *For Whom the Bell Tolls* and *Spellbound*.

After Brighton we played for nine months at the Cambridge Theatre, naturally to full houses. Ingrid could fill a theatre if she was reading the telephone directory. The play is not one of Shaw's best. Ingrid could never be an English aristocrat, I could do little with Brassbound – a very dull man whom Shaw based maliciously on Laurence Irving – and the eccentric, brilliant Kenneth Williams was more at sea with Drinkwater than his character could ever have been. John Robinson as the doctor was truthful and accurate. Frith directed meticulously – too meticulously for Ingrid, who wanted movement and romance. We found a little in our last scene – more perhaps than Shaw intended.

Every evening, in the interval, Kenneth Williams would leap into my room and we would have a glass of wine.

'Don't you ever knock?' I said.

'Why, I know you're there.'

I grew very fond of him.

And Ingrid became a great friend and remained so until her death. On Sundays she would come out to Ravenswood for the day and go cycling with the children in Richmond Park.

It was a glamorous run and, thanks to Ingrid, Pukk and I spent some fascinating evenings. Through her we met Alfred Hitchcock who was in Britain to make the movie *Frenzy*. He was so meticulous in his preparation that as far as he was concerned the film was completed – and he had yet to cast anyone in the picture.

1973: *The Collaborators by John Mortimer – Duchess Theatre*

Not a happy experience. I felt that – despite having a good director, Eric Thompson – Glenda Jackson, John Wood and I never did justice to the play. John was far too demented and extrovert and Glenda and I were forced to lose balance and underplay. Glenda was a pleasure to work with, but this was a real example of boredom of repetition and each time we left the stage, she and I would put a little tick on the wall as we approached the end of our three-month contracts. One satisfaction was working with my daughter Melanie who was on stage management. Strangely enough, I heard that

Diane Cilento, Peter McEnery and John Thaw, who replaced us, were if anything more miserable than we were.

1974: A Streetcar Named Desire by Tennessee Williams – Piccadilly Theatre

I was filming in Madrid and staying with Pat and Michael York at their borrowed villa. One morning I was sitting outside a café drinking coffee when a small tubby man appeared, looked around, gave an exasperated sigh and walked away. A taller, younger man appeared on the scene. He also looked around, made a sound of annoyance and made his exit. Then the tubby man appeared again, vanished; the tall man arrived and departed, and this farce continued for some time until, at last, they met, gesticulated furiously at each other and then left together. That evening Pat, Michael and I were having dinner when two surprise visitors turned up – the tubby man and his friend. They turned out to be Tennessee Williams and Bill Barnes his agent.

Tennessee insisted on swimming twenty-one lengths of the pool every night and so after the meal he put on his little bathing cap and dived in. He tried to persuade me to join him, but at one in the morning the water was like ice. I told him how some years before I had much enjoyed playing Mitch in *A Streetcar Named Desire*, and he informed me that there was going to be a production in London the following year with Claire Bloom as Blanche.

When I returned home I rang my agent, Michael Anderson (Philip Pearman had sadly died suddenly in 1964) and told him that I would like to have another stab as Mitch. So I played the same role exactly twenty-one years after the production at Coventry. Despite being too young the first time and too old the second time, it proved a most enjoyable experience. It was a very honest, gutsy production by Ed Sherrin, who was a twin to Pukk because they were born at the same time on the same day in the same year. The chemistry between Claire and me was rich and Martin Shaw and Morag Hood had a brave shot at Stanley and Stella. Morag is a fine actress, but seemed prim and very Scottish, and Martin was vegetarian and liked to play the guitar with incense burning.

Although I do not believe it necessary to live one's role there is no way that Stanley could be a vegetarian and the two roles require a strong basis of animal. However, the audience liked it, the critics liked it and Tennessee showed immense satisfaction, and that meant a lot.

It is very difficult for an actor to be satisfied with anything he does, but there are rare moments when something inexplicable occurs, not possible to explain, but you know it is right. There was one of these moments in *Streetcar* when alone with Claire – and she was desperate that Mitch should propose marriage – I tentatively said: 'Blanche . . . Blanche?' and then held a pause while the audience strained forward, waiting for the question to be popped. After going through a confusing agony of mind I could only say, 'Guess how much I weigh, Blanche', and the audience would break into a wave of sad, sympathetic laughter. I knew then that they had climbed inside my shell.

There had been a similar moment in the second production of *Twelfth Night* at the Old Vic, years before. In the first production in America, at the end of the kitchen scene, John Neville as Aguecheek and myself as Toby Belch were high on drink, and with a jovial roar of ''Tis too late to go to bed now' from Belch we stomped upstairs and offstage with John's left leg and my right leg inside the same boot, while the audience laughed and clapped.

During rehearsal of the second production I awoke in the middle of the night with a new idea. We worked it into the show. At the end of the same scene Tom Courtenay as Feste had passed out, and Stephen Moore as Aguecheek dropped asleep with his head on my shoulder. Suddenly the drink turned sour and my wasted life passed before my eyes. I felt naked and alone and I picked up Aguecheek and held him tight. With quiet desperation I said, ''Tis too late to go to bed now' and walked slowly up the stairs, holding Aguecheek close in my arms as a cock crowed quietly in the distance. The audience turned from laughter to a breathless silence and you could feel that magical tremor sweep through the theatre. It is moments like these that more than make up for the depressions and repetitive boredom.

Claire and I had been students together at the Central School, but we had never really met. *Streetcar* was the start of a working relationship and friendship which has continued to this day.

1975: A Little Night Music by Stephen Sondheim – Adelphi Theatre

One evening Glynis Johns phoned me from New York and told me she was going to do a new Stephen Sondheim musical based on *Smiles of a Summer Night*, the Ingmar Bergman movie. Would I like to do it with her? 'That would be great,' I said, but I felt the side of my hair go a shade whiter. Much as I loved and admired Glynis I trembled at the memory of the unhappy period in *Come As You Are*. I quickly changed the subject and we talked of other things.

When the show opened in New York Glynis had a great success and was the toast of Broadway.

Many months later Harold Prince, whom I had met when he was an admirer of *Jorrocks*, telephoned and asked if I would be interested in playing Frederic Egerman in the London production of *A Little Night Music*, and would I try out the songs with Ray Cook, the English musical director, to see if I could hit the notes correctly. This I did but found the very complicated score was too high for my untrained base baritone. Various messages were passed on to Stephen Sondheim in the States, but eventually when I insisted that the key of nearly every number be lowered, Stephen came up with the perfect solution. 'Fuck him.'

And that was that.

Some time later Pukk and I were having dinner with the American producer Jack Levin and his wife Clorice, when Jack said, 'Have you heard? Jean Simmons is going to play Desirée in *A Little Night Music*.'

The next morning, as a joke, I rang Richard Pilbrow, who was presenting the show in London and said, 'I've suddenly discovered that I can hit high C.' This message was delivered in all seriousness to New York and a few days later, while I was in Prague filming, I received a telegram asking if I could meet Harold Prince in Vienna, where he was directing the show. Of course they had to change the title there, as it would have been foolish to have a musical called *Eine Kleine Nacht Musik* in Vienna. The locals would have been very confused. Instead, Ingmar Bergman had been so impressed by the show, he allowed it to be called *Smiles of a Summer Night*.

So I flew from Prague and saw Hal Prince who was busy watching rehearsal in the auditorium.

'Would you like to play Frederic?'

'Yes,' I said.

'Good,' he said. And I flew back to Prague.

And what a joy the show proved to be. The piece was a meringue soufflé and Stephen had kept the feel and delicacy of the enchanting movie and added his own extraordinary magic. His working relationship with the brilliant Hal Prince who loved danger and achieved the impossible was, I believe, the peak of musical theatre.

The cast was superb and we all worked well and played well together. Every evening I would dash into the theatre with excitement. Toby, our young son, watched the show from the wings about sixty times. At the end, when Jean and I walked slowly towards each other while the chords of 'Send in the Clowns' swelled into a great romantic crescendo, beyond the orchestra we could hear the sobs from the audience. Manipulative – yes. Sentimental – yes. Truly theatrical – yes. And I loved it.

1977: The Madras House by Harley Granville Barker – National Theatre

Granville Barker was an extraordinary genius and this episodic play was satisfying, although the National Theatre, that concrete jungle with Big Brother having a field day over the Tannoy while the various companies become part of the same brew, is not my cup of tea. But then I did not enjoy school either and could never get rid of the feeling that I was acting in the labour exchange. And the labyrinth of corridors defeated me. I did put in a request for a guide dog. I missed one curtain call because I found myself locked outside in the auditorium. Another curtain call resulted in my making my entrance through the fireplace. William Gaskill was an interesting director, laid back to the point of reclining, and it was fun working with the two Pauls again – Scofield and Rodgers.

Much as I hate the rigid discipline of eight performances a week, I found playing intermittently, sometimes with a break of nearly a month, terrifying. The only chance of recapturing a show was a word rehearsal, but how do you find the rhythm and the ability to be on top of an audience and manipulate them like a conjuror, after so long a break?

1977: The Taming of the Shrew by William Shakespeare – national tour

Later in 1977 my old friend Frank Hauser asked me to play Petruchio in *The Taming of the Shrew* which he was about to direct for Duncan Weldon. I thought that this might be my last chance to play Petruchio and it would be good to work with Frank again, so I agreed. Wendy Craig, fresh from a successful TV series, was to play Katherine. Two days before the first rehearsal Don Siegel phoned from Hollywood and told me that Max von Sydow had to drop out of a new movie that Don was directing and could I play the role. I said that I was about to do the tour. 'That's okay,' said Don, 'we'll buy you out.' I explained that it was too late. I was no longer a fledgling and the show had been cast accordingly, and I had given my word. Much as I would like to do the movie, it was impossible. Some months later, when the tour was well under way and we were playing at Richmond, Duncan Weldon came to tea at Ravenswood and I told him the story.

'You should have told me,' said Duncan benignly, 'we could have got anybody.'

I had not toured for years and felt, for the first time, that outside London the theatre had lost its magic. However, the production was exciting, Wendy was a delight to work with and I made a friend of Johnny Dennis who played Grumio.

1978: Evita by Tim Rice and Andrew Lloyd Webber – Prince Charles Theatre

Bob Swash from the Robert Stigwood Organisation phoned me to say that Harold Prince was going to direct a musical by the pair who had written *Jesus Christ Superstar*. It was not a big show, there was not much money, but Hal would love me to play Perón. What was unusual was that a recording had been made of the complete score, and 'Don't Cry for Me, Argentina' was already a hit. The prospect of working with Hal was always exciting, so I agreed. A short time after, David Essex, the king of the bobby-soxers, was signed to play Ché Guevara. But the long, exhausting role of Evita was yet to be filled. On the day that Hal was to fly back to New York and I was to fly off to Singapore to do a movie, Hal told me that he had reached a decision. As Evita was such a difficult role he would have the part played by three actresses, all conveying different facets of Evita, and at the end of the show they would all expire together.

Some time later, in Singapore, I picked up a copy of *The Times* and saw that a young, unknown Elaine Paige was going to play Evita. Who are the other two? I wondered. On my return I discovered that there were no other two. Elaine insisted that she could cope with the whole caboodle. From the beginning I had a strange conviction that *Evita* was going to be an enormous hit. For the first time ever I decided to buy shares in the show and Bob Swash promised to get five for me. Later, when I asked him for the shares he pressed his hand to his mouth and said, 'Oh gosh – I forgot.'

'Can I get some now?'

'No, it's too late – they've all gone. I am sorry,' and he did his impersonation of a crestfallen cherub. When I told Eddie Kulukundis, the good-natured Greek impresario who has remained a firm friend since *A Little Night Music*, he immediately sold me half of the one share he had in the show, and even that has proved quite useful in the survival stakes.

Before rehearsals began, Pukk and I went off to Argentina, ostensibly to do some research on Perón. We thought that we would get there cheaply as I had arranged through Robert Stigwood to do some publicity shots as Perón, for British Caledonian Airways. However, they were cautioned that if one photograph was taken of Perón for the airway, British Caledonian would never be allowed to land in Argentina again.

We paid full fare!

En route we stopped off at Iguazu, with its majestic cascade of falls, and we stayed the night. Our next step was Rio in Brazil, where the carnival was just getting under way. The extravagant costumes created a mass of colour and the air sizzled with excitement and joy of life. As we walked in the street people would grasp our hands and lead us off to the beat of the samba.

Buenos Aires in Argentina was very much an anti-climax, and also rather awesome. The Stigwood office had arranged for me to meet various people who had connections with the Peróns, but at the appointed hours of meeting not one of them turned up.

In the course of time I made my own connections, but they would either leave abruptly when I said the magic word 'Perón', or they would close the door before speaking. I began to feel like Holly Martins in *The Third Man*.

Pukk and I found ourselves an interpreter – a 'warm-hearted, sweet-natured' girl. One day I pointed to a statue in the middle of a square and asked her who the imposing fellow was. 'Oh, he was a very great general,' she said, smiling happily. 'He started at the bottom of Argentina, and made his way to the top, getting rid of all the Indians.' She gave a sweeping gesture with her arm and made a sound like a machine-gun.

She took us to Lobos, the small town where Perón was born. With the exception of Franco, Perón had ruled his country as dictator longer than anyone this century, yet here, in his birthplace, it was as if he had never existed. Even the children in a small kindergarten were ignorant that their school had been the house in which their godlike leader had been born. And this was only a few years after his death.

Under the pretext of writing a book about the general I managed to interview a surgeon, once his best friend. I discovered little, apart from the fact that Perón, who politically was right of Mussolini, had grown weaker after meeting Eva – of whom the surgeon thought little – and their friendship had waned.

Pukk and I cut short our time in Argentina and returned to Rio, where we were in time for the last, uplifting days of the carnival.

Of one thing I was certain: there was no way that I wanted to appear in another version of *Springtime for Hitler*, and was determined to bring a touch of the monster to the man so lightly presented in the script. Hal agreed, and he was in great form in rehearsal, weaving new patterns, taking his usual risks, creating huge changes of emotional colour and turning the ordinary into gold. Rehearsals were enjoyable, and the cast worked hard. I was the only actor in the company (I had the only unsung line in the show: 'No'). The others were all part of the new rock world, and I felt occasionally like a Martian, but we all got on well together and the work was satisfying.

Two reporters from the *Daily Mail* sat through all the rehearsals, ate with us, drank with us and laughed with us. Their article appeared just before we opened. On that same day the happy couple disappeared for ever. The article covered the four centre pages of their newspaper, describing rehearsals as utter chaos and saying that there was no way that the show would work.

The sheer size of the musical convinced me that naturalism was not the most appropriate approach to the extravaganza, so I set out to exaggerate everything, from movement to make-up. To create a vivid picture of Perón I wore a dark wig, dark brown contact lenses and had a number of false noses made. I had great trouble with the noses. Each one had its own personality and often refused to stick to my face. Eventually I phoned Laurence Olivier for advice. He of all people would be the expert. He told me that with the exception of the movie *Richard III* he had always made his nose himself, from putty. So had I, but in the first scene I appeared as myself, and the change was too fast.

'Have you tried lining it with cotton wool?'

'Yes,' I said.

'Have you tried pricking it with a pin?'

'Yes.'

'Well,' he said, 'you have a problem. If you're not careful this is going to be a musical about a nose.'

The nose problem was never completely resolved, and it required attention throughout the show. The previews went smoothly. Half-way through the first night, which seemed the same as any other night, I thought, "My God – I'm bored." And I had a year to go.

Of course it was a fantastic success. Perhaps the most successful show ever. And for Elaine it could have been a fairy tale. 'Chorus girl becomes star overnight' screamed the headlines.

But every evening was the same. The music started and the great machine rolled into action, the audience sat in silence, the show finished and then there was an ovation. Always the same. Nothing varied. Except the artists, who dropped in and out like cogs in the machine. Being an opera, we were controlled absolutely by the orchestra. Without freedom on a stage the actor's ego suffers. Not able to control an audience with natural timing and, because of so much visual imagery, unable to control attention, I began to feel superfluous. Years of hard grind had left their mark and I still believed that if you are advertised to perform – you perform. After only a few days Elaine began to miss performances and soon other actresses would appear in the role of Evita. This break in discipline soon spread to the rest of the cast and before long there would be up to seven people off at a time. None of this seemed to upset the Stigwood Organisation. Theirs was a new world of musicals presenting neat, wrapped-up packages with the word 'success' stamped on the covers. A different world. But my world and my ego had taught me to believe that it was important to appear every night or the show would suffer.

Eventually so many people were off that I rang Hal Prince in New York. He flew over and got the company together.

'This is a delicate matter,' he said. 'We have the same problem now in New York, but today artists are not as dedicated or professional as they used to be. They miss performances when they do not need to miss performances. Let me give you an example. Mary Martin was doing a show – *I Do, I Do* – in New York when she got ill, so the ambulance would take her to the theatre, she would do the show, and then the ambulance would pick her up and take her back to the hospital. That's what I'm talking about.'

There was a long pause – and then a chorus of voices said, 'Who's Mary Martin?'

Hal looked at me, raised his eyebrows and said, 'What can you do!'

David Essex was never off. He had great charm on stage and even though more like Alan-a-Dale than the dedicated revolutionary Ché Guevara, the facile script did not encourage him to do otherwise. But again, he belonged to another world – the pop world, and was always surrounded by his entourage. We hardly ever made contact.

1981: The Cherry Orchard by Anton Chekhov – Chichester

It took some time after *Evita* before the theatre bug started nibbling away at my system. The prospect of working with my old chum Claire Bloom in one of my favourite plays for a relatively short run at Chichester did the trick.

Some years before I had done a broadcast of *The Cherry Orchard*, playing Lophakin to Edith Evans's Ranyevska. It was a time when I was doing three jobs at the same time, and I shall always remember the first rehearsal with the lovely, fastidious director Charles Lefeaux, when I walked up to the microphone, picked up my script and went to say my first line to the formidable Edith. 'My God – it's *Z Cars*,' I burst out. I had brought the wrong script.

In that same production, Peter Copley, who played Gaev, told me that when he was in the play before with Charles Laughton as Lophakin, Charles used to get him to whirl him around several times before he went on, so that as he made his entrance and banged his head he actually was dizzy. 'Brilliant,' I said. 'Will you do the same for me?' Peter did. The only trouble was I had forgotten it was a broadcast, and I was so befuddled that I could not see the script.

While I was at the National Theatre I had several discussions with Peter Hall regarding further work at the National. Peter would always come flying in with a smoked salmon sandwich, and we would have a glass of white wine and talk about the future. On one occasion *The Cherry Orchard* was brought up. I suggested Lophakin. 'Albert Finney is playing that,' said Peter.

'What about Gaev?'

'Oh no, you are quite wrong physically for Gaev,' said Peter. Gielgud had left his indelible print on the role.

'But Gaev could be a lost teddy-bear of a man.'

'Let's think of something else,' said Peter.

So I played Gaev at Chichester, and Claire was Ranyevska. The director Patrick Garland is a sweet-natured man whom I have known since I was working at the Oxford Playhouse, but he declared he was not too happy with Chekhov. A good cast played with a hodgepodge of styles and the piece was only partly successful; but Gaev could be, and was, a lost teddy-bear of a man.

1982: The Dresser by Ronald Harwood – national tour

I had been asked to play Sir in *The Dresser* before, but unfortunately had been working at the time. So when Robin Lefevre asked me to do a national tour of the show I could not resist. When Kenneth Haigh was suggested as Norman, the dresser, I was none too happy. Kenneth was well known as having a chip on his shoulder. As it turned out he was brilliant in the role and we struck up a very good relationship. Robin directed superbly and it could have been one of the most satisfying shows of a lifetime. There was only one problem: non-existent audiences. We played to empty houses throughout Britain. Most people thought *The Dresser* was a piece of furniture!

It was this show that convinced me that TV had really made its mark, and good live theatre was dead in the provinces. London and all the local critics gave it rave reviews, but nothing could induce people to buy a ticket. In most towns we followed an Agatha Christie play, which in the West End had come off almost before it opened, yet on tour it played to full houses everywhere. Halfway through our tour the notice went up: we were to finish in two weeks. However, the Arts Council representative came to see the show and offered to guarantee our losses. They thought it was important the play should continue. So we played on – still to empty houses. At Edinburgh the local critic wrote in to his own newspaper asking why no one was taking their advice to go and see *The Dresser*, but to no avail.

A very frustrating experience. I still have one theatrical ambition: to play Lear in a Wolfit-type production in the afternoon, followed by Sir in *The Dresser* at night.

1982: Henry IV by William Shakespeare, Parts I and II – Opening of the Barbican Theatre

From time to time Pukk and I would fly to New York to discuss various projects. Work in the States always posed a problem, because I did not possess the invaluable green card. This small object is vital to spare you the rigmarole of having to prove that only *you* can play a role that would go to a local actor. This petty bureaucracy has gone on for many years. British Equity started the ball rolling. In the fifties most movies, however English the subject, would have to have an American star to sell the product abroad. The William Holden role in *The Bridge on the River Kwai* was written into the movie for this reason. Often the star was only a very small satellite. So the theatrical Iron Curtain came down. Lack of freedom is as wrong in the theatre as it is in the political world. It all equals out in the wash. The pendulum of popularity swings one way and then the other. Today it is the turn of English acting to command the greatest respect. Even musicals, once considered to belong to the United States, are now respected more if they are English. In my opinion, quite wrongly. The Emperor's clothes' syndrome has taken hold of the musical world. On one occasion Pukk and I were in New York to see Robert Anderson, the author of *Tea and Sympathy*, as he wanted me to play his father in a fine new play he had written. Rosemary Harris was to play my wife. Rosemary had gone to the States at the time I was there with the Old Vic in the fifties.

We had travelled to the States by way of the West Indies, where we stayed with the impresario Eddie Kulukundis in a lovely home in Barbados. Eddie was like an excited bear because he wanted to ask Susan Hampshire to marry him, so just before he flew back to England, Pukk and I decided to tour the islands. We stayed at the lovely, unspoiled island of Bequia where we had to carry our suitcases through the sea to reach our hotel, and then went on to St Lucia where the only other English couple were Jeremy Isaacs and his wife Tamara. He was taking a breather before embarking on running Channel Four with such extraordinary success.

We had to return to Barbados to catch our plane to New York. Eddie had left, the English cricket team were playing in a Test match and we could find nowhere to spend the night, except for a run-down room where the bed was stained with blood from cockroaches and squashed mosquitoes. We had therefore slept – if that is the right word – in the sizzling heat with all our clothes on and our faces covered in order to avoid being bitten to death. A steel band played outside our room throughout the night. On arriving in New York next day we took over an elegant suite just vacated by the Oliviers at the Wyndham Hotel, which had been arranged for us by my ebullient American agent Milton Goldman.

There was no luck with the play, which was to open at the Kennedy Center in Washington and then go to New York.

American Equity refused to give me permission, saying it was like getting an Englishman to do *Death of a Salesman*. Bob Anderson wrote to me when I returned to England, and told me the news. He said Elia Kazan had argued on my behalf and finally Bob had thrown the script down in disgust and swept from the room. After all, it was his play.

When we saw Stephen Sondheim's *Sweeney Todd* in New York it was with the possibility of me playing the demon barber in London. The music and score were stunning, Hal Prince had done a brilliant, imaginative job creating a weird Dickensian London, with great steam hammers beating away in the auditorium alongside the audience. Angela Lansbury was quite superb as Mrs Lovett and Len Cariou did good, solid work as Todd.

There were two major defects. Steve had made it almost impossible for Todd, by giving him too much to do; to my mind he had fallen into the Andrew Lloyd Webber trap. Todd was controlled completely by the complicated music, always on the run so that he never was able to – as I remember Todd Slaughter doing so brilliantly with tatty sets in a small theatre when I was nervously in the flies – stand quietly in control and terrify that audience as a man dominated by evil. Hal, who always wants to create something important, instead of allowing the piece to be simple, frightening melodrama, had tried to turn it into an important sociological document, showing the miseries and deprivations of the time. In one number, when Todd sang lovingly and sexily about the attractions of the razor, the audience were spellbound. But mostly he was cavorting around the stage chasing the music.

Steve phoned me the next day while we were visiting my sister-in-law Zena and Ken, her husband, and asked me what I thought of the show. I told him I had enjoyed it but Todd was very difficult to sing. When the show opened in London at Drury Lane we were Hal's guests on the first night. Denis Quilley, who like myself is primarily an actor, was excellent, but the show was not a success.

On another occasion Pukk and I had arranged to go to New York to see another Sondheim-Prince show *Pacific Overtures*. The day before we left, Ingrid Bergman phoned and we told her our plans.

'Good,' she said. 'Can I come and join you?' And she did.

The three of us sat one afternoon and had a magical experience. Steve and Hal had created something quite beautiful and the number 'Someone in a Tree' gave me perhaps the most extraordinarily satisfying experience I have ever had in a theatre. Youth and age together created the sad and funny spectrum of life, portrayed here with exquisite sensitivity. At the end I sat in my seat, with tears pouring down my face, while New Yorkers rose from theirs saying, 'Okay, I guess, but very slow.' That evening we went to see *Chorus Line* which was a huge hit in New York. A good Broadway bouncer, but after *Pacific Overtures* it was an unwanted dessert after a real meal.

When Hal asked me to do *Pacific Overtures* in London I was elated. He had revised the show and we were going to do it without an interval at my old home, the Mermaid Theatre. I was to play the Reciter who tells the story to the audience and double it with the Madam in the Japanese whorehouse. However, the Mermaid ran out of money and the show was cancelled. Free and out of work I thought of taking time off for the first time for many years, when Trevor Nunn asked me to play Falstaff in the opening production at the Barbican Theatre, a double header, *Henry IV*, Parts I and II.

I must confess to a blind spot about the RSC. After my disastrous season at Stratford in 1947, Peter Hall crept in, started the Royal Shakespeare Company and gradually the actors' theatre died and the director became the star performer. When Trevor Nunn took over from Peter, the director was in full command. Actors in the company became puppets and even their 'star performers' were usually extrovert exhibitionists who disappeared when they entered the real world. Those who succeeded did so in spite of, rather than because of, their work in the company. When Richardson and Olivier virtually ran the Old Vic, the company included George Relph, Joyce Redman, Alec Guinness, Margaret Leighton and Sybil Thorndike, all of whom could light up any stage, but not many flickers of brightness have come from the RSC stable. Helen Mirren, Ian Holm, Ian Richardson are fine performers who left in time. But surprises do happen. Eddie Kulukundis almost had to force me to go and see *Nicholas Nickleby*, which was a wonderful theatrical experience.

So I leapt into *Henry IV* with the same director, Trevor Nunn, and the same designer, John Napier. We rehearsed for six months. Timothy Dalton was playing Hotspur in Part I, and he and I were the only two who were not regular members of the company, so we followed them around wherever they were playing. First in Stratford-upon-Avon, where as in 1947 the snow lay thick upon the ground, and then when the company moved to Newcastle, Tim and I would fly there regularly to rehearse. Well, when I say

With Richard Burton in *Villain*, 1971; and, below, in *England Made Me*, 1972

Hook in the musical of
Peter Pan, with grandson
Gianluca; and, below, as
Sir playing Lear in *The
Dresser*

The whole family in Greece

Melanie

Penny

Toni and David

Sammy and Paolo

Kirsty

Toby

Paul: a favourite photograph at Bodmin Road Station, Cornwall; above right, with Irene; below left, with son Ben; and, right, his daughter Kandy

More grandchildren: Pukk with Gianluca; and, right, Penny's son Daniel

As Perón in *Evita*

As Goering in *The Man Who Lived at the Ritz*

Don Masino in *The Sicilian*

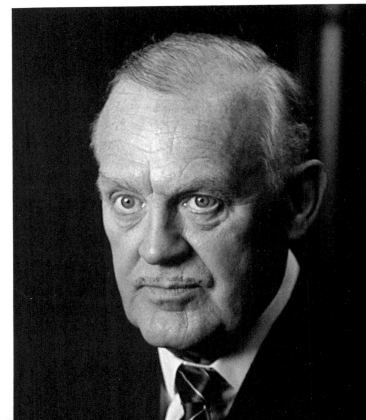

Jock Delves Broughton
in *White Mischief*

With Pukk in Paris

rehearse – that was the official rehearsal period. In fact, for the first four months we spent most of our time sitting around in a circle playing games. It was back to school in earnest. We had to write essays about the period, discuss the sanitary conditions and the results of the Black Death, then we would read out our efforts to the rest of the class while Trevor sat nodding sagely. We had to speak each other's lines and run inanely from one side of the room to the other as we did so. Everything was together, by numbers, nothing was left to the individual imagination or trusting to the intelligence of each performer. The company quietly moaned about anything or everything but no one ever said, 'The Emperor has no clothes.' Secretly, I think, many quite enjoyed being controlled and manipulated. By the time we did get down to rehearsing we had to go at it like the clappers. And we all had to understudy each other. At first I refused, saying that for a heavily padded Falstaff to understudy a gatekeeper in Part II was a hypocrisy: it was not practical, and then again, it cancelled individuality.

Nicholas Nickleby had opened with the cast walking among the audience and chatting. In the episodic piece with actors playing many roles this was a bit like the school play, but it worked quite well. Trevor decided to do the same thing with *Henry IV*. My own mental preparation was complicated enough, convincing an audience that Falstaff and I were one and the same person, let alone running around the auditorium saying, 'Hello, old chap, or madam, I am just an actor really but let's have some topping fun together!' I declined. But I did give in to his heartbroken, anguished plea for me to move a stool three feet across a stage during a scene change. 'Hello,' I could hear people saying in the audience, 'what is Falstaff moving that stool for?' I shrivelled inside. It was not Falstaff. It was me. It was agony.

Early in rehearsals at Stratford the snow was so thick we were told that it was impossible to drive to London, but I wanted to be with Pukk for the weekend so I set out anyway. Trevor had an appointment in London so he decided to risk coming with me, together with his co-director John Caird. Halfway to London we were stuck in a line of traffic which could not continue. Whereas most cars turned back, "To hell with that," I thought, and drove through side roads until I came upon a tractor crossing a field. I drove into the pressed-down tyre marks made by the tractor, crossed the field and continued my way to London. Suddenly Trevor said, 'Please stop the car for a moment.' I did so and Trevor then said, 'I think that effort deserves a round of applause', and quite seriously sat next to me in the car and clapped me. "Hell's teeth," I thought, "I could have trouble here."

The Barbican proved a disaster acoustically. The auditorium was covered, but above the stage was a never-ending void and the audience could have been sitting in the Haymarket Theatre while we acted in Regent's Park; so the entire production had to be altered and moved downstage. John Napier had designed the brilliant sets for *Nicholas Nickleby*, so he did something similar for *Henry*. Sadly, the great maze of girders and planks did not help intimacy of playing, or assist the actors in relating to the audience.

I loved playing Falstaff and enjoyed the sheer physical excitement of becoming the man. And it was a marathon. On the days we did both plays, Part I would start at two p.m. and with a one-and-a-half-hour break between the plays, Part II would end at eleven p.m. I sweated so much I had to have four baths during the two shows.

It was the time of the Falklands, and the 'Honour' speech seemed to have an extra dimension. I was very touched one evening. When I had played Falstaff in *Merry Wives* many years before at the Old Vic, Caryl Brahms gave me the worst notice that I have ever received, calling me 'an empty vessel of lard who in no way resembled Falstaff' – or something like that. For years I was bruised; often bad reviews are like water off a duck's back, but this one dug deep. At the Barbican, Caryl came backstage and told me that up to that night Falstaff, in her mind, was Ralph Richardson; only he had found the dignity in the man. But now I was equally impressive. I could receive no finer compliment. It meant a lot, and I was exorcised.

A few weeks later Caryl was dead.

Our son Paul came to see the show, and was very chuffed. Afterwards we went to Joe Allen's, where he had once worked, and had a great evening together. Two men at a nearby table came to blows and Paul, good-humouredly and effortlessly, jumped up and restrained them.

The following Sunday Pukk was hearing my lines for Papa Barrett for a BBC TV version of *The Barretts of Wimpole Street*. The phone rang. It was Paul. 'Shall I come for lunch?' he said.

'Of course,' I said, 'but Mum is just going through lines with me.'

'Then I'd better not come.'

'Do come,' I said.

'We'll see,' said Paul. But he did not arrive.

The next morning, while I was filming *The Barretts* at Television Centre, Paul dropped in to see Pukk. He was restless. He had been going to see his son Ben and Ben's mother, Irene, but that had not been possible. Nor could he go and see his daughter Kandy and her mother, because he had no money. He picked Pukk up in his arms and yelled, 'I love you – I love you – I love you,' and left.

The following evening I had finished my work on *The Barretts* and went home. My scenes had been shot first because I had a performance of *Henry* the next evening. I paused for a second outside Television Centre, wondering whether I should pop in and take Paul by surprise at Randolph Road, my father's old home in Maida Vale. But I was tired and quickly rejected the idea.

The next morning, Pukk left for Brooklands College, where she was doing a law and secretarial course. I was sleeping late, getting rid of Barrett and getting ready for Falstaff, when my daughter Penny knocked on my door. 'Dad,' she said, 'could you go downstairs? There is a policewoman and she says it's important.'

I threw on a dressing-gown and started to move briskly down the staircase. A long, thin policewoman stood at the bottom of the stairs. 'Sorry to trouble you,' she called out, 'but your son is dead.'

The insensitive, callous broadside caught me full sail. I almost fell down the rest of the stairs and then went completely numb. Penny was standing with her eyes wide open, transfixed. Then we clasped each other and sobbed together, as the policewoman looked on in mild surprise.

I drove to Brooklands College to break the news to Pukk.

'No – it's a mistake,' she said. 'It isn't true.'

But it was.

I do not want to go through the torment of that time again, so I will not go into too much detail. The previous evening Paul had decided to make a meal for some chums who were sharing his flat with him, and he cooked a spaghetti bolognese. Apparently he was in high spirits, so they all went out to the pub, where Paul started chatting to two young men who came in. Back at the flat, later that evening, the bell rang.

'It's for me,' said Paul, and ran down to collect five pounds' worth of heroin from one of the young men. By the morning he was dead.

It was not a big dose that killed him, but the quality was poor and Paul had not touched anything for a very long time. It was a big shock to his system.

For many years the family had suffered agonies trying to save

Paul from himself. But now that he was gone, by God we missed him. We will never lose sight of the loving, friendly, fun-loving boy he really was. Nor were we allowed to go through a private tunnel of grief. The media descended on us. Not for the purpose of exposing the drug scene but simply to exploit a newsworthy item to sell newspapers. I arranged to have a private interview with the *Guardian* and the *Observer*, and they obliged by writing columns full of tact and understanding. But the *Sun* wrote a long interview with me, about Paul, without ever seeing me – because I refused to talk to them. Roy Hattersley was so incensed he tried to expose them in *Punch*, but the cheap bad taste continued to fill their pages, and people continued to read the drivel. If I had not been so confused and bruised I should have taken them to the Press Council, but at the time life was too black to offer any form of incentive.

And it wasn't only the newspapers. Having missed one performance of *Henry* the night after Paul died, I had to continue with the show. Not for professional reasons – simply because it seemed the only way to survive and get through the tunnel of grief. During one matinée, a TV team waited outside my dressing-room door for *News at One*. Assuming that it would be an attack on the ever-growing drug scene, I agreed to be interviewed. As I returned to my dressing-room at the end of the show, they entered the room, a camera was pointed at my face, and an ambitious female reporter stuck a microphone an inch from my mouth and said brightly, 'How responsible do you feel for the death of your son?' The TV team looked embarrassed. I pushed her from the room. Later her boss apologised, but moments like that make life – and death – very difficult to cope with.

Shortly before Paul's death Ingrid Bergman had also died, after a long, painful fight with cancer. Despite her illness, which made it impossible for her to lift her right arm, she had come to see both *Henry*s, as she had gone out of her way to see every play I had done since *Brassbound* – even driving to the north of England to see *The Dresser*. We used to exchange favourite video tapes, and when she was ill I took her a copy of *The Little Prince*. Knowing she was dying she identified with the prince and his approach to death as something beautiful. She played it several times and showed it to her family. The day before her birthday she telephoned and said, 'You had better have the tape back now.'

The following day she celebrated her birthday with champagne – and died. I promised to read an excerpt from *The Little Prince* for her memorial service. This turned out to be the day of Paul's funeral. With my family we went to a quiet funeral service at Roehampton. Then I went on to St Martin-in-the Fields and read for Ingrid. After a brief greeting to her family I drove back to Ravenswood and then our family drove off in several cars to Paul's favourite spot in Cornwall, taking Paul's ashes with us. There we met dozens of Paul's friends, who walked with us to the Gannel estuary at Crantock which Paul so loved. We all stood on the bridge and I threw Paul's ashes into the flowing water and everyone flung armfuls of flowers which floated in a long, colourful stream out towards the sea. Then I toasted Paul with the cider he loved and threw that also in the water. A mass of solid love was there that day and, strangely, our spirits lifted as the procession of flowers gently disappeared from view.

FOURTEEN

There was a big gap in the middle of the *Henry*s while the RSC
did their Christmas show, *Peter Pan*. Of course, being the RSC
this had to be the definitive *Peter Pan* and Trevor Nunn and John
Caird would explore every nook and cranny to find the psychology
behind Barrie's great work. Fascinated by Barrie's stage directions,
they decided to include them and introduced a pipe-smoking Barrie
wandering around among the action, describing what was going
on. Peter Pan was a boy, not a girl, so they cast a man to play the
role. They also wanted adults to play the children, because only
grown-ups could understand what children were really like. I had
visions of Miriam Karlin leaping around with a teddy-bear as
Michael, but they finally settled on younger members of the
company. It seemed that every idea rejected from the original
production and those that followed was back in, so that the show
now ran for three and a half hours instead of the usual two.

I played Mr Darling and Captain Hook.

John Napier's sets were stunning and the lagoon was a visual
treat, with mermaids appearing to leap around in cascades of
water made of canvas. Animals of all kind and description moved
realistically around the huge stage and the crocodile devoured two
agile young actors who controlled the huge, fearsome monster.
Tinker Bell became a major role, with a young actress wearing
headphones in a tent speaking dialogue in a charming bell-like
whisper getting laughs and tears as a laser light leapt over stage
and auditorium. A new form of organised flying had to be used
for Peter Pan and the children. Of course everything was very
complicated, and the flying was not the greatest success, what with
actors dangling helplessly as wires caught on scenery or one small
cog did not work. Several previews were cancelled, which was very
tough as several thousand children, possibly visiting a theatre for
the first time in their lives, and who had come from all parts of
Britain, were turned away from the theatre.

At the first rehearsal the cast gathered in the usual circle and
Trevor said, 'This is a children's play and you all have to think
and feel as children, so for the first week I want you to become

children again. We will play games and you must do what you would do if you were under six years old.' The cast leapt into action with a will and the rehearsal-room became a nursery of thumb-sucking ugga-wuggas.

Quietly I said to Trevor, 'How does it help me being under six? I am playing Hook.' Trevor grinned happily and nodded, but he did not reply. 'I tell you what,' I said, 'I am going home. When you start rehearsing give me a ring.' He smiled again. I went home. A week later the stage manager telephoned and we started to rehearse.

I had done my pre-production work as Captain Hook for nearly twenty years playing monsters with Melanie, Paul, Toni, Penny, Samantha, Kirsty and Toby, when I would roar and roll my eyes and chase them until they leapt on top of me and finally subdued me.

The production, after many delays, finally opened and was a great success with the adults. It was indeed magic to behold, but to my mind it was too clever by half. It was presented brilliantly, but it did not open up its heart for the children to enter the world of magic that Barrie had created. They did not enter wonderland, they just caught sight of it. Three and a half hours is a long time for a child to sit in a theatre seat with only one interval. Lots of youngsters were leaping up and down, not with excitement, but eager not to pee in their pants.

Back to the *Henrys* and then I left. The detached scholastic approach to plays was not for me. Relationships were good and friendly but there was always a void. I wondered how our leading actors, Richardson and Gielgud and Olivier and Guinness, would have coped with the company – I could well imagine Coral Browne's reaction, but I dare not print it.

Peggy Ashcroft and Judi Dench love the system, but then I would not mind betting that they were prefects at school – perhaps even head girls. When I was asked to stay on in other plays I said, 'Sorry, Trevor – I prefer the theatre.'

He just grinned.

After Paul died we decided to sell Ravenswood, our home for sixteen years. Melanie had married and divorced and was living at Denham with her three children. Toni had married David Yardley and with their first child moved to Kent, commuting to the Moving Picture Company in London where they both worked. Penny was a doctor with a house in Peckham. Samantha was at Exeter

University, expecting a baby by Paolo, an Italian she met abroad, Kirsty was about to embark on a foundation course in Manchester before going to St Martin's School of Art. Only Toby was still at home, shortly before leaving King's College at Wimbledon.

Our extraordinary friendly home, which held such happy memories, was difficult to leave. There were still the echoes. The laughter and wit at the dinner table, the parties carrying on through the house and into the gardens, rehearsing for plays and TV shows. And the mad moments: Pukk and I waking one morning to find Mai Zetterling lying on top of us in bed, with a camera six inches from my face. She was making a short movie about us for the BBC programme *One Pair of Eyes*, and with her husband at that time, David Hughes, was staying with us for two weeks. And one November afternoon when I arrived home to find log fires in every grate, the house strewn with decorations, a Christmas tree and an enormous TV unit occupying every room. All this, I thought, for a TV interview about children at Christmas? I was very incensed at this invasion of privacy and was about to explode when Santa Claus came into the house, pulled down his beard and said: 'This is your life!' It was Eamonn Andrews.

But the house also revived sad memories. We decided to make a complete break and moved to a lovely flat in the heart of London in Covent Garden. Leaving Ravenswood was not easy; we had to slip away without telling it. On earlier occasions, when we had talked of moving, the house had got very upset. Things went wrong, articles disappeared; on one occasion we heard a noise upstairs and found that Penny's harp had exploded. As we left the large, empty rooms, the house appeared hurt and resentful.

In Covent Garden we walk everywhere. I did three shows which were only footsteps away. The first was *Pack of Lies*, at the Lyric, where I took over the mysterious inspector for a few months. Later I was asked to do the role on Broadway, but again I had green card problems. Anyway, I did not think the show would work there because the plot concerned the dilemma of conscience of two people who discover that their good friends are spies. I always thought that the Americans would not understand the dilemma: 'For God's sake, what's the problem – they are commies!' As it happened I was right. Pat McGoohan played the inspector, but the play closed after a few performances.

Then I did a musical which proved disastrous. Originally *Jean Seberg* had been directed by Peter Hall as a workshop at the National Theatre and it was a success. So I joined the company as

Romain Gary, the show transferred to the Olivier and it was disaster. The show never found its shape. Music and lyrics were by the warm, frenetic Marvin Hamlisch and the young Christopher Adler, who tragically died shortly after the show ended. The moment the piece left the rehearsal-room and moved into the Olivier one sensed that it would not work. And it was beset by more accidents than the Scottish play.

My next appearance in the theatre – and as I write, the most recent – was one of my favourites, and the theatre was less than three minutes' walk away: the Aldwych, the home of my first play ever, *The Hasty Heart*. This time I played Hook and Mr Darling again in the musical *Peter Pan*. When I was a disc jockey in South Africa in 1956 I was perpetually playing numbers from the cast album of the first production of the show, starring Mary Martin and Cyril Ritchard. It was a great favourite of mine. Little did I think that I would be in the first English production thirty years later! The superb scene with Peter Pan flying over the audience was arranged by Foy, the same people who had worked on the original production of so many years before. The show, presented by Mark Furness, was assembled at Plymouth and directed by the ever-active professional Roger Redfern, who has made such a success of that theatre. Bonnie Langford played Peter. She was a delight to work with, eager, dedicated and professional to her fingertips. What she lacked in the acting stakes she more than made up for with her energy and exuberance. Although fairly cheaply mounted, this time I felt the show really related to the audience. I played Hook very camp as a diabolical coward – a monster with sequins, and sensed that wonderful combination of fear and excitement, love and hate from the children that I think Barrie intended, and is so satisfying. At that time we only had eight grandchildren, but they were all transfixed by the show. The three youngest, Emily, Tom and two-year-old Gianluca, were all spellbound and they talk of the piece with awe and excitement to this day. Not Chekhov. Not even quite Barrie, but theatre at its most fulfilling.

The only time I ever met Donald Wolfit was at the Mermaid Theatre, when he swept into my dressing-room after a performance of *Treasure Island*, flung his arm around my shoulder and said, 'Well done, my boy – now you have given yer Silver yer don't have to bother with yer Hook.' Then he turned on his heels and he was gone.

And he was wrong!

Fifteen

For someone who entered the acting world in order to make movies my career had gone very well – for someone who wanted to do theatre and television. Most actors long for the chance to tread the boards and have little respect for the cinema. Not me. I love the lunacy and the danger and the apparent confusion, with always the possibility of creating that elusive butterfly – a good movie.

Movie directors used to avoid using television actors like the plague, but sometimes they would take a risk with someone in the theatre. I had almost given up hope when Fred Zinnemann, the superb director of *High Noon, From Here to Eternity*, and *A Man for All Seasons*, came to see Paul Scofield, who had starred in the latter film, and in *The Hotel in Amsterdam*. He was about to direct *Man's Fate*, an adaptation of the André Maurois fine novel, *Man's Estate*. He offered me the role of Konig described in the book as short with dark hair. It was a 'Harry Lime' of a character, who does not appear until late and then proceeds to ruin everyone's lives. I held my breath because I did not believe it would happen – maybe I would be replaced on the first day. Fred had worked on the script with Han Suyin for three years. Ten thousand civilian costumes had been made, three thousand army costumes completed, Lord Mountbatten (as Chief of the Defence Staff) had set aside half of Singapore Harbour, two young Japanese boys had been cast as the young heroes, Liv Ullman was the heroine and the leading character men were Peter Finch, David Niven and Max von Sydow.

We rehearsed for two weeks and had temporary costumes for rehearsal. On the last day before shooting I was torturing David Niven. It was after lunch and Fred was five minutes late. During that five minutes the always meticulously punctual Fred sent down two notes of apology. What we did not know was that he was busy on the telephone trying to raise three million dollars. Four million had already been spent. This was the time of the big clamp-down on big budget movies by MGM. The phone calls were to no avail. As we rehearsed the studios were being pulled apart. Everyone was stiff upper lip: Liv Ullman cried a little; David Niven went off to do his Christmas shopping; Fred Zinnemann had the quiet strength of a man used to disappointment. I could not believe we would not be saved at the last minute. But no cavalry appeared. Not one foot of film was ever shot. I got the role but they took away the studios – and the film.

Some years later John Huston offered me the role of a transvestite who was really a tough CIA agent in the movie *The Kremlin Letter*. At the last moment, after I had renewed my passport to go off to Norway and California, the producer Bob Falkenburg insisted on a transatlantic name and George Sanders got the role; his last, before his tragic suicide. As it turned out, he was the best thing in the movie.

I did get a couple of horror movies. The first, exactly twenty years after *Seven Days to Noon*, was *Crescendo*, directed by my friend Alan Gibson, which we shot partly in the Camargue and in which I ended upside down in a swimming pool.

John Mortimer and his first wife Penelope had invited us to lunch at their house near Grasse as soon as we arrived in the Camargue. We hired an open jeep and set out across the South of France. The sky was blue, the weather was hot, and we decided not to travel along the motorway but to take a small coastal road. We left reasonably early in the morning and thought that we should be at Grasse in a couple of hours. We arrived at nightfall and John and Penelope came out to meet us with torches.

'Sorry about lunch,' we said sheepishly.

'Never mind,' said John. 'We'll have dinner, and you must stay the night. You are not filming tomorrow, are you?'

'Good Lord – I don't know,' I said.

'You had better find out,' said John. 'What number should you ring?'

'I don't know,' I said.

'But you must know where you have come from.'

'I don't.'

Eventually I phoned my daughter Penny in London and asked, 'Do you know where we should be?'

John and Penelope were in quiet hysterics.

Luckily Penny had got the number written down, so I phoned and fortunately was not wanted, so we tootled back the next day.

In the next horror movie, *The House that Dripped Blood*, I finished up with my head on a plate.

Later that year, 1970, I went to see Michael Tuchner, the director, and Alan Ladd Jr, the producer, about a movie, *Villain*, that they were about to shoot, starring Richard Burton as a Cockney who was roughly based on the Kray brothers. I said I wanted to play Edgar Lowis, the rival gangster who was a bit of a slob. 'Not your part at all,' they said. 'You're no Cockney. You could be right as the detective, but Nigel Davenport is doing the role.'

I left the office and went home. Then I thought, "The movies is a lunatic business – if you can't lick them, join them." So I put on a black shirt and a white tie, plastered down my hair, relaxed the muscles in my face and returned to the office. Then I swept past the secretary and burst in on Alan Ladd Jr who was seated behind a desk, grabbed him by the lapels, thrust my face into his and said, 'If you don't give me this bleeding part I'll break your bloody neck!'

For a moment Ladd looked shaken, then he recognised me, grinned, and said, 'The part is yours.'

At last I had broken into the movie scene, and for the next sixteen years I played good supporting roles in some interesting movies. I also played good supporting roles in some dull movies. I also played good supporting roles that were cut right out of the movie, and leading roles in movies that were never shown.

One of these was *The Happiness Cage*, which we shot in Denmark. It was an anti-war piece about Vietnam, but before it had a chance to surface in New York it disappeared as if it had never happened. Ironically, Christopher Walken played a similar role to the part he played later in Michael Cimino's *The Deer Hunter*, for which he won the Oscar. At the end of the movie I had reduced him to a robot-like zombie hero.

England Made Me, directed by Peter Duffell and shot in Yugoslavia, was a good stab at a Graham Greene novel. I admired Peter Finch on screen and grew very fond of him off screen. It was also the first of three movies I did with Michael York. In this one I killed him, in the others I played his father and his guardian. The editor was Malcolm Cooke. He and his wife Jenny Mclaine, secretary to Dick Lester, are still great friends of ours.

The year 1973 brought a bonanza of five movies, four of which I actually worked on at the same time. I was on first call for *The Black Windmill*; the director – the lovely, wicked, laid-back, old-time professional Don Siegel – described my role as the dullest part ever written. I remember one sad scene – where a young boy was dying in hospital – when Michael Caine and I got the giggles. So did Don. He left the room. 'Action,' he yelled from afar. We played the scene. After a while from the next room came Don's voice: 'Have they finished?'

'Yes,' called the first assistant.

'Okay,' boomed Don. 'Cut.'

I was on second call to Irwin Kershner's *S.P.Y.S.*, in which I played the third lead, an American comedy villain. The two stars were Donald Sutherland and Elliott Gould, who were capitalising on their success in *M.A.S.H.* ('S.P.Y.S.', get it?). This was the first time I experienced young American actors being given too much freedom and control while their egos run wild. The first day was wasted when they insisted on switching roles.

After the usual three or four takes for a shot, Don would nod his head sagely and say, 'That's the take for me' – and meant it. I was reminded of the story of John Wayne as a young man, walking off the set after a shot was completed, looking very unhappy.

'What's the matter, John?' asked his friend, Ward Bond.

'I wasn't happy with that last take and John Ford is using it.'

'Well, tell him you are not happy,' said Ward. 'You are a star now. Go on, tell him.'

'Do you think I should?'

'Of course – after all, it's your movie.'

So John Wayne walked up to Ford and said, 'John, I am not happy.'

'Waddya mean, you're not happy?'

'I wasn't happy with that last take,' said Wayne. 'I want one for me.'

'You want one for you?' Ford's one good eye gleamed.

'I want one for me.'

'Okay,' said Ford. 'Set up the shot again.'

The scene was replayed. 'Cut!' yelled Ford. 'How was that, John? Was that the one for you?'

'Yep, that's the one,' said Wayne, feeling good.

John Ford walked up to the camera, pulled out the strip of celluloid and handed it to Wayne. 'All right, John, you take it,' he said. 'Now let's move to the next shot.'

Working on *S.P.Y.S.* and *The Black Windmill* at the same time was fascinating because Kershner and Siegel, the two directors, could not have been more different – and both had considerable talent. I was delighted when Kershner asked my daughter Melanie to play my daughter in *S.P.Y.S.* In the film she gets married in Denham Church. A year later she married and went to live in Denham.

The Black Windmill was being shot in London and Paris, and *S.P.Y.S.* in Paris and London. Two weekends I spent outside Madrid, fighting Michael York for the sequence over the credits in *The Three Musketeers*, in which d'Artagnan's father teaches his son his 'secret thrust'. There were two stuntmen dubbing for us, but as far as I can remember they were never even used. Michael actually flaked out for a second when I was giving him a bear-hug and my ribs were bruised black and blue.

My fourth film at the time was Stanley Donen's *The Little Prince*, which I was post-synching at MGM's Borehamwood studios. The delicate story had a full cast of eight and could not convert into a big MGM musical, despite the lovely score written by Lerner and Loewe.

Working simultaneously on the four films involved twenty-four air flights in one month because I was determined, whenever I had a few hours free, to join the family in Cornwall. Eventually the complicated schedule slipped out of gear when we got behind on *The Black Windmill*. I had one more scene, when I died in a car crash in Paris, and was due back to shoot *S.P.Y.S.* in London. The sympathetic Don Siegel said, 'All right, we don't see you die – you're just dead. No one will notice.' And I caught the plane.

In *The Little Prince*, as the king, I had a song and dance on top of my planet. The planet was the upper part of a sphere which filled a large studio. The prince flew in on wires but I was on terra firma, and if I took more than a few steps from the top I would slide all the way down. This had happened to two men during construction. One broke his leg and the other his arm, so I was saved from the dancing and only the singing remained.

Great Expectations was intended to be made as a musical. At the last minute the songs were cut and we did a straight version. The brilliant Freddie Young was lighting cameraman as he had been on the famous David Lean version which had taken seven months to make. We had seven weeks. We had a fine cast. Michael York was Pip, Sarah Miles played Estella – child and grown up. James Mason was Magwich; Anthony Quayle, Jaggers; Robert Morley, Pumblechook; Andrew Ray, Herbert Pocket and Margaret Leighton in her last role was Miss Haversham. I played Joe Gargery and Rachel Roberts and Heather Sears were my two wives. Joe was a great character, a good man to his marrow. It is always much more of a challenge to portray goodness, without appearing dull, than it is to portray villainy, but I enjoyed the experience and the cast were a delight. Robert Morley, as my uncle, asked me on the first day, 'Are you going to use that funny dialect?'

'Yes,' I said.

'Well, I hope you don't expect me to use it, too. The trouble with you is nobody ever knows who you are.'

'And the trouble with you,' I said, 'is they always do.'

We both smiled. We got on very well.

This was the first time that I worked with the divine Sarah Miles. I could sense that beneath her brittle madness was a warm, understanding creature always balancing on a knife edge . And she could not put up with any affectation. On our last day of shooting she and I went to see the rushes. As we left the dubbing theatre I gave her a farewell kiss. She burst into a peal of laughter and leapt up like a gazelle and entwined my neck with her legs and kissed me on the forehead. At that moment one of the money men from the States walked in with some of the production team. He gave a stern, pompous look of disapproval. One of the entourage nervously introduced us to him. He gave us a cool nod. Without ado, Sarah leapt up, flung her legs around his neck and kissed him on his purple face.

After a Walt Disney movie about a missing dinosaur I went off to Czechoslovakia to film *Operation Daybreak* for Lewis Gilbert. This was about the killing of Heydrich in 1942 and the tragic aftermath at Lidice. We used the actual locations and I was the leader of the resistance who was the only survivor. I met him during filming. The church was still riddled with bullet holes where the young Czech assassins flown over from England met their sad end. An aura of sadness still hung in the air. The beautiful city of Prague was also low in spirit. In the late sixties a sense of freedom had begun to take wing and the people rediscovered their rich pride and passion. But after the crushing by the Russians they lost all meaning and purpose and life became grey and bleak.

There were exceptions. Jan Verech had been Prague's leading theatrical light. He and George Voskovic ran a famous theatre together but they would not toe the party line so it was made impossible for them to work. George Voskovic left for America, where his success continued on stage and in films like *Twelve Angry Men* and *The Diary of Anne Frank*, but Verech refused to budge. His presence in the city caused embarrassment to the authorities. He was so popular it would be better if he had left. Unable to work he would have to leave. But he stayed, and existed by help from friends and admirers. The affection shown for this extraordinary man frustrated any effort to subdue him.

One day I sat with him in a crowded café. He looked around, his eyes gleamed. We were very close but he yelled at me with his huge theatrical projection, 'Do you know the real meaning of Russian roulette?'

'Tell me,' I said warily.

His voice boomed, 'It is a game for Russians!' and he roared with bellowing laughter as people all around hurriedly left their tables.

Later, back in England, I was about to send him some books when I heard that he had died.

Royal Flash was a Dick Lester romp – an adaptation of one of the Flashman novels by George MacDonald Fraser, his version of *The Prisoner of Zenda*. I played C. Aubrey Smith. Bavaria was beautiful and the people less so. Nationalism was as strong as ever, purity could still only be found in true Aryan stock, humour was humourless and loud, and I remember a taxi driver who carried a gun 'in case one of those niggers in the US army tried to run off without paying his fare'.

I remember Pukk and my getting locked by mistake in Ludwig's fairytale castle of Hoenschwangau while eight-year-old Toby crawled under the trellis and ran a mile through the snow to get help.

The other vision I still have is seeing Britt Ekland through the open door of her room studiously hoovering her mink.

The Silver Bears was directed by the Czech, Ivan Passer. It was through the gentle Ivan that I met two more Czechs, Jan and Lyda Brychtas, both artists with whom we made friends.

Thanksgiving took place during the movie, and there was a private Thanksgiving dinner at Walton's in Knightsbridge. An American chef was flown over for the occasion. Cybill Shepherd was offered a table and she invited Louis Jourdan and his wife, Michael Caine and his wife, Pukk and myself, and the zany Tommy Smothers of the Smothers Brothers. Cybill, Michael, Louis, Tommy and I were all in the movie. After a great meal we dispersed. Pukk and I were going to drop Tommy in Hill Street in Mayfair and then Cybill at her hotel.

Tommy was well away. He entered our car still clutching a glass of brandy and when we reached Hill Street I offered to give him a hand upstairs. He refused and stood on the pavement two yards from his front door. Two attractive prostitutes moved straight up to him.

'Tommy,' I said, and started to get out of the car.

'G'night,' he said, waving his glass.

'He's okay,' said Cybill.

Tommy disappeared inside his front door with one girl on each arm.

The following morning at the studio a pale Tommy arrived.

'What happened?' I asked.

'Well,' he said, 'it's a funny thing. I went upstairs with the two girls, and they sat on the bed. I paid them sixty pounds each, and they asked "What do you want to do?" and I told them – You do just what you want to do . . . "' Tommy paused.

'. . . So they left.'

After 1976 my film career almost ground to a halt for nearly a decade. I appeared in a number of movies but the theatre took up most of my time and I only managed brief appearances in films, which invariably were not successful. In *The Greek Tycoon* I played the Norwegian skipper of a fleet chasing Anthony Quinn across the seas for a long pre-credit sequence that eventually was cut right out of the movie.

For a TV movie, *The End-of-Civilization-as-we-know-it Affair*, a very funny script, I played two presidents of the United States. Could they be Ford and Carter?

The Carter sequence was particularly funny, but was cut. Sadly the script lost its magic on film.

In *Someone is Killing the Great Chefs of Europe* I wandered around as the English chef, drinking champagne and getting slowly pissed. I went to Singapore to appear in *Saint Jack* (adapted from Paul Theroux's novel) for Peter Bogdanovitch. He had lived with Cybill Shepherd for some time. 'You must work with Peter,' Cybill had said. 'You two will get along just fine.'

Wrong!

We had nothing in common. I had read his excellent appraisal of moviemakers (including a piece on John Ford that was intelligent, sensitive and moving) but found it difficult to relate the author with the cocky, egotistical, bumptious young director in Singapore. And he appeared to show little interest in his surroundings and ambience, which were the basis of the book.

When working, he would walk around, always closely followed

by his leading man, Ben Gazzara, both smoking large Monte Cristo Especiale Number Three cigars. Peter would blow a cloud of smoke through clenched teeth. 'I want a twenty-three here,' he would call to the lighting cameraman.

'That's it,' puffed Ben. 'Let's have a twenty-three here.'

Jimmy Villiers, Mark Kingston, Rodney Bewes and I were playing weary, embittered planters who were only there to provide the atmosphere for Ben and Denholm Elliott, but Peter insisted that we play them like a mixture of Arthur Treacher and Derek Nimmo. Much to my surprise the movie was quite successful, but only Denholm, who put his head down and did his own thing, was really convincing.

My favourite moment occurred during rehearsal. Jimmy Villiers was a few minutes late.

'I'm so sorry,' he panted.

'That's okay,' said Ben, 'I've only just arrived.'

This was my first trip to the Far East and I loved the people and their philosophy. When filming finished I flew to Bangkok for a couple of days and stayed at the Oriental, now my favourite large hotel in the world. I was determined to go back to the East with Pukk.

During the same year I had made two other movies, *Rough Cut* and *The Apple*. Don Siegel directed *Rough Cut* and for a time I hoped for the role eventually played by David Niven. I ended up as a Belgian detective, a part that had as much meat in it as a vegetarian breakfast. But it was good working with Don again, and I got to know the enchanting Niven, with his unspoilt, twinkling humour. Anecdotes poured from him non-stop, always made funnier by his vibrant relish of life. Back at Ravenswood with the children, he gave them concentrated, undivided attention. Always interested – always interesting.

We shot *The Apple* in Berlin. It was a rock musical and I played God. Here is what I took to be the plot.

God carves Adam out of a rock. Adam goes down to earth where he meets Eve. The Devil gets her into a nightclub and tempts Adam into evil. God comes down to earth disguised as an old hippy to keep an eye on things. The old hippy turns around three times, becomes God again and leads Adam and Eve, lots of young hippies and Miriam Margolyes back to heaven with the help of Kirby's Flying Ballet.

The director was Menahem Golan of Cannon Films fame. The

cast was a bright bunch of eager youngsters, and Vladek Sheybal was the Devil.

The day before we started shooting I went across to East Berlin by underground and succeeded in losing my passport. I did not notice until I put my hand in my back pocket at passport control, before getting the train back. The passport was not there. Sweating a little I retraced my steps and searched. "This could take three months," I thought. "The movie could be over. I could be kept in jail. Bad enough to lose a passport in Moscow – but in East Berlin! Details would have to go back to Moscow before the ball could start rolling."

As a last resort I went into the main overground station where I had stopped earlier to ask my way. It was a crowded mass of people. There was a long empty table – empty except for my passport, the most coveted item in East Berlin. It was so conspicuous that it must have looked like a KGB plant. I picked it up and walked back to the passport control.

Filming began in Paradise. There were a lot of animals – some real, some phoney.

I was stuck in a crevice, hacking away at a canvas rock, dressed in white tails and top hat, smoking a pipe, Bing Crosby fashion, and singing,

> Behold the wonder I've created
> The first of all humanit-ee.

There was no room for the camera to edge in amongst the scenery. A tiger escaped. The dinosaur and brontosaurus collapsed because midgets inside their skins were fainting with the heat.

> Behold the wonder I've created
> The first of all humanit-ee.

The elephants became embedded in the fragile scenery and were stuck for ever, while their trunks flailed at all who came near.

Vladek and I did a song-and-dance routine over the complicated set, which ended with him falling into a stream. We did not look like Fred Astaire and Gene Kelly. Menahem was yelling, 'Bring back the tiger – bring back the tiger!'

Paradise was a large portion of the movie. Paradise never made the movie. Menahem was an endearing early-Hollywood Gregory Ratoff of a director. I never saw the end result. As far as I know it has never made England in any form. I could work again.

West Berlin was fascinating and the Berliners had a great sense of humour and humility. Cut off from the rest of the world, it was like a decadent village. I enjoyed it.

Peter Greenaway was going to shoot *A Zed and Two Noughts* in Berlin, but he had to shoot it in Rotterdam because of the one-legged gorilla. He needed a shot of a one-legged gorilla, and the only one available was in Rotterdam. You cannot transport a one-legged gorilla.

I went into the movie with my eyes wide open. Peter is a painter on celluloid, without humour and with a strong, bizarre approach to his work, which I suspect evolves from some strange Freudian hang-up. He regards actors and normal human emotions dis-passionately, and almost invariably in long shot. However, there is an honesty in his work and a fanatical sense of dedication. He is his own man and he makes his own movies.

Anyone who can have a static shot with two actor brothers playing twins sitting uncomfortably on either side of a bed and staring at the camera while the audience have to listen to the full version of 'The Teddy Bear's Picnic' on a wind-up gramophone for several minutes, deserves to get away with it.

Frances Barber as the zoo prostitute (and you don't find many of those) had the right sense of humour for the occasion. In the film she comes to a sticky end when I send her to have it off with a zebra.

The film was the first for the comic Jim Davidson, who played my side-kick, and I suspect that he found it a little confusing. He did get one moment of relaxation when he dropped a small crocodile which snapped at my testicles as it fell, missing them by a couple of inches.

'My God,' I roared, 'it nearly got my cobblers!'

At the end of the movie the leading lady, who has both legs severed, has it off with the twins who have become one person because they get into the same pair of trousers. Then she dies and the boys strip, lie down, and after listening yet again to 'The Teddy Bear's Picnic' not unnaturally allow themselves to be covered by snails.

Lady Jane was Trevor Nunn's inauguration as a film director. Tentative at first and then gradually taking control as his confidence grew, he appeared to have the situation well in hand. But the film was a talkie rather than a movie, and the piece was observed rather than lived. When you have a film about a fifteen-year-old girl who becomes queen and has her head chopped off, and she is never for a second moving – then there is something wrong.

It was a jokey cast to work with, but the film bombed with a heavy thud.

Sixteen

My father never really liked Ravenswood. The first time I took him there I stood back with pride and waited for his reaction. He wandered silently through the rambling house with suspicious eyes, sat down on a chair in a bathroom and told me a story about a girl he once knew. I don't remember the story.

He never drove a car in his life. He had no dreams – only memories. If he enjoyed a meal it was simply the best meal in the world. If he liked a story it was the best story ever written. Wherever he happened to be his mind was somewhere else, as if he could hear the strain of some mysterious pipe calling to him from some distant place.

Jane idolised him and cosseted him. He was her lover and the child she never had. When his legs grew weak she kept him in a wheelchair. He relied on her for every movement, for every function, and she loved it. But then fate played a cruel trick and upset the applecart. Jane died suddenly of cancer. Dad was desolate and lost. He left Randolph Road and came to live with us at Ravenswood. A nurse moved in to help him through the night. We arranged for him to go to a nursing home at Cheam and Pukk visited him nearly every day. She understood that faraway look in his eye and he was aware of her understanding. I would sit with him and tell him all the news and sometimes he would listen. Then he died. I would like to have known my father. I wish he had kissed me.

In 1985 I had a dilemma. I was asked to appear in the movie *Out of Africa* and at the same time I was offered the role of C. S. Lewis in *Shadowlands* on BBC television. There was no script for *Out of Africa* and Lewis was a great part in a very moving, intelligent script. I chose the television and it was the right decision. It turned out to be a little jewel and one of the most successful TV films ever, winning awards all over the world. It was the love-story of the middle-aged, confirmed bachelor, C. S. Lewis, Oxford don and author of *The Screwtape Letters* and *the Lion, the Witch and the Wardrobe* and Joy Davidman, 'a Jewish, ex-Communist, atheist

American'. She dies and he has to fight his way back through 'the tunnel of grief'. Everything about it worked. The delicate threads of a tight web of a script were spun superbly by William Nicholson the author, Norman Stone the director and David Thompson the producer. The fine cast responded magnificently and once again I was united with Claire Bloom as Joy.

The film, of course, had to be shot out of sequence in Oxford and Wales, and the interplay of fine emotions had to be gauged and measured throughout. The most difficult moment for me was towards the end when Lewis and Joy's young son are alone in the attic, confused, bitter and resentful at the loss of the one they loved so deeply. Suddenly the dam bursts and a flood of grief pours out in an outburst of emotion. We had to record this one morning fairly early in the filming and we did several takes, but I could not live the moment.

'Do you mind if we try it again after lunch?' I asked.

Ever sympathetic and understanding, despite the tight schedule, Norman and David agreed. You cannot lie to a camera. It fights its way through the layers and always noses out the truth. It is no good performing for the lens. Nor can you paint a colourful clever picture. You cannot work beyond your own emotions and under-standing. You can only recapture what you have experienced yourself in some form. I had been there – I knew I had to go there again.

After lunch I did.

After *Shadowlands* was shown on the box I received hundreds of letters, most of them from people who had lost someone very close and many said that at that moment of breakdown they too were released.

Ever since 1971 my agent and friend has been Michael Anderson. Irwin Kershner (with whom I worked on *S.P.Y.S.*) once said to me, 'Never have a friend for agent – a friend is a friend, and an agent's an agent.' But I think that a good relationship is a good relationship. One day in 1985 Michael phoned and said that Rose Tobias Shaw, the casting director, had arranged for me to see Dino De Laurentiis about a new mini-series that his daughter was producing, starring Richard Chamberlain. A script arrived at Covent Garden. The part was a pirate chief – Anthony Quinn style – who captures Richard Chamberlain on the high seas and only agrees to let him go on condition that he takes the pirate chief's daughter back to England to be educated at Roedean. Good rich stuff – I thought. Posh English schools must be packed with pirates' daughters.

So the next day I went to Claridges to meet one of the moguls of the movies. He was in his suite and Rose was with him, having done her thing that she does so well, giving a brief recent history of each prospective actor's work, invariably unknown on the other side of the Atlantic.

'How do you do,' said Dino after a cursory glance. 'Please sit down.'

I sat down.

'Thank you very much,' said Dino. 'Nice to meet you. Goodbye.'

I stood up, left the room and went down in the lift. When I reached the ground floor, I thought, "What am I doing?" I had gone through too many wasted interviews. So I went up in the lift and back to the suite. The door was ajar and a young actor was nervously reading a few lines from a script. I went in. Dino looked up. 'Yes?' he asked.

'Sorry to interrupt,' I said, 'but is that it?'

'Is that what?' asked Dino.

'The interview – our little chat – is that it?'

'Why, yes.'

'A little perfunctory,' I said. 'Don't you think it a trifle rude?'

Rose sat silent and still, but her lips quivered slightly. The boy looked confused. Dino's manner changed abruptly – he became humble and full of apologies.

'Forgive me. I am so sorry. You should have been told. We had a script conference last night and the pirate chief has been cut out of the movie.'

'Don't you think that it would have been courteous to tell me,' I said, and then I quoted Spencer Tracy: 'Quite frankly, I'm too old – too tired – and too talented.' Then once more I left the room.

The following day Rose rang me. 'Dino felt really bad,' she said. 'He wants me to send you a script for another part.'

The script arrived. You can never win in the movies. The part was a one-eyed Norwegian dwarf.

Michael Cimino was in England casting Mario Puzo's *The Sicilian*. Michael Anderson told me that Cimino wanted to see me and suggested that I read the book as a script was not yet available. I had a conflict of emotions. I did not want to go through any more humiliating 'nice to meet you – goodbye' interviews and after reading the book there seemed to be no suitable role for a fair complexioned, originally fair-haired Englishman in the all-Sicilian cast. I had experienced too often the 'always casting to type' in the cinema. But on the other hand Puzo's *The Godfather* had resulted in two magnificent movies and Cimino had directed *The Deer Hunter* superbly. He was also a very controversial creature. He had made *Heaven's Gate*, closed United Artists, and Hollywood was still rocking. There was another incentive. I had heard that Marlon Brando was going to be in the film. I perused the book. One interesting character was a red-bearded middle-aged bandit. This could be a possible role.

I went to see Cimino. When I arrived at the Atheneum Hotel in Piccadilly, Deborah Brown, the American casting director, was there to meet me. 'I am delighted to see you,' she said. 'I am a great fan of yours.' "I like it," I thought. 'But,' she went on, 'Mr Cimino has got a little behind. Would you mind waiting?'

I felt like saying I was not interested in the size of Michael Cimino's posterior, so I had better go, but she was very charming. "Here we go again," I thought. 'Not at all,' I said.

I sat in the lounge and had a pot of coffee. I assumed that Cimino was up in his suite. I finished my coffee. I was getting up to leave when an actor I knew came up to talk to me. Deborah Brown arrived and asked would I like to see Mr Cimino now? She led me towards a small swarthy man a few yards away. He looked Roman but sounded American. Cimino asked me if I had read the book.

'Yes,' I said, 'but one thing confuses me. I hear that Brando is going to play Don Masino Croce and yet Don Corleone is also in the book – the part he played in *The Godfather*.'

'For one thing,' said Cimino, 'this is going to be a very different movie to *The Godfather*. I am cutting out all references to the Corleone family. The second thing is it is all nonsense about Brando playing Don Masino – why do you suppose you are here?'

I laughed, I patted my mouth simulating a grotesque yawn, and I laughed. 'You wanted to see me for a swarthy Sicilian god-father?'

'Many Sicilians are fair with blue eyes. It has been that way for centuries.' We talked for nearly an hour. He talked very quietly. He told me later that if you talk very quietly people have to bend towards you to listen. Then I left and forgot all about it.

A few weeks later I was filming a television piece in Wales when I got a message. Could I fly to New York for a reading of *The Sicilian* with Michael Cimino? Pukk went with me, we could see old friends, catch up on a couple of shows and the trip was paid for.

One morning a group sat around a table in New York and read the movie. A mixed bunch. Barbara Sekova from Germany. Christophe Lambert from Switzerland, John Tuttoro from New York, Julia Boschi from Italy and me. Ian Holm was also supposed to be there, but had not turned up. An American stage actor Richard Bauer read his part. Michael Cimino was there and his co-producer and mentor Joann Carelli. I was reminded of a similar scene in *Final Cut*, the book by Steven Bach on the making of *Heaven's Gate*.

We broke for lunch. In the afternoon we sat in our circle and read it again, except now there was a clean-cut, very good-looking, all American hero reading the part of the bandit Giuliano. Christophe Lambert had gone.

After the reading Cimino and Joann Carelli picked up their coats to fly off to Los Angeles.

'What do you think of Lambert?' Cimino asked casually.

'Fascinating,' I said. 'Seems very talented.'

I heard nothing for two or three days. Pukk and I were in limbo. We went to see Woody Allen's *Hannah and Her Sisters*, which we adored, and half of Jonathan Miller's *Long Day's Journey* which we hated.

One afternoon I was in Hal Prince's office. There was a message to phone Michael Anderson in London. 'It is moments like these,' he said, 'that make my job worthwhile. You have been offered the part of Don Masino Croce in *The Sicilian*.' The tension within me was released and I yelled with delight. Pukk, Hal and I went out for a glass of champagne to celebrate and he confided in us that he was about to do a production of *Phantom of the Opera* with Michael Crawford. I thought, "That sounds like hell to me," but I was feeling too chuffed to care. Anyway, I was wrong. When I eventually saw the piece in London it was Crawford's performance and Hal's direction that made the show.

I went to Sicily several weeks ahead of the rest of the cast. Cimino had agreed that I could soak in the atmosphere of the place and find the character – and there was an old man he wanted me to meet. He arranged a car for me and sent me off to live in a quiet, dull little fishing port where the houses sloped down to the lovely coast. Nothing much ever seemed to happen in Castellammare where the young boys from dingy homes put on their fancy clothes and rode their motorbikes while they wooed the pretty young girls and bought them ice-creams, until they married and the men would sit inside the bars and drink beer while their wives made the pasta, until the old men sat outside the bars, drank coffee and ruminated and the old ladies peeked at the outside world through net curtains.

Nothing much happened at Castellammare, but this had been the home of Lucky Luciano, Frank Costello, and Joe Banana.

Before going to Castellammare I had stayed at a lonely, elegant, decadent hotel in Palermo. The Villa Igiea was large and rambling and its location in one of the poorest quarters of Palermo emphasised the decadence and it still reeked of the turn of the century. I met various members of the Sicilian aristocracy, including the count who was captured by the bandit Giuliano and the adopted son of Lampedusa who wrote that great novel *Il Gattopardo – The Leopard* (which Visconti had filmed with Burt Lancaster in 1963). A local baron was presented by Cimino with a beautiful handmade saddle from Montana. One small sadness – the baron did not have a horse.

The man Cimino wanted me to meet in Castellammare came from a different world and the contrast between the social butterflies and the earthy peasants was extreme. Diego Plaia was not a baron or a count; in his world he was a king. Humorous and wicked he created complete respect. All the other men would kiss his hand and step two paces back. Carved from concrete he had great character. Old now with sleepy, wandering, twinkling eyes, behind the heavy paunch and the slow movements could still be seen a man of steel. I would drive him to the sea for the day and, always physical, he could clutch my elbow with a warm, affectionate, challenging vice-like grip. At lunch he would devour his langoustine like a scavenger dog.

His grandson Leonardo was flown in from New York and was sent to act as my interpreter. He had lived in a tight Sicilian community in the Bronx and the English language was still strange to him.

Pukk flew over with our daughter Sammy and her young son Gianluca. Sammy had studied and lived in Italy, which was now her second home. She helped interpret and then got a job on the movie. Technically she was a personal assistant, but she rarely left the office, except to transport film and actors to and from the airport, and she saw little of the actual shooting.

Diego Plaia had a little friend of great charm who lived half the year in Rome. He was a dead ringer for Hector Adonis, Don Masino's friend in the novel. His real name was Vincenzo Sabella but he was known to all as 'the teacher' or 'the Englishman'. He did not teach and could not have looked less English but, in his natty colourful expensive finery, the locals thought he did. He had great love for English movies and English actors, especially 'Ronnarld Collmarn'. He fluttered around Don Diego. When they walked together they looked like Pooh and Piglet. 'The Englishman' had an exquisite house overlooking the sea next to a small jutting castle on a rock, which was to be my home in the film. He was eighty-five and ran everywhere, talking incessantly with superb recall.

Diego had a cousin who had lived in Brooklyn for a short time and was very proud of his English. He sounded like a poor man's Chico Marx. He was very kind and always eager to help but he was very voluble, very effusive and very physical and I would eventually have to beg him to 'cool it'. He was everywhere. I could not turn a corner without coming across his welcoming arms and his broad grin. One day I was at a greengrocer's, desperately trying to think what apricot was in Italian. As if by magic the exuberant face appeared. 'Wassa matter?' he said. 'You wanta some 'elp?'

'Apricots,' I said. 'I want some apricots.'

His brow furrowed. 'Why – you wanta clean your shoes?'

One day I mentioned to Diego that I thought his cousin was a lovely man, but a little claustrophobic. I never saw him again.

I asked Diego if he had ever travelled. 'I went to America once but I did not get in. Another time,' he continued, 'I went to Sardinia.'

I said that I had only passed through Sardinia once and had not been very impressed.

Diego half closed his heavy lids and shrugged impassively. 'Sometimes you go to places you do not wish to go.'

My relationship with Diego grew even more *simpatico*. He and his large family would always kiss Pukk and me on both cheeks. One day he held my face after the two kisses and then kissed me firmly on the lips. He did the same with Pukk. There was nothing sexual. He smiled, but nothing was said. I felt I would not have to lock my car again.

The actors arrived and I would drive to Palermo to rehearse. They were the same group who had sat around the table in New York. Christophe Lambert was playing Giuliano, not the good-looking young American. We sat around another table in the basement of the Villa Igiea and read and re-read the script and quietly found our way and each other. Christophe was impatient to get on with the filming. He was not used to analysis and preparation and would get up from his chair and stride around the room. Barbara Sekova's eyes flickered. 'Are we boring you?'

'No, no,' said the guileless Christophe, and would seat himself uncomfortably in his chair.

My friend from *The Madras House*, Oliver Cotton, came from England to swell our ranks but we were well into filming before the count was cast and Terence Stamp came to join us. All through rehearsals Cimino was quiet, patient and understanding. At the end of the final rehearsal I walked with him from the room. 'Tomorrow we shoot the movie,' he said. 'Now, directing a movie is like being a general in wartime. You have to make big decisions quickly so don't be surprised if I shout and upset people. You cannot make a big movie without making a lot of noise.'

'Well,' I said tentatively, 'Fred Zinnemann did.'

'Fred's the old school,' said Cimino.

During filming, as he frenetically sought to make an epic movie on a tight budget, he did shout a lot. Not at the leading actors because he needed each close-up to be relaxed and unruffled, but technicians, make-up, small part actors and particularly photographers were perpetually under fire.

The hours were long and Alex Thompson was having to do two men's work as lighting cameraman operating the camera himself. One of the American TV networks sent a unit to shoot an hour-long documentary on the making of the movie for peak showing throughout the States. They were going to interview a few of us, but Cimino refused to be photographed so they went back with unused cameras. A complicated lonely man, sometimes a strutting Mussolini, sometimes lost and defensive, I found him nonetheless helpful and understanding to work with. 'Remember less is more,' he would say before a shot. And of course he was right. But he was intolerant. One actor arrived a few minutes late from Rome, because he got the wrong plane, and from that moment he never stood a chance. Cimino would not let him off the hook. One day in front of eleven hundred Sicilian extras Cimino yelled at the Italian second assistant who was so humiliated that he grabbed the side of an armoured tank and banged his head in frustration and was in hospital for some time. After shooting, watching rushes, and planning the next day Cimino would disappear into his room leaving a 'Do not disturb' sign and refusing any calls, but I believe he rarely slept more than an hour or two at night.

Despite the considerable influence of Joann Carelli on Cimino his chauvinism knew no bounds, unless it involved minor aristocracy, and his rudeness and antagonism were so strong that they indicated complete lack of understanding of the opposite sex. The benevolent, rasping Aldo Ray, a big star in the fifties, arrived to play a don, and introduced his wife. Cimino ignored the out-stretched hand. 'What the hell did you bring her for?' he glowered, and strode away. One evening he ignored Pukk so rudely that I rose from my chair to ask him why. Pukk held my arm and said, 'Don't bother. How can you worry about someone who wears five-inch heels?'

We set one record for the Guinness book. The scene towards the end of the movie when Giuliano and Don Masino finally meet was shot in one day. During that day Cimino shot twenty thousand feet – twenty cans of film, longer than *Gone with the Wind* – and nineteen thousand feet were of close-up shots of Christophe and myself, and he printed the lot. After each take Alex would adjust the lens a fraction one way and then the other. Eventually our words came out like hot bubbles of glue. Françoise Bonnot, our clever sophisticated editor, nearly collapsed when she heard the news – but the scene was good.

Before the filming had started I drove to Palermo for a voice lesson with Elizabeth Percy. Normally I try to avoid voice lessons. Working on an accent phonetically is not my scene. It is painting by numbers. Dialect springs from within from background, en-vironment, and speech is developed from character. Find the man and the words find themselves. If you work on a speech phonetically you have to act the speech. The truth is I just do not like acting. An American once asked me in London, 'Where do I go to see some acting around here?' I suggested the RSC because, by God, you certainly see it. But in Elizabeth Percy I recognised a fellow spirit. An essentially English 1930s eccentric who looked as if she had just come from tea with Virginia Woolf or Edith Sitwell, she helped me to 'think peasant' and 'think Sicilian' and my face muscles gradually changed shape as I relaxed into character. This was also helped by the fact that I was gradually putting on thirty-two pounds in weight, much encouraged by Cimino's wicked smiling, 'More wine, Joss, more pasta.'

On my way to see Elizabeth Percy at the Villa Igiea, I bumped into Gore Vidal whom I had known since appearing in his play *The Long March to the Sea* on television in the late sixties and he was a close friend of Claire Bloom. The original script for *The Sicilian* was written by Steve Shagan, then Michael Cimino took a hand and finally Michael approached Gore for his version and his was the final script. Over lunch Gore told me how I got the role.

Cimino had approached Albert Finney in London. Finney was unhappy that no script was available and he was not sure a play in which he was appearing in the West End would be off in time for the movie. Michael was eager to get on and see a few other actors while he was still in London. I was one of them.* Then Cimino flew to Rome to discuss the script with Gore, and they went out to dinner with Anna Steiger, Claire's daughter; they talked about *Shadowlands*. Claire had sent a cassette of the film 'to show off' as she told me later. Michael saw *Shadowlands* and wired me to go to New York for the reading. He offered me the role, we signed and the following day Finney contacted Michael to say that his play would be off in time. The wheel of fortune had spun in my direction at last. I had a great part in what should be a distinguished movie.

The filming was exciting. Always adventurous, Cimino used the Sicilian panorama with giant sweeping flourish: a thousand peasants carrying colourful red and white banners made an awesome procession through the countryside before the massacre, a car raced over steps and up to the front of Monreale's cathedral. Cimino squeezed every ounce of juice out of the budget to try and fill the screen. But after *Heaven's Gate* the brakes were on and today Hollywood is run by nervous, avaricious accountants, not by movie lovers.

One day three locals to whom Cimino had given work riding in the movie went to the production office for their day's pay. When they opened their brown envelopes they said, 'Mr Cimino promised us twice as much as this.'

'Mr Cimino made a mistake. That is what we pay.'

'But Mr Cimino promised.'

'Mr Cimino was wrong.'

A few hours later two men walked up the stairs to the production office. They wore masks and carried double-barrelled shotguns, stripped the accountants of their jewellery, opened the safe, took the money and left.

* This was the suggestion of the director Claude Watham, whom I hardly knew.

SEVENTEEN

For all its madness the movie world is very conservative. A youngster can achieve instant stardom but play a number of supporting roles and one goes on playing supporting roles. That is how the machine works.

Purely by luck I had broken the mould. A hand had reached out and I did not want to let it go. In the theatre a character actor can command – and on television. But not in the movies. Destinies are formed by young couples canoodling in the backs of cars in drive-in cinemas in the mid-west of America and today their heroes and heroines shine and disappear as rapidly as their favourite numbers in the charts. The spadework of movie performance is done by the professionals but they have to keep their place. How many movies have been held together on the backs of Lee J. Cobb, Thomas Mitchell, Walter Brennan, Cecil Parker and Alastair Sim or Ethel Barrymore, Jane Darwell, and Beulah Bondi? Yet as far as I know they never starred in a movie.

During the forties most of the big studios had their own repertory companies with an abundance of talent. Warner Brothers led the field. *Casablanca* will last for ever. The chemistry was rich between Bergman and Bogart (who also broke the barrier between supporting roles and stardom), but would the movie had reached the same heights without Claude Rains, Conrad Veidt, Peter Lorre, Sidney Greenstreet, Paul Henried, and S. Z. (Cuddles) Zakall? Most of them had achieved one burst of stardom – Rains as *The Invisible Man*, Veidt in *The Cabinet of Dr Caligari* and *The Passing of The Third Floor Back*, Lorre as *M*, Greenstreet in *The Maltese Falcon*, Henried in *Now, Voyager* – and then they were pushed into their slots as good, strong reliable support. Audiences relaxed with them as their names below the title discreetly guaranteed talent and professionalism.

The short burst of brilliant films written and directed by the young genius Preston Sturges all had the same supporting casts, always led by William Demarest, Raymond Walburn and Franklyn Pangbourne.

Charles Laughton and Orson Welles started big and stayed there, but like rockets their genius fizzled out in mid-air. Even they were in and out with the fashion. Anthony Quinn was an exception – he was lucky; after many years in supporting roles, like Bogart he broke the mould. Everything in its place is Hollywood's motto. When Jack L. Warner was told that Ronald Reagan had become governor of California he frowned and said, 'No, you're wrong – Errol Flynn for governor, Ronald Reagan for best friend.'

Lee Marvin, Joan Collins and Charles Bronson fluttered around the edges for years until they built their own creature, solid and always identifiable, and gave their audience what they wanted and knew they would get.

In my late fifties I had been given my opportunity to break the mould. How to hang on to it? First a great deal hung on the success of *The Sicilian*. I heard conflicting reports from the States. 'Great, it's going great. Keep this under your hat, but how do you feel about an Oscar nomination?' . . . 'There are problems with the movie. I hear there are lawsuits pending. Everybody is suing everybody else.'

I felt the ground slipping away. I got myself a press agent, Theo Cowan, jovial and pipe-smoking, solid and reliable, who had seen it all and knew this topsy-turvy business inside out.

There were problems with the movie. Wounds were still smarting in Hollywood. The knives were out for Cimino. He had agreed the film should not run longer than two hours ten minutes. His completed version ran two hours fifty minutes. *The Professionals* ran two hours fifty minutes and did well enough, *Gone with the Wind* was three hours forty. The point was made that if a movie ran two hours ten you could get in an extra showing each day. Cimino dug in his heels. Then he sued David Begelman, the producer. He lost. The movie was taken out of his hands and forty minutes were sliced out of it. Gore also sued – his name was not on the movie, but Steve Shagan was back. Steve Shagan had been president of the Screenwriters' Guild. Gore said to me, 'Somehow I don't think I'll win.'

I played a moustache-twirling villain in a colourful piece of hocus-pocus, *Queenie*, a mini-series based on the Michael Korda novel and well directed by the warm and friendly Larry Peerce. Two of my favourite ladies were around, Claire Bloom and Sarah Miles. Sarah was my wife, but Claire and I did not even meet on this one.

Pukk had read *White Mischief* by James Fox. We had been fascinated by the decadent Happy Valley crowd since our tea-planting days in the fifties when stories of the trial of Jock Delves Broughton for the murder of Lord Erroll still filtered through from Kenya to Nyasaland.

'Broughton is a fascinating mass of contradictions,' said Pukk. 'A wonderful part for you to play.' I read it. It was.

I made enquiries about the rights only to discover that Michael White had acquired them before the book was written. There was also talk of the BBC doing their version of the same events for television. Then I heard that Michael Radford was going to direct the movie. How to get it? Michael Anderson contacted Michael Radford and told him I was keen to play Broughton and could I talk to him. 'There really is not much point,' said Radford. 'He is not my idea at all of the character, but if he wants to see me let him see me.'

I had seen Radford's movies *1984* and *Another Time, Another Place* and had hated the first and loved the second. *1984* starred John Hurt and Richard Burton and I felt that Radford had tried too hard to recreate the book on screen. Both the book and the film were relentless, but with the book one could occasionally look up and gulp fresh air. And in the book I identified with Winston Smith, the John Hurt character, and I wanted him to live as I wanted to live myself. But Radford detached me from the character and I kept wishing he would jump out of a window and save himself any further agony.

On the other hand *Another Time, Another Place* with Phyllis Logan as the lonely, repressed Scots housewife who gets involved with Italian prisoners of war to me was a gem of a movie.

Michael Radford had a boyish charm and a nervous attacking vulnerability. He had seen me play Kirilov in *The Possessed* at the Mermaid when he was a schoolboy and the image had remained, but he was sorry, I was not his idea of Broughton. Anyway the money-boys were insisting that the part be played by an international star.

"How to get a return of investment with a guaranteed profit?" think the money-men. Pay a huge sum to a reliable draw at the box-office and get back an even bigger sum.

At the time there were a few stars who could guarantee high returns. Sylvester Stallone was perhaps a trifle limited, but Clint Eastwood, Jack Nicholson and Dustin Hoffman could play anything. And they were asked to play everything.

But Radford was stubborn. He wanted the right people for the right roles, but he was obviously not averse to having a big draw.

'I have just played a lead in *The Sicilian*,' I said. 'It's a big picture and the word is good.'

I suggested that Michael Radford telephone Michael Cimino for a reference. This was arranged and I do not know what he said but he came up trumps. Radford agreed to let me have a screen test. The test was sent across the Atlantic and there was approval. But big movie names continued to be juggled in the air. The young Greta Scacchi was to play Diana Broughton and Charles Dance had been asked to play Lord Erroll a year before. He had already starred in two or three movies and appeared set. One morning Michael Radford phoned me and said that across the Atlantic they wanted to see a test of Charles in the role. Charles was none too pleased.

'And you would like me to do it with him?' I said.

'Would you really?' said Michael. 'That is very decent of you.'

Garth Rabinsky is a mogul who runs the Cineflex chain of cinemas throughout Canada and the States. He is a tough cookie who makes Harry Cohn look like Shirley Temple. He had a big piece of the movie and wanted to make sure his money was returned with considerable profit. He probably would have liked Clint Eastwood to play Broughton and Robert Redford, Lord Erroll. I could imagine him talking to his minions,

'On second thoughts Redford was not so hot in *Out of Africa*.'

'Maybe Hoffman in lifts?'

'No, that movie he did with Beatty bombed.'

'Maybe John Travolta?'

'Who the fuck is John Travolta? Now Nicholson is still hot . . .?'

But Michael Radford could be stubborn; after all, he was the director and he had written the script with Jonathan Gems. So could Simon Perry the producer. And by this time they were on our side. Meanwhile an extraordinary cast was assembled as rich as Warner Brothers in its heyday. Sarah Miles, John Hurt, Geraldine Chaplin, Susan Fleetwood, Murray Head, Catherine Neilson, Ray McAnally, Alan Dobie, Hugh Grant and (our casting director Mary Selway announced with glee) Trevor Howard.

I had been talking with John Dexter about doing a new play by William Douglas-Home. It was scheduled to open at the Malvern Festival in the New Year and then move to the West End. There was still no decision about the movie. I did not know if I could get the part that I so longed to play or even if the film would ever be made. Simon and Michael were flying backwards and forwards non-stop in their efforts to raise the money to get *White Mischief* off the ground.

Christmas 1986 and New Year went by quietly. At home with the family and then still at home with my sister Barbara, her husband Ron and friends Annie and Chris Hancock. Then suddenly a starting date was announced, but the money was still not in the kitty. I went to costumier Maurice Angel and had fittings for many suits, dinner-jackets and tropical outfits. Pukk and I had all our vaccinations for the tropics, and I had to turn down the play with John Dexter, but I still did not know if I would play Sir Jock Delves Broughton. I had not been given the green light.

At the last moment it came, and Pukk and I boarded the plane for Kenya.

Then *The Sicilian* opened in America. In its shortened version with forty minutes cut from the film it made no sense and sadly Christophe did not have the underlying anger or the charisma for the title role. Cimino was the prey and the vultures pounced. All the expectations and high hopes came to nothing. *The Sicilian* bombed. I got some great reviews but it made no difference. If your ship sinks you go down with it.

But fate had saved me. I was playing the lead in *White Mischief*. The only reason that I had got the role was because of the prospect of my having a big success in a big success. If *The Sicilian* had opened a few weeks earlier I would not be playing Broughton. Fate had given me another throw of the dice.

It did not seem to land too well. I arrived in Nairobi to start my first scenes with Greta at the same time as my costumes arrived in Manchester. Desperately our shy and sensitive costume designer Marit Allen grabbed costumes from all directions and managed to tog me up until the right ones arrived.

We filmed in or around Nairobi for three or four weeks. The company was a bizarre group of strong personalities, every one quite individual, and we all got on very well together and made a good team. Michael Radford was on a high the moment shooting began and beavered away with frenetic energy.

An unusual number of the company were born under the sign of Pisces and sought to go in opposite directions at the same time. Michael and I were included in this which created a slight problem, being both supremely confident while we were both desperately unsure. Broughton was very satisfying. The major difficulty was to make a man without personality interesting, but cast and crew began to treat me like a decent old buffer and I felt at least that I had become the man. What was exciting was to play someone who betrayed no emotions and concealed everything behind a respectable façade. But as the movie progressed a turmoil was building inside the man like a volcano, until it erupted into madness. Shooting out of context meant each scene had to begin with the correct balance of unseen torment and I had to be sure to betray nothing to actors or the camera and at the same time arrange that future audiences would sense what was really going on. Another complication was that Michael had travelled a new road in film making. Normally there is someone in a movie with whom the audience can identify and travel with in the story. They become Clint Eastwood or Meryl Streep and laugh and cry and suffer with them. But *White Mischief* was concerned with a group of selfish unsympathetic characters who could be observed, but never joined. I believe we all instinctively became the characters we played.

I discovered that Trevor was really not well when he arrived and I went to meet him in Nairobi. I said, 'Of course, you have been to Africa many times,' and he looked around in surprise and said, 'Is this Africa?' He had trouble learning lines, but the moment he was in front of the camera the old magic returned and he lived his role with that unique richness that has always bewitched millions.

John Hurt missed his connecting plane and arrived as we were about to shoot a scene with him at Nairobi racecourse. As he travelled to the set he was changing his clothes, helped by two Masai warriors (his in the movie), as he moved through the crowds by the track. He reached the set and went straight into his opening line.

One night we were shooting a scene in which I arrived tipsy at my house helped by Catherine Neilson as June Carberry. When I play a drunk scene I always like to psyche myself into a state of drunkenness and then say the lines. Anything to avoid acting. I thought they would reach the scene by midnight and worked myself up accordingly. Some of the cast and crew became quite concerned and tried to protect me because they thought that I was really pissed. I had not touched one drop of alcohol. Unfortunately the previous scene ran over and by two a.m. I began to feel quite sick and lay down to sleep. When I was awakened in time for the shot I had recovered except for a hangover.

We moved up north to Lake Naivasha where one hundred and eighty tents had been set up, each one with a separate baby tent at the back containing a loo and a shower – a basin with a piece of string.

We worked long hard hours and used the actual locations belonging to the Happy Valley set – including the 'Gin Palace', the house owned by Lord Erroll which Broughton bought for Diana and himself after Erroll's death. Invariably we were held up in the afternoons when it rained heavily – the long rains had come early.

By nine or ten in the evening we would stumble exhausted into a large tent, our dining-room and bar, where we would have a good meal and a bottle of wine, watch the rushes and then, by torchlight, find our way to our individual canvas bedroom, light our anti-mosquito coils and sleep. Nothing could be heard except the sound of the crickets and the zipping and unzipping of canvas.

Living together as one community helped us become a close, tight team. Usually, location work involves splitting the company into groups with actors in one hotel, technicians in another, make-up and wardrobe in another and so on. But on *White Mischief* we became a family, there were no complaints about the long hours and on the word 'action', concentration was complete.

On one occasion we were doing evening shooting. I had to wait for the last shot, which involved me driving emotionally and erratically through the bush. The unit were working miles away. John Dodds, our second assistant, kept in touch with them by walkie-talkie, and remained with my Somali driver and me at base camp. It was dusk when I was called.

'They are nearly ready,' said Doddsy to my driver and me.

'Where do I go?' asked the driver.

'Take that turning to the left. It's a small track but just drive straight on. After thirty miles you will run straight into the unit, and they will flash you to stop.'

We drove for thirty miles. We drove for thirty-five miles. Nothing. After forty miles I said we had better turn around and go back. Still nothing. We reversed once more. Then we saw a small light from a lantern by a Masai hut.

A lone Masai was there. He had seen nothing. We drove on. Suddenly my driver freaked out. We were travelling at fifty miles an hour and I was in the back seat. He clutched at his head with both hands and moaned as the car sped forwards. "Look, no hands," I thought, but said quickly, 'Steady – put your hands on the wheel. What is the trouble?'

He continued to grasp his head. 'It is not my fault,' he cried. 'As God is my judge, it is not my fault.'

'Don't worry,' I said, 'it is only a movie.'

'But they will sack me from my work. Oh my God, it is terrible.'

And he wept copiously as the car jerked onwards, skidding from side to side.

'Let me drive,' I said.

'No, it is my work. I will drive,' cried the driver, and he swerved into a ditch.

I hoped that we were not stuck. We were in the middle of the bush, miles from anywhere and I was wearing a tuxedo with a stiff collar. Three days previously a bus had been stopped by Masai bandits and thirteen people had been massacred. I really did rather hope that we were not stuck.

I climbed out of the back seat. The driver was rigid and shaking. He could not move. I pulled him limb by limb and eased him out of the car. Then I lifted him up in my arms and deposited him on the back seat. I climbed into the front. The car started and I drove forty miles back to base camp. I passed Doddsy and waved. He waved back and did a double-take. He did not expect to see an actor in evening dress driving a screaming driver through the bush. The driver leapt out and started to run off. I ran after him and placated him. Michael Radford had decided it was too late for the shot and they had all left for dinner and the walkie-talkies rarely work. After I had persuaded my driver he would not lose his job he became my friend for life. I had done my shot driving emotionally and erratically through the bush pretty well. Unfortunately there was no camera. When we did it next it was at Shepperton Studios.

Pukk and I loved our little tent. It took us back to our tea-planting days at Likanga. And we loved the camaraderie. I shall never forget night after night seeing Sarah Miles sitting in front of Trevor Howard's tent writing out his lines on large pieces of card and going over and over them with him ready for the next day's shooting.

Garth Rabinski was now out. David Puttnam sailed in to the rescue just in time before his brief reign ended at Columbia.

The last three days' shooting in Kenya were of Greta and Charles wading sexily in the sea at Mombasa so Pukk and I went off on safari from Little Governors camp. We spent the days in an open jeep and saw every form of wild life: herds of elephants coming from all directions to attend a great meeting, leopards, lions, even a pair of the rapidly diminishing rhino. We went up in a hot-air balloon which worried me because we had to crash land and I was nervous of Pukk being able to protect her broken back. However,

231

nothing would deter her any more than it had some years before in Acapulco in Mexico when she had insisted on paragliding and I had to run across the sand to break her fall.

She has always been adventurous and her disability has made her all the more determined to try the unusual. A few years ago we flew with our young son Toby to Kashmir, stayed on a houseboat on the lovely lakes at Srinagar, went on a pony trek for three days through the mountains attended by three Sherpa guides and then up the Himalayas to Leh, the highest point of civilisation in the world. We were driven by a crazy character called the Ladakhi cowboy in his open jeep and he played music on his horn all the way up. Halfway up the fourteen thousand feet we stayed the night in a little hut without water. The scenery was like the moon, awe-inspiring and the light was a cameraman's paradise. Breathing was difficult and any violent movement dangerous. When Toby ran down one of the mountain peaks he got mountain fever and we had to send a runner to Leh to get a doctor. When he arrived we were amazed to find that he had been educated at Edinburgh University and then moved back to his mountain peak to practise. Leh itself was known as Little Tibet because after the lamas were sent away from China they settled there. The place was paradise, a Shangri-la, but I had to be back in England to rehearse *The Dresser*. We could not return by car because there had been a rare fall of rain which had caused two landslides and the bridge across the river had collapsed. Panic time, but I discovered that a plane flew down to Srinagar every weekend.

On Saturday at nine a.m. we waited in a small aircraft hangar in a field outside Leh. At midday we were still waiting. A Ladakhi soldier told us to be patient. At two p.m. he informed that there would be no plane that day. Come back tomorrow. The next day we returned and waited until midday. We were then told that there would be no plane until the following Saturday. We discovered that only one pilot could manage this particular take-off and he would only go if the wind was absolutely right. It had been six weeks since the wind had been absolutely right. The runway was short and as soon as the plane was in the air it had to make a sharp turn to the right in order not to hit one mountain and then it had to travel along a narrow pass between two other mountains. We decided not to wait for the plane. But how to get back?

The rehearsal-room seemed a long way away. We found the Ladakhi cowboy and persuaded him to take us down as far as he could. Somehow he managed to wind his way past the two landslides, although we drove pretty close to eternity, but even he had to give up when we reached the gushing river and the broken bridge. Someone had attempted to cross and the empty car could still be seen in the middle of the river. The Ladakhi cowboy left us and drove back up the mountain. A group of men arrived with makeshift planks which they placed haphazardly over various parts of the rushing water. An Indian bus was going to try and ford the stream. Unbelievably, it was crowded but the driver allowed us on, and it set out on its perilous journey with half-naked men running alongside, heaving planks under the wheels. By the time we had reached the middle of the river the water was halfway up the locked windows beside us, but somehow we made it and had time to relax on our houseboat again before returning. Even then our adventure was not over. On our return to Delhi, to change aircraft, our plane hit a small bird and we were forced to land in the Punjab. The heat and the humidity were so bad that outside the waiting-room one could only move in slow motion. Luckily, despite rumours to the contrary, we only had to wait a few hours before another plane arrived and we continued on our journey.

But I digress. We were on safari in Kenya. Little Governors was charming and our tent luxurious, but at night we could not take a step without being joined by an armed African with a rifle. At first we thought that it was because of the animals. One night an elephant brushed through the camp. On another day we had a hippo in the stream immediately outside our tent. 'The poor old thing is dying,' said Pukk, because it was moaning and groaning and huffing and puffing. Then indeed it appeared to be on its way to heaven because it rose from the water and continued to ascend. Beneath it was another hippopotamus.

Then we found out why we were so protected. A few weeks before, raiding Tanzanian bandits had crossed the border in the middle of the night and robbed some European guests of their jewels and left them out in the veldt.

Sadly our time in Kenya was up. When I say sadly, we had loved our time there, but neither Pukk nor I was eager to return. Life had not changed all that much since the Happy Valley days – despite independence. Years of subordination had left their mark on the Africans. Many still were naturally subservient and encouraged to be so by some of the whites who still lived in an isolated glory of escapism at the Matheiga Club. When I entered the bar there accompanied by an African actor, Blimp-like, the members mumbled disapprovingly to themselves and left the room.

233

Back at Shepperton we remained a unified company. There was a cross-dressing scene with the women in tuxedoes and the men in drag. This was made much easier by the fact that when the artists were called down to the set, all the technicians, make-up and wardrobe were also cross-dressed. Mike Radford wore a particularly fetching little number.

We finished on schedule. Sadly, lack of funds had meant cutting a couple of scenes during the air-raids in London at the beginning of the film but the movie was otherwise complete.

I went off to Paris to make another film, *To Kill a Priest*, written and directed by Agneska Holland about the murder a few years ago of the Polish priest, Father Popieluszko. Agneska was a Polish tiny ball of concerted energy and the movie was her apotheosis. She protected it like her child, perhaps with too much love and concern, but had the ability to create natural respect. Christophe Lambert was the priest, but this time we did not meet on the movie and he had finished before I began. *The Sicilian* had opened in France while he was filming and what he saw on screen must have been quite a shock because with Agneska's help he straightened his shoulders and ploughed on industriously and well. Too much too soon is always one of the great traps of our profession. Christophe has a beguiling innocence, a lot of energy and great charm. His only weakness is that when he kisses you on the cheek I think he assumes that you will never wash your cheek again.

Another person that I did not meet on the movie was Cheri Lunghi which was a shame because I am a great fan, but I did work a lot with the young American actor Ed Harris whom I found most impressive.

White Mischief opened at the Curzon Cinema, Leicester Square, and easily broke all records and the reviews were good. For me they were wonderful – better even than *Shadowlands*. Greta and I flew all over the place to promote the movie. Always fun to be with, a free spirit, Greta resented her beauty and used it. There were three premières in England, one for AIDS, one for the royals, in this case the Duke and Duchess of York. Fergie looked lovely but was wearing an extraordinary creation with a mass of bunched-up material sticking out behind. 'She shouldn't have opened it before leaving the aircraft,' I whispered to Sarah Miles, as the handshakes approached.

The third première was in Cromer in Norfolk. Simon Perry had tried to revitalise interest in a small cinema there. John Hurt, Murray Head, Michael Radford and I travelled there to join him for the opening. After the film we were invited to stay the night at various homes. Pukk and I went off with a very pleasant couple, Sarah and William Bulwer Long of Heydon Hall. His family had lived there since Cromwell. Indeed their walls were covered with Roundheads on one side and Cavaliers on the other, like football teams. Another couple came in for drinks that night. They reminded me of Broughton and Diana, and there was the same age gap. We mentioned that we had been staying at Little Governors camp.

'Oh, really,' said the young wife. 'We were there recently, but we had a beastly time. We were woken by some armed men in the middle of the night and they took all our money and jewels. Isn't that right, dear?'

'Yes, dear,' her husband nodded.

'And then they took us outside and walked us for miles in the bush,' she went on languidly. 'Then they made us strip and lie down on the ground. My dears, for one fearful second I thought they would rape me. Jolly unpleasant. Isn't that right, dear?'

'Absolutely,' her husband nodded.

'And then of course we had to find our way back to camp – completely starkers and with all those beastly animals around. It could have been quite messy. If we had not seen the light of a fire we would never have found our way back.'

'But we did, old gal,' said her husband.

'But we did.'

Later she said, 'I like Kenya, but one can't live there for ever. And you can't buy anything. One always has to go abroad for one's jewels. Isn't that right, dear?'

'Absolutely,' said her husband.

I flew to San Francisco to promote the movie for their film festival. In Britain, Columbia had bent over backwards in their efforts to sell the picture but *White Mischief* was a Puttnam movie and Puttnam did not live there any more. I sensed a certain lack of enthusiasm when I got off the plane after a long flight and a publicity girl was there to meet me. 'Hi,' she said. 'Greta Scacchi should be here in an hour or so. Do you want to wait for her or go straight to your hotel?'

'I think the hotel might be a good idea,' I said.

The festival opened with *White Mischief*. It was the big movie, but the organisers were worried. 'The other day,' said their chief, 'we had a press showing for all the critics, but not one critic was invited so the movie played to an empty room.'

I got the impression that somebody at Columbia was sulking. This was made even more clear when our Columbia publicity lady said, 'Well, there is nobody here for you to see. What would you like to do?'

"And I crossed the Atlantic for this?" I thought.

I made a fuss and in Los Angeles it was all points go. Interviews in my suite, by telephone, over meals. I also discovered how different was their world to ours. I know that work is hard to find but unemployed actors are really treated like dogs. No wonder they become so arrogant when their hand is on the greasy pole of success. My agency, ICM, asked if I could manage to see a certain lady. I presumed this certain lady was producing a certain film. With all the interviews, timing was difficult but I managed to just slot it in with the help of the Columbia car. There was a secretary in a front office.

'Could you sign your name here?' she said.

'Why?'

'Actors always sign their name here. If you are kept waiting for more than an hour it is reported to Equity.'

'I don't think I will be here that long,' I said.

The door opened and a young woman ushered me into her office. 'What is all this about?' I asked.

'Oh, nothing specific,' she said, 'but I haven't managed to catch your work and I just wanted to know what you looked like.'

'Buy a ticket,' I said.

When David Puttnam was fired from Columbia he had three parting shots and they all found their mark. The wonderful *Hope and Glory*, that most accurate, moving and funny account of life on the home front during the war, and *The Last Emperor* were both nominated for Oscars and the latter swept the board. *White Mischief* opened too late in the United States, after the glossy Oscar shenanigans were over, but the reviews drew in the audiences, who were intrigued by the decadent Brits.

When I was working with Bernard Hill and James Fox in a BBC film in Wales just after playing C. S. Lewis in *Shadowlands* and was then called to New York about Don Masino in *The Sicilian* they said, 'That's natural, Cimino thinks you always play dons.'

I had managed to carve a niche in the movies as a Mafiosa boss

236

and now as a stuffy Englishman. Offers naturally came in to play stuffy Englishmen and various forms of Mr Big. Now I had two identities – but at least there were two.

When the opportunity came to play something quite different I leapt at the chance. Desmond Davies was directing *The Man Who Lived at the Ritz* as a four-hour mini-series and Hermann Goering was a colourful contrast to my previous roles. Monster, child, charmer, high on drugs, sensual and transvestite, the character as portrayed in the script was a bonanza for an actor. Once again I put on weight although this time I did have the assistance of padding. I thought the script was a great improvement on the book which had been a bestseller a few years ago. The Ritz was the famous hotel in Paris where Goering stayed for some time during the war. The young hero was Perry King, well known on American TV, but new to me, and the French contingent included the still gamine Leslie Caron as Coco Chanel, Patachou as Madame Ritz and Mylene Demôngeot. The two girls were Cheri Lunghi and Maryam D'Abo, David McCallum played Charlie Ritz, Brigitte Khan was Goering's mistress or rather *maîtresse* and Barry Houghton was Goebbels.

So not long after completing *To Kill a Priest* I was back in Paris for three months, and Pukk was with me. We had an elegant suite at the Hotel Raphael on the avenue Kléber. One night we had a good Chinese meal and discussed going off to Italy as soon as I had the chance. Our six children and eleven grandchildren were all well and happy and life had really begun to straighten out. Content, we strolled home through a drizzle of rain.

When we reached the avenue Kléber we crossed at the lights. Just before we reached the other side a small car sped along the bus lane and knocked us down. I was angry but unhurt apart from a few bruises. A young girl and boy got out of the front seats. 'We did not see you – it was not me driving!' cried the boy.

Pukk could not move. She was in great pain. The police arrived and questioned the youngsters merrily inside the ambulance for twenty minutes with Pukk lying in agony. We then drove to the General Hospital and it was four hours before she was given an X-ray. She was given nothing to relieve the pain. By now our line producer Serge Touboul had joined us to help. We explained that she was paraplegic but they insisted on trying to straighten her legs. The pain was too much. We told them to stop and they walked out in a petulant huff. A young doctor arrived with a yellow mop on his head and two balloons emerging from his dress like large boobs. 'We're having a party,' he said. 'I hope you're not going to spoil it for us.'

The accident occurred at nine p.m. At one a.m. the X-ray revealed a broken femur. Pukk was put in a room where there were two beds. I asked to go in with her. This was agreed. Serge, very upset and angry, went home.

Early in the morning a nurse and a male orderly entered the room. 'What are you doing here? Get out – get out!' roared the orderly. This was too much. The nurse restrained me. During the night, with the help of my daughter Melanie, I had contacted Stoke Mandeville Hospital. They recommended a top surgeon, Professor Roy-Camille at the 'La Pitiée' Hospital on the other side of Paris. He was abroad, but he arranged for his team to do the operation.

It was midday before another ambulance drove Pukk painfully to 'La Pitiée' where she was given an immediate painkiller and the operation was performed. The break was joined by a plate and three screws. Four days later Pukk needed blood and I had to be the donor. I went to the blood bank after filming. It was closed and only open between nine a.m. and five p.m. I was filming from six a.m. to seven p.m. and was in every shot. There was a lunch break from one o'clock to two fifteen and my large friendly Yugoslav driver, Boda, volunteered to drive the thirty-minute journey to the hospital so that I could give three litres of blood, and then drive me back, still in my padding and make-up. But the production could not take the risk so our son Toby was flown over from Newcastle as donor and then flown back again. During the week Kirsty flew over to help interpret and keep Pukk company while I worked and then Sammy, Toni and David and their children all arrived.

Back in England our doctor daughter Penny and teacher daughter Melanie helped plan Pukk's future and after two weeks, when I had a break from filming, Pukk and I flew by air ambulance back to Heathrow, to be met by a comfortable ambulance which took us to Stoke Mandeville where she had spent such a long time twenty-five years before. I stayed at a nearby small hotel. It was thought that Pukk would be on her back for three months before she could learn to walk again. Having to learn to walk twice in a lifetime is difficult enough – but three times. What had gentle, loving, caring Pukk done to deserve this?

If our life were the Grand National, Pukk fell at Becher's Brook twice and, both times, got up and remounted. This time it was even more difficult to complete the course and it was only her gutsy determination that drove her on. I am still too frustrated and angry with the cruel arrogance of the Parisian bureaucracy to write clearly or talk dispassionately of this period of time and the pain with which Pukk had, once more, to cope. Like a boxer hit below the belt, I am still confused and dazed.

I returned to Paris but flew back to Stoke Mandeville at every opportunity. As for the eighteen-year-old girl who drove the car that hit Pukk, apparently she got her driving licence in November and the police informed our solicitor that this was her eighth accident in five months. Each visit to France became a trip into enemy territory. *The Man Who Lived at the Ritz*, which could have been such a joyous occasion, became an effort. The production helped in every possible way and they did have other problems. A fire burnt part of a set and young Maryam D'Abo had developed a skin infection abroad which could not be cured quickly and she had to drop out of the movie.

Pukk left Stoke Mandeville and went to stay with Toni and David in Kent. There she had physiotherapy and moved around with the aid of a walking frame. By the time the shooting finished we were back at home in Covent Garden and she was on two sticks. Then we went by motor rail to Italy to help her recuperate in the sun while I completed this book. On the way over many passengers were robbed of money and jewellery as they slept. We thought ourselves lucky until I went to collect our car. The seal had been broken, the car ransacked and my cameras and some luggage stolen. Pukk is still on two sticks but not for long, she says. Life goes on. Up and down. A helter-skelter ride. Next year I go to film in Hollywood for the first time, playing the villain in *Lethal Weapon II* for Warner Brothers. But first I go to New York for a three-day role as a Mr Big for the BBC. Then I start another four-hour mini-series of an Eric Ambler spy story as a middle-aged hero. Today a costume designer flew over to Italy to measure me for my three-day role – from the BBC. Things must be really swinging.

My apprenticeship is over. Now for the big stuff.

Christmas 1988

INDEX

247